SAN ANTONIO

SAN ANTONIO

 NANCY HASTON FOSTER

Lone Star Books®
An imprint of Gulf Publishing Company
Houston, Texas

*This reprint was reviewed by the author,
updated, and reprinted April 2000.*

LONE STAR GUIDES:
SAN ANTONIO

Lone Star Books®
An imprint of Gulf Publishing Company
P.O. Box 2608 □ Houston, Texas 77252-2608

10   9   8   7   6   5   4   3

Library of Congress Cataloging-in-Publication Data

Foster, Nancy Haston.
    Lone Star guide—San Antonio / Nancy Haston Foster.
       p.   cm. — (Lone Star guides)
    Includes index.
    ISBN 0-89123-022-X (alk. paper)
    1. San Antonio (Tex.)—Guidebooks.   I. Title.   II. Title:
San Antonio.   III. Series.
F394.S23F66   1999
917.64'3510463—dc21   98-49240
                                           CIP
Printed in the United States of America.

Printed on acid-free paper (∞).

Front cover photo of the Alamo by Laurence Parent.
*Back cover photos of the River Walk by Christina Ybarra and Hemisfair Park by
Jean Higgins/Unicorn Stock Photos.*
Lone Star Guides series cover design by Senta Eva Rivera.

To my family,
who has always been there
with encouragement and support

CONTENTS

ACKNOWLEDGMENTS

Thanks go to the folks at the San Antonio Convention and Visitors Bureau for their helpful maps and info. And to many other local organizations plus friends for their input on what makes San Antonio tick. Thanks also to my editor at Gulf Publishing, Kelly Perkins.

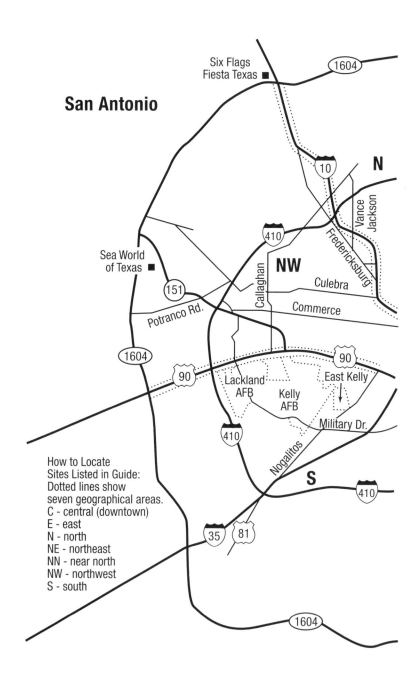

San Antonio

Six Flags
Fiesta Texas ■

1604

N

10

Vance
Jackson

410

Fredericksburg

Sea World
of Texas ■

NW

Culebra

Callaghan

151

Commerce

Potranco Rd.

1604

90

90

East Kelly

90

Lackland
AFB

Kelly
AFB

Military Dr.

410

Nogalitos

How to Locate
Sites Listed in Guide:
Dotted lines show
seven geographical areas.
C - central (downtown)
E - east
N - north
NE - northeast
NN - near north
NW - northwest
S - south

S

410

35

81

1604

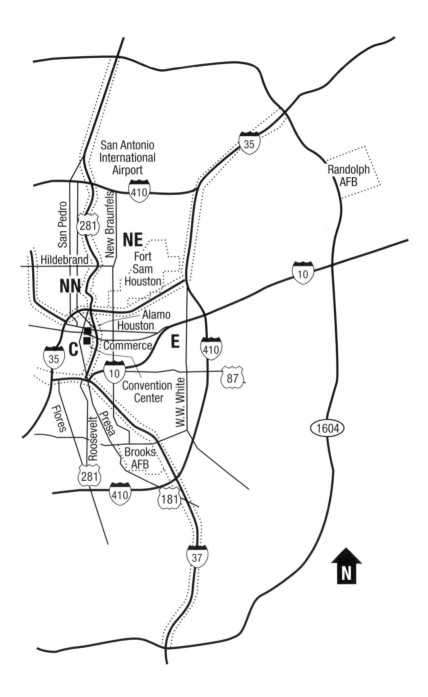

San Antonio International Airport

Randolph AFB

San Pedro

New Braunfels

281

410

35

10

NE

Fort Sam Houston

Hildebrand

NN

Alamo Houston

C

Commerce

E

410

35

10

87

Convention Center

W.W. White

Flores

Roosevelt

Presa

Brooks AFB

281

410

181

1604

37

N

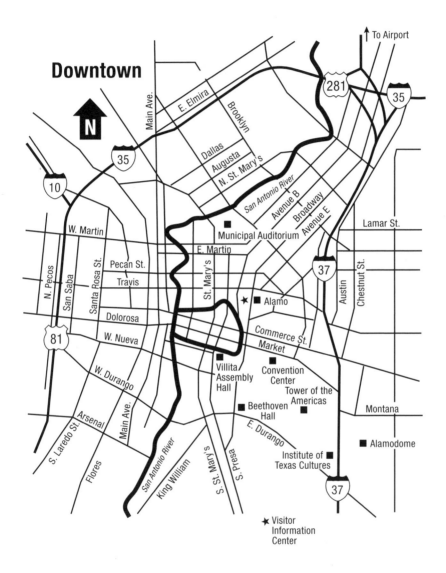

Downtown

N

To Airport

281

35

10

35

Main Ave.

E. Elmira

Brooklyn

Dallas

Augusta

N. St. Mary's

San Antonio River

Avenue B

Broadway

Avenue E

Lamar St.

Municipal Auditorium

E. Martin

W. Martin

N. Pecos

San Saba

Santa Rosa St.

Pecan St.

Travis

St. Mary's

Austin

Chestnut St.

37

Alamo

Dolorosa

81

W. Nueva

Commerce St.

Market

W. Durango

Villita Assembly Hall

Convention Center

Tower of the Americas

Beethoven Hall

Montana

Arsenal

Main Ave.

E. Durango

S. Laredo St.

San Antonio River

King William

S. St. Mary's

S. Presa

Institute of Texas Cultures

Alamodome

Flores

37

★ Visitor Information Center

INTRODUCTION

Ask a card-carrying Texan what Texas cities are most dear to his heart of hearts, and you can safely bet the ranch that he'll mention San Antonio—after a few obligatory genuflections to his own hometown, of course.

That's the way it is with the city the Alamo built. It has a certain independent, show-me spirit that defies urban fads and an indefinable, old-fashioned charm that sets it apart from other southwestern cities. Even other Texans trek here on vacation, enough to make it the No. 1 destination in Texas both for Texans and for out-of-state visitors.

After all, why go to *Fortune* 500 Dallas and Houston for mere fun? They may have more petroleum and banking dynasties, but they simply don't have the character, ethnic texture, or plain old soul that San Antonio has, particularly in its downtown areas.

Despite being the nation's eighth largest city, with the usual metropolitan trappings, San Antonio still has an almost small-town attitude and friendly natives whose outlook on life allows them (sometimes at least) to let business slide and have a Fiesta-snortin' good time. The fiesta lifestyle—one of many San Antonio traditions borrowed from Mexico, whose flag long flew over the city—blends in comfortably with the historic buildings and sites to give San Antonio a certain aged patina you can't get with the plastic and steel of most urbana.

The legendary Alamo and Spanish missions attract a lot of tourist attention and generate much marketing hype, but there's something very real here too. San Antonians venerate the past and appreciate the patriotic values that the Alamo represents. They can identify with a little healthy cussedness and have cared enough about their roots to the land and past to do something about saving and restoring the missions.

Although San Antonio maintains ties with the past, this is still a modern, growing city with a population of around one million. Most of the growth is evident in the city's two most dynamic areas, the downtown section and the north side. The far northwest, the home of Sea World, Six Flags Fiesta Texas, and a fledgling biotechnology research park, has particularly grown.

DOWNTOWN AND RIVER WALK ARE EASY TO ACCESS

As the downtown areas of many southwestern cities quietly succumb to suburban shopping malls and the culture of the automobile, San Antonio's downtown thrives, as hotels and office buildings continue to multiply. Although freeway feeders and parking garages are features of downtown, pedestrians feel welcome, and the downtown area is compact enough that most places are within walking distance of each other. If you don't feel like walking, opt for the inexpensive trolley that loops through the downtown area.

Nowhere is walking more pleasant or more fitting than along the River Walk, a real focal point of San Antonio. For strolling, shopping, or simply feeling the pulse of the city, a visit to the River Walk is absolutely required. Several hotels and a major cluster of shops and galleries line the River Walk, and it is the center of downtown nightlife. Festivals and fiestas take place here, and during the Christmas season the trees of its central section are decked with lights.

But the Alamo and River Walk are only two of many attractions in San Antonio. As the various sections of this guide show, the richness and diversity of attractions in San Antonio explain why it is one of the most popular spots for travelers in Texas. Sea World of Texas, Six Flags Fiesta Texas, museums, historical sites, universities, a major medical center, and a selection of charming nearby towns that invite side trips all contribute to San Antonio's appeal.

CLIMATE AND LIFESTYLE

The pace of life is slower here than in other Texas cities, and most San Antonians would not think of changing that. Numerous influences seem to have created this placid lifestyle—the mild winters, the South Texas summer heat that in the days before air-conditioning made a siesta at midday not a luxury but a necessity, the genial mix of diverse cultures, and an economy geared to the dependable flow of federal payrolls (there are five military bases in and around San Antonio, though one will be closed after 2000) rather than to the vicissitudes of a highly competitive industrial environment. Longtime residents, however, say the pace of San Antonio has been quickening as new faces and attitudes have moved into the city's leadership.

As alluded, the Alamo City's industries aren't of the smokestack variety. Rather, the significant ones are tourism, military, insurance, health care/research, oil and gas, and communications.

San Antonio is a threefold meeting ground. Here, the culture of Mexico meets that of the United States. The history of San Antonio cannot always be separated from the history of Mexico because, for almost 150 years, San Antonio was part of colonial or independent Mexico, although it differed in important ways from the rest of Mexico. The chapter called **Mexico in San Antonio** shows the extent to which the two cultures of Mexico and Anglo-America are intertwined. Second, in San Antonio, the culture of the West meets that of the South. East of San Antonio, the flavor of Texas is largely southern, while the area to the west is generally characterized by ranching and wide-open spaces. San Antonio has elements of both. Finally, the Hill Country and plateau lands come together in San Antonio, making it a geological as well as cultural meeting ground.

Part of the exuberant San Antonio spirit finds its expression in the city's numerous fiestas and festivals. The major ones are listed in **Annual Events** and in the special section about Fiesta, the citywide, annual ten-day extravaganza in April. Lesser events can also be fun. Almost every week, there is a celebration or fiesta in Market Square, which fills with music, food vendors, and a throng of good-humored celebrants. Somehow, Mexican food rarely tastes better than it does fresh off the grills or out of the kettles in the booths at Market Square.

Some of San Antonio's character can be vexing. For example, many of the city's old streets meander unpredictably, and street signs are not always provided. Businesses sometimes lack street numbers. While most intersections are marked with street signs, the most confusing ones do not give a clue as to which streets meet there. The city also throws up other unintended barriers to navigation—newcomers may require months just to learn how to get around via the downtown freeways. If, as a newcomer or visitor, you do not sometimes lose your way, you are probably in the minority.

Other hazards to navigation include streets that change names without warning, blocks in which a street simply vanishes and then reappears some distance away, and easily confused street names. For example, Military Road is not the same as Military Highway. Similarly, W. W. White is not White, and Wurzbach is not Harry Wurzbach Highway, even though freeway signs might have you believe otherwise. A map is a necessity in getting around. Adequate maps are sold throughout the city, but one of the most detailed is *Ferguson's San Antonio Quickfinder Mapbook,* a set of street maps covering the entire county, complete with approximate street numbers for the major streets.

San Antonio's numerous attractions are balanced between those that are free (the River Walk, the McNay Art Museum, the missions) and those that are not (the San Antonio Zoo, the Spanish Governors' Palace). Where admission fees are specified, this book has indicated the prices current at the time of this printing. But remember, they're ever changing.

All information in this book is as accurate as possible at the time of printing and is subject to change.

HOW TO USE MAP FOR LOCATIONS

To help readers locate the numerous businesses, parks, museums, restaurants, and other places in this guide, this book divides the city into seven areas. The listings indicate the area in which the attraction is found. More for convenience than for geographic appropriateness,

I have let the freeways determine most of the divisions. The divisions are defined as follows and are shown on the San Antonio map (pp. x–xi):

Central: Generally, this is the downtown area. I-10 forms its southern and western boundaries, I-35 is its northern boundary, and Pine Street is its eastern boundary.

East: East of I-35, Pine Street, and I-37.

Near North: The area north of the Central district bounded on the south by I-35, on the west by I-10, on the north by Hildebrand, and on the east by US 281.

North: North of Hildebrand, east of I-10, and west of US 281.

Northeast: North and west of I-35 and east of US 281.

Northwest: West of I-10 and north of US 90.

South: South of US 90 and west of I-37.

SYMBOLS OF WHEELCHAIR ACCESSIBILITY

W: This building or area is accessible to wheelchairs: The entry is a least thirty-two inches wide, and there are no steps. Not all facilities (rest rooms, elevators, etc.) are accessible.

W+: This building or area and all major facilities are accessible.

W call ahead: The management will make special arrangements to admit persons in wheelchairs.

W variable: This building or area is accessible only in part.

(No symbol): This building or area is not accessible.

FOR YOUR INFORMATION

GETTING AROUND

You're in luck—San Antonio is user friendly. Its neighborly inhabitants, with their blend of southern Tex-Mex hospitality, are more apt to respond to visitors with a civil "howdy" than with the usual urban indifference.

Ask and you shall usually receive if you need help getting around. They will either show you or point you in the direction of one of the visitor information centers listed below.

San Antonio has a genuinely fun downtown that contains many of the spots visitors (and natives) want to explore, from the historical (the Alamo) to the more up-to-date (the Alamodome). Better yet, downtown is very walkable. Many of the attractions and sites, such as the Alamo and River Walk, are within walking distance of hotels and reasonably priced parking lots. Parking lots and garages are scattered around the downtown area, and finding one is not a problem unless there is a large special event going on downtown. If you plan to go downtown when there is an event in the Alamodome, consider taking the bus.

Once downtown, you can either walk or hitch a ride on one of the handy streetcars that run continually between points of interest. (For streetcar and city bus routes, call VIA Metropolitan Transit at 362-2020.)

Whether you're a resident, visitor, or newcomer, this book provides a crash course about San Antonio and where to find its unusual sites, restaurants, shops, and entertainment. This chapter starts you off on your trek to discover San Antonio by giving you resource information (including tourist) centers and listing numerous publications and books about the city. Now you, too, can learn the history of the San Antonio River, where to find wild bull riding events, and how to keep a lawn alive and well through San Antonio's dry summers.

INFORMATION CENTERS

SAN ANTONIO CHAMBER OF COMMERCE

602 E. Commerce at Alamo St. • Central • 229-2100
Monday through Friday 8:30–5 • W side entrance

While some of the organization's reports are business oriented and available only to members, many are sold to the public. Directories of office buildings, shopping centers, industrial parks, employers, government agencies, and organizations are available, as are a newcomers' guide and media list.

SAN ANTONIO CONSERVATION SOCIETY

Anton Wulff House, 107 King William • Central • 224-6163

Many of the historical sites mentioned in this book have been owned, restored, managed, or saved by the society. The Steves Homestead, the Navarro Home, the Espada Aqueduct, and the Yturri-Edmunds Homestead are, or have been, Conservation Society properties. As its main fund-raising activity, the society each year plans, organizes, and manages A Night in Old San Antonio, one of the most popular of all Fiesta attractions. Information about the King William area is available here at the society's headquarters, as is other information about historically significant aspects of San Antonio.

SAN ANTONIO CONVENTION AND VISITORS BUREAU

203 S. St. Mary's at Market • Central • 207-6700 or
(800) 447-3372 • Monday through Friday 8:30–5 • W

If you're planning to visit San Antonio, write P.O. Box 2277, San Antonio 78298. The helpful bureau not only provides free information about the city's events, accommodations, and attractions but also offers assistance in planning conventions.

SAN ANTONIO RIVER WALK ASSOCIATION (PASEO DEL RIO ASSOCIATION)

213 Broadway at Travis • Central • 227-4262 • Monday through Friday 9–5

The association's office can supply information about the many things to see and do on the Paseo del Rio (River Walk). The association also publishes a monthly magazine, *Rio*, with current information about River Walk shops, lodging, restaurants, and entertainment. Each issue includes a handy map pinpointing River Walk establishments and is distributed free in most hotels and shops along and near the river.

VISITOR INFORMATION CENTER

317 Alamo Plaza at Houston • Central • 207-6748
Open daily 8:30–6 • W

The staff members of the Visitor Center aim to please. They'll give you directions, free maps, and brochures about the city and nearby sites as well as a handy calendar of events.

AREA CODE

Dial 210 as the prefix when calling a San Antonio number from out of town.

BOOKS

These are some books currently in print. For a list of books with a more directly historical slant, see the end of the **History** chapter. Or check the library.

ALAMO
Written and published by Mary Ann Noonan Guerra
San Antonio

A softcover about the Alamo, with historical pictures and data.

ALAMO LONG BARRACK MUSEUM
Daughters of the Republic of Texas • Taylor Publishing
Company • Dallas

Full of historical photos and facts about the Alamo and its exhibits.

EYES OF TEXAS TRAVEL GUIDE
Ray Miller • Gulf Publishing Company • Houston

The San Antonio/Border edition contains a section on San Antonio and a lot of helpful material on surrounding counties. Both history and photographs supplement the descriptive text.

FLAVORS
Junior League of San Antonio • San Antonio

This eclectic cookbook, like many similar Junior League volumes, can give one an idea of how local chefs cook at home. There are also recipes that had been featured at the Junior League's restaurant. From Spanish *paella* and Creole gumbo to *sopapillas* and Mexican coffee, it's all *sabroso*. Available at local bookstores.

A GUIDE TO SAN ANTONIO ARCHITECTURE

Prepared and published by San Antonio chapter of American Institute of Architects • San Antonio

This takes a historical look at San Antonio's commercial and residential architecture. Some of these old buildings have tall tales behind them. Many photographs.

THE MISSIONS OF SAN ANTONIO

Mary Ann Noonan Guerra • Alamo Press • San Antonio

Interesting historical photos of the missions, with appropriate background material. Useful chronology.

ROADSIDE GEOLOGY OF TEXAS

Darwin Spearing • Mountain Press • Missoula, Montana

Painless way to learn geology while cruising down Texas highways. Don't try to read while driving, however; it's best to take a friend along. Contains a section on areas and terrain around San Antonio.

SAN ANTONIO CUISINE: A SAMPLING OF RESTAURANTS & THEIR RECIPES

Karen Haram • Two Lane Press • Kansas City, Missouri

Illustrated book by *San Antonio Express-News* food editor, who knows the foodie scene.

SAN ANTONIO MISSIONS NATIONAL HISTORICAL PARK

Louis Torres • Southwest Parks and Monuments Association Tuscon, Arizona

Beautiful color photos, along with the history of the local missions.

SAN ANTONIO MISSIONS NATIONAL HISTORICAL PARK, A GUIDEBOOK

Compiled and published by Junior League of San Antonio

Designed for schoolchildren, with worksheets. Contains historical photos and background on the missions in the park.

SAN ANTONIO ON FOOT

Diane Capito and Mark Willis • Texas Tech University Press Lubbock

The authors seem to have walked every interesting section of town and reported each in loving detail. Two dozen walks, from five downtown strolls to four rambles through local parks, make up the bulk of the book, but appendixes and introductory material extend it further. Each walk is described with historical and cultural notes, and each includes a detailed map.

SAN ANTONIO: PORTRAIT OF THE FIESTA CITY
Susanna Nawrocki and Gerald Lair, photography by Mark Langford
Voyageur Press • Stillwater, Minnesota

Beautifully done with excellent color photos, this book shows the color and character of San Antonio. The book is heavy on photos of historic sites, architecture, and festivals, with good explanatory text dovetailing the history and background of all. Few books do as well in showing the texture of the city and its people.

SAN ANTONIO UNCOVERED
Mark Rybczyk • Wordware Publishing • Plano

This book on San Antonio covers the offbeat, the funky, the little-known, and the trivial, but it also has historical information on such topics as the River Walk, the Municipal Auditorium, and the stories of various ethnic groups. No matter how much you know about the city, you'll find something new here, and all the material is presented in a light and engaging style. The book concludes with a droll chapter of San Antonio lists, including "Fourteen Terms that Every San Antonian Should Know" (e.g., NIOSA, Gucci B).

SOUTH TEXAS GARDEN BOOK
Bob Webster • Corona Publishing Company • San Antonio

Gives ample instructions on growing grasses, trees, shrubs, plants, and lawns in this area. The author, a local nurseryman, has distilled years of experience in local gardening and horticultural problems into this book.

TEXAS, A LONE STAR GUIDEBOOK
Various writers • Gulf Publishing Company • Houston

An authoritative guide to all of Texas, for the traveler, newcomer, and lifelong resident. Hundreds of entertainment, dining, and hotel listings. Available at bookstores.

TEXAS MISSIONS, A LONE STAR GUIDEBOOK
Nancy Haston Foster • Gulf Publishing Company • Houston

An easy-reading travel guide to Texas missions, with emphasis on the Alamo and other San Antonio missions. Photos, maps, history, and tips on touring them.

13 DAYS TO GLORY: THE SIEGE OF THE ALAMO

Lon Tinkle • Texas A&M Press • College Station

The siege and battle of the Alamo are described in a dramatic way, day by day.

WHY STOP? A GUIDE TO TEXAS HISTORICAL ROADSIDE MARKERS

Claude Dooley and Betty Dooley Awbrey • Gulf Publishing Company • Houston

Here are reprints of the actual inscriptions on more than 2,500 of Texas' most interesting historical roadside markers. Also provides useful highway and mileage information.

MAGAZINES

FIESTA

San Antonio Express-News • Avenue E and Third
San Antonio 78297 • Monthly

Fiesta is a glossy magazine distributed without charge where visitors are likely to find it—mainly at hotels and city attractions. While it is heavy on advertising, it also includes articles and has up-to-date information on museums, galleries, performances, and new attractions. It also includes a good map of the downtown area showing the locations of major attractions for the month.

OUR KIDS—SAN ANTONIO

For a descripton of this magazine, see the chapter **Kids' Stuff.**

RIO

Paseo del Rio Association • 211 Broadway • 227-4262 • Monthly

This magazine tells what's going on along the River Walk and in the city. Distributed mainly in hotels and shops by the San Antonio River Association, it includes an excellent and handy map of shops and other establishments located on and near the river.

TEXAS HIGHWAYS

P.O. Box 5016, Austin 78763 • (512) 483-3689 • Monthly

A useful magazine if you like travel articles. Beautiful color pictures featuring the state's parks, scenic places, and history, with a monthly calendar of events for all sections of the state. A good buy.

TEXAS MONTHLY

P.O. Box 1569, Austin 78767 • (512) 320-6900 • Monthly

Each month the Around the State section details what's going on in Texas cities (including San Antonio), and there is a lively dining guide. The articles, by some of the best authors currently writing about Texas, often cover topics related to San Antonio.

TEXAS PARKS AND WILDLIFE
4200 Smith School Rd., Austin 78744 • (800) 792-1112 • Monthly

This is another good state publication, with excellent color photographs.

NEWSPAPERS—DAILY

DAILY COMMERCIAL RECORDER
17400 Judson Rd. • 453-3300

This business and legal newspaper, published each Monday through Friday, contains current courthouse notices and records, plus local business news.

SAN ANTONIO EXPRESS-NEWS
Avenue E and Third • 250-3000

The biggest newspaper in town and now the only surviving regular news daily in town. This morning paper is a part of the Hearst chain. Also publishes a weekly community-oriented suburban edition.

NEWSPAPERS—WEEKLY AND SUBURBAN

CURRENT
8750 Tesoro Dr. • 828-7660

This lively weekly alternative paper is a giveaway but is better written and produced than most such papers. It tackles both light material and serious San Antonio stories and provides a weekly guide to the fast-changing club and music scene. Its general orientation toward the arts and entertainment sectors includes film and art reviews as well as critical essays on local performances.

LA PRENSA DE SAN ANTONIO
113 Lexington • 242-7900

Written bilingually for the Hispanic community, this weekly paper is distributed widely in South Texas.

MEDICAL GAZETTE
17400 Judson Rd. • 453-3300

Distributed free at major medical and research facilities in the South Texas Medical Center, and other city locations, this publication has ads and articles oriented to the extensive San Antonio medical community.

METROCOM HERALD
122 E. Byrd, Universal City • 658-7424

Free suburban weekly paper for the Universal City area.

NORTH SAN ANTONIO TIMES/NORTHSIDE RECORDER TIMES
8603 Botts Lane at Cheever • 828-3321

These suburban editions emphasize matters important to area residents but perhaps too parochial to find space in the city's daily paper. In addition to the expected ads for local businesses, readers often find a particularly helpful listing of local craftspeople and tradespeople—electricians, garden workers, painters, and whatnot.

SAN ANTONIO BUSINESS JOURNAL
8200 W. I-10 • 341-3202

As the name implies, the accent is on business, with news of companies, trends, executive appointments, and transactions. Well written and researched, this paper often comes up with stories before the daily paper.

SAN ANTONIO REGISTER
235 St. Charles • 222-1721

This news weekly covers the African-American community.

SOUTHSIDE REPORTER
2203 S. Hackberry • 534-8848

This weekly covers the south side and emphasizes classified ads, especially those offering goods for sale. And it's free.

BROCHURES, BOOKLETS, ETC.

CALENDAR OF EVENTS IN SAN ANTONIO

Visitor Information Center • 317 Alamo Plaza • 270-8748 • Free

Lists festival, sporting, musical, and other events for the year.

CALENDAR OF TEXAS EVENTS

Travel and Information Division, Texas Department of Transportation • P.O. Box 5064, Austin 78763 • Free

This calendar lists what's going on all over the state; it includes fairs, armadillo races, fiddling contests, wildflower trails, balloon races, and rattlesnake roundups.

CITIZENS' GUIDES

League of Women Voters • 109 Lexington • 226-3530 Usually free

For every major local election, the league compiles a free voters' guide listing all the candidates. It also offers for sale a *Local Government Handbook*, explaining the myriad city bureaucratic organizations.

SAN ANTONIO—SAVE ON HOTELS AND ATTRACTIONS

Visitor Information Center • 317 Alamo Plaza • 270-8748 • Free

This brochure usually comes out annually. Pick up one or write to the center; it can save you money. It lists many hotel/motel special packages and includes coupons that help save on admissions at some local attractions.

Points of Interest

MAIN ATTRACTIONS

This section includes places to see that aren't easily pigeon-holed or covered in other sections, such as **Historical Places,** where you'll find the *Alamo.* For example, the San Antonio River Walk (Paseo del Rio) is part park, part historic place, yet a unique phenomenon all to itself. Because the River Walk and Market Square are the downtown heart-beats of the city, we'll begin with them and follow with Six Flags Fiesta Texas and Sea World. The other listings in this section are arranged in alphabetical order.

RIVER WALK (PASEO DEL RIO)

Downtown • Central • 227-4262 • Open at all times • Free • W ramps on W. Crockett across from La Mansion del Rio and at Casa Rio; elevator at Hilton Palacio del Rio

Here's one place that lives up to its advertising hype. The River Walk really is the essence of San Antonio. This little pip-squeak of a river is what visitors remember and natives keep going back to. The San Anto-nio River runs right through downtown, so you can't miss it. In fact, it meanders and turns so much you're forced to cross it frequently.

Part Bourbon Street, part Europe, the River Walk is one and one-half miles of delightful sidewalk cafes, shops, art galleries, bars, hotels, and landscaped parkland. This is the busy riverbend stretch, but actually the River Walk extends much farther along both sides of the river, about ten or fifteen feet below street level, among tall cypress and oak trees. You'll find steps leading down to the River Walk at various bridges, such as the one at Commerce and Losoya.

On a sunny afternoon, amid hustle and bustle, you can forget the cares of the world and sip spirits along the River Walk. At night, the River

River Walk Area (Downtown)

Houston

★ Visitor Information Center ■ Alamo

College

Crockett

San Antonio River

Losoya

Alamo St.

Commerce

■ Rivercenter Mall

St. Mary's

Navarro

Presa

San Antonio River

San Antonio River

Market

■ Arneson River Theater   Convention Center HemisFair Park

Walk romantically lights up and takes on another life, with jazz, country and western, mariachi, disco, and Irish music escaping from the bars and clubs. Also throw in the Hard Rock Cafe and Planet Hollywood.

Visiting celebrities wander about, with river groupies eyeing them. Riverside apartment dwellers, artsy individualists, and politicos converse at riverside cafes. Even a subculture of street people frequents the River Walk.

National urban planners and architects point to the River Walk as a classic example of what a city can do to revitalize its downtown area and attract people. The attractive, comfortable River Walk invites foot traffic and interaction. The river area is intimate. Of course, part of the River Walk's appeal is due to San Antonio's cosmopolitan heritage. The blending of several cultures, particularly the festive and exuberant Mexican culture, contributes to the relaxing, fun-loving atmosphere.

The River Walk is appealing precisely because it is *not* modern. The old rock walkways and walls blend in with the tropical greenery and old mercantile buildings—they even seem at home with the modern hotels, perhaps because the hotels were designed to fit into their River Walk niches. San Antonio really hasn't grown with haste, as the tourist ads say. And thank goodness.

Throughout the year, special festivals and entertainment occur along the River Walk. The river is even dyed green for St. Patrick's Day. The more popular annual River Walk events, most of which are free, include:

Mud Festival	January
River Walk Mardi Gras	February
St. Patrick's Day Festivities	March
King's River Parade (Fiesta)	April
Fiesta Mariachi	April
Nightly musical entertainment at Arneson River Theater	June–August
Great Country River Festival	September
River Art Show	October
Holiday River Parade	November
Fiesta de las Luminarias	December
Las Posadas	December

For more details, see **Annual Events**; for precise dates, which vary from year to year, see *Rio* or other publications for visitors. Many of these entertainment shows are held at the open-air Arneson River Theater on the River Walk.

Christmastime on the River Walk shouldn't be missed. At night, the lights in the trees and the candles in paper sacks lining the river's edge are really beautiful. Local carolers, often on river barges, add to the festive atmosphere.

The San Antonio River Association (see **For Your Information**) is a good source of what's happening along the River Walk with its free monthly magazine, *Rio*. Also, check the **Restaurants** and **Bars and Clubs** chapters for more details about dining and nightlife on the river. For people-watching, the Kangaroo Court is popular. They don't mind your ordering only a beer to while away the time. For a Mexican bar experience, the Esquire Tavern is marvelous. Bankers and blue-collar workers alike frequent this place after work, where what must be the longest old wooden bar in town is one main fixture, and another is the mariachis. Both the Kangaroo Court and Schilo's (the latter is above the River Walk at street level) offer reasonably priced lunches.

For a comprehensive view of the River Walk, you can board a river barge that takes you upstream to view the natives and shops. (The Rivercenter Mall is full of upscale stores.) The main "dock" is across from the Hilton Hotel, at the Market Street Bridge (see the listing for Yanaguana Cruises in the **Sightseeing Tours** section of the **Tours** chapter). Another dock is at Rivercenter.

Way back in antiquity, the Indians called the river Yanaguana, meaning "refreshing waters." Then the Spaniards arrived in 1691 and named it San Antonio de Padua (for Saint Anthony of Padua) when they camped out near the river. The Alamo, or Mission San Antonio de Valero, was built near the river. And naturally, Santa Anna's troops fought around the river in 1836 during Texas' fight for independence from Mexico. In later years, Teddy Roosevelt set up camp on it to recruit and train his Rough Riders for the Spanish-American War in 1898.

When we look at the tiny river today, it's hard to believe it once was difficult to ford and often flooded the town. Before the 1890s, when the drilling of artesian wells cut down on its flow, people even used the river for swimming. In the early 1920s, local business leaders, tired of their places being flooded, wanted to cover the horseshoe bend in the river and make it into a sewer. Fortunately, some astute women protested, thus saving it. They were the forerunners of the San Antonio Conservation Society, formed in 1924 as a result of this fight.

In the 1930s, the real aesthetic potential of the river was finally recognized, and WPA funds were used to beautify it with walkways, footbridges, and an outdoor theater. Ever since then, the city has had the good sense to treat the river like the gem that it is, occasionally extending it—such as with the branches that go to Rivercenter Mall and the Theatre for the Performing Arts at HemisFair Park. And there is always speculation about extending the landscaping all the way up to the San Antonio Museum of Art.

MARKET SQUARE

W. Commerce at Santa Rosa • Central • 207-8600 • Open daily

This festive square is usually jumping at all hours, particularly if there's the excuse of a holiday. It encompasses a large block of restored historic buildings with a promenade in between. The large building is El Mercado, a Mexican-style market crowded with small shops featuring imported Mexican goods. It's the largest Mexican market in the States. Mexican restaurants, cantinas, art galleries, and clothing shops round out the square. The square makes a perfect spot to drink *cerveza* at an outdoor cafe table or listen to Mexican entertainment.

(See Shopping section under **Mexico in San Antonio** for more details.)

SIX FLAGS FIESTA TEXAS

17000 I-10 W, northwest of intersection of I-10 and Loop 1604 Northwest • 697-5050 • Open daily in summer, weekends only in spring and fall; hours vary • Adults $36; children $17 W+ but not all areas

Six Flags Fiesta Texas, San Antonio's second major theme park, seems to be trying to have it all—music (lots of music), a water park, rides, and food. Fiesta Texas is an exuberant, varied, beautifully situated, huge attraction that can entertain, even enthrall, visitors from about three years old on up to grandparental age. The park, started as a cousin of Opryland, is now run by Six Flags. Set in an old limestone quarry with towering cliffs and dramatic views (at least from the top of the roller

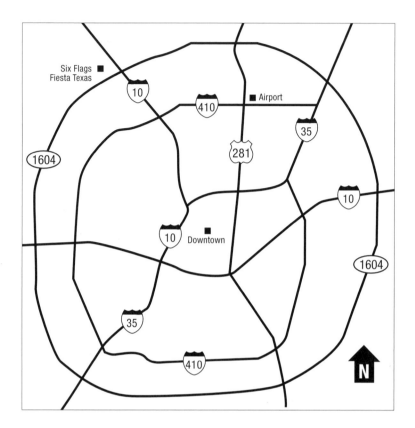

coaster), Fiesta Texas has the advantage of a splendid location. Even the cliffs have been engineered to contribute to the park—piped-up water cascades over them in several places.

Music is a big attraction, and each of the park's main areas has its own musical theme. Spassville features German music, food, and *gemutlichkeit* (which roughly translates as "amiable German enthusiasm for life"). Rockville re-creates, with a fidelity startling to some, a Texas town of the 1950s, complete with rock-and-roll music and burger palaces. Los Festivales represents a Mexican village with its own music, food, and shops. Crackaxle Canyon, a Texas boom town of the 1920s, is the place to go for barbecue, country music, and a convincing sense of time warp. There is also Fiesta Bay Boardwalk. The various areas lie only a short walk from each other.

One of the park's most visible attractions is the Rattler, a roller coaster that is one of the world's largest wooden coasters. It definitely is not for the faint-of-heart, in either the literal or the figurative sense of that expression. There is often a long line to ride the Rattler. This is a BIG coaster—enough wood went into its construction to have built almost 100 small houses. In addition, the Joker's Revenge, a steel roller coaster, twists and turns you upside down. Many other rides, including some just for the very young, are scattered throughout the park.

Also scattered here and there are all kinds of fast food stands, soft drink vendors, souvenir shops, stores with more extensive offerings, and arcade and midway games. While the admission fee covers music and rides, the games and, of course, food and drink, cost extra. Because of the hot summer weather in San Antonio, the Ol' Swimming Hole, in the water park, is especially welcome. Families planning to make full-day excursions to the park can reserve the hottest part of the day for a visit to the water slides, tube chutes, and pools, then return, refreshed, to the rest of the park. A quicker and only slightly less wet way to cool down is on the Gully Washer—a raft trip down simulated rapids, where a good splashing is guaranteed. The Power Surge is another cooler—rather like a roller coaster on the water that ends its plunge with a huge splash into a pool.

A good way to start a visit is with a ride on the narrow gauge railroad that circles the 200-acre park—it gives a good view of every section and will get you oriented. Most visitors let the musical performances determine their schedules. Some performers are park employees, but "name" entertainers are featured from time to time. The different the-aters have entertainment appropriate to the section of the park in which they are located.

Not all the music is in the theaters. You may round a corner and come upon a strolling band, such as a small brass marching band, or a German band, or singers outside the buildings. Because of such surpris-es, allow plenty of time just for strolling around the park.

SEA WORLD

Mailing address: 10500 Sea World Dr., San Antonio, TX 78251 Located at Westover Hills Blvd. and Ellison Dr. • *Going west on TX 151, exit west on Westover Hills Blvd., which runs to the main gate* **Northwest** • **523-3611** • **Open weekends in spring and fall, daily during summer. Seasonal hours vary—call ahead** • **Adults $33, children 3–11 $23. Admission ticket covers all attractions. Season passes available** • **W+ but not all areas**

San Antonio may be landlocked, but that didn't keep Sea World from planting its sea legs firmly in a 250-acre complex in the western fringe of the city. Billed as the "world's largest marine-life family entertain-ment park," Sea World of Texas is the largest of four Sea Worlds in the nation. Those who have not visited since the park's first year or two will find Sea World has added rides and diversions to the earlier mix of whales and other sea creatures, with the result that it now combines some of the best features of an amusement park and a theme park.

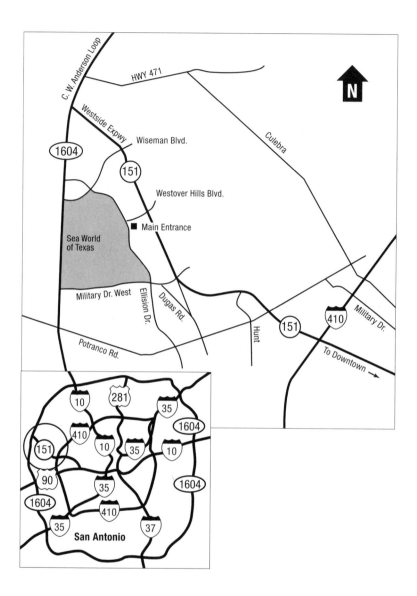

Sea World certainly lives up to its billing. Never fear, mates, there's always something going on here, with all the scheduled shows, zippy water rides, restaurants, and even big-name entertainment for special concert events during the year.

Overlooking San Antonio at the edge of the Texas Hill Country, Sea World of Texas is worth a full day's visit, particularly for families with energetic kids. The place offers plenty to amuse, entertain, and educate everybody, no matter what age: Shamu the killer whale; dolphin, beluga whale, walrus, sea lion and otter shows; a penguin exhibit; a Clydesdale horse exhibit; lake water ski performances; hands-on feeding of marine life; avian exhibits; water theme rides; a water adventure area; and a Texas history walk to boot.

Restaurants, food carts, and snack bars are scattered throughout the park, as are gift and souvenir shops. If you plan to see the whole thing in one visit, which probably will take a full day, plan on having a meal and taking a rest stop or two, if only to let the feet recuperate a bit.

SHOWS, EXHIBITS, RIDES, AND ATTRACTIONS

Shamu Show. Star Shamu and other killer whales show off their tricks in a 4,500-seat stadium. Beneath the geodesic dome roof, the multi-ton Shamu swims in a multimillion-gallon pool of man-made seawater. Spectators at poolside, especially at the end opposite the whales' entry chutes, can expect to get wet. Very wet. When you are a killer whale you can demand, and get, a big splashdown.

Beluga Whale and Dolphin Show. The world's largest oceanarium (that's what they call it) population of beluga (or white) whales and acrobatic Pacific white-sided dolphins cavort in this show. In spite of its 3,000 seats, the popular show fills up early on crowded days, so give yourself plenty of time.

Sea Lion, Walrus, and Otter Show. Sea lions, walruses, and otters perform with trainers in another large theater. This show, as befits its ungainly and naturally droll performers, emphasizes comedy rather than grace, but the skills of the animals (and their trainers) are as impressive here as elsewhere in the park.

Water-ski Show. Sea World dug and dammed its own twelve-acre lake where water-skiers do trick skiing and jumping. Some performances are laced with comedy and teenage music themes.

Penguin Exhibit. You can really cool off in this re-created Antarctic environment exhibit where four species of tuxedoed penguins dwell among rocks and snow. Just step onto the moving walkway that takes you first by the penguin habitat, then into a learning hall with multimedia displays. Alcids, or aquatic birds of the northern hemisphere, are on display nearby.

Shark and Coral Reef Exhibit. This marine-life exhibit comprises several aquariums. One 450,000-gallon aquarium houses an array of sharks, including hammerheads. Others display sea life as diverse as moray eels and grouper. A re-created coral reef displays thousands of colorful fish typical of an Indo-Pacific reef.

Water Adventure Area. This area features high water slides and an impressive wave pool, plus an alligator exhibit and walk-through aviary. If you make an all-day visit to Sea World of Texas, spend the hottest hours of the afternoon here.

Shamu's Happy Harbor. Let the kids romp in this creative three-acre playground. A clutch of paraphernalia with nautical and tropical themes offers ample opportunity for play. Climb aboard the Funship, get soaked at Virgil Pelican's Waterworks, or take in a show at Banana Cabana outdoor theater.

Water Theme Rides. The meek need not apply. Raft down the raging Rio Loco rapids ride or zoom down the Texas Splashdown log flume ride (sort of a roller coaster on water) that has a drop equivalent to that from a five-story building.

The Great White. More recently, following its competitor Fiesta Texas' lead, Sea World has added a steel roller coaster to its fun and games. It's an inverted hang-ride one.

Clydesdale Exhibit. These statuesque horses stand a full six feet tall and weigh almost a ton when full grown. Since the 1930s they have been associated with Anheuser-Busch, the current parent company of Sea World.

Texas Walk. Sixteen life-size bronze statues of famous Texans (including Alamo defender William Barret Travis) line a garden pathway, making possible a quick study of the main actors in Texas history.

Summer Night Magic. Those who visit in the summer will have a chance, if they stay until closing, to see a fireworks show and laser presentation.

Miscellaneous notes. Foreign currency change is available, wheelchair access is virtually complete, strollers, lockers, and wheelchairs can be rented, and behind-the-scenes tours are available at extra charge. There's also an in-park tram to help keep down the tramping aspect. An education department provides a variety of educational programs. Nearby is the Hyatt Regency Hill Country Resort hotel.

OTHER ATTRACTIONS

ALAMODOME
I-37 at Market • Central • 207-3663
Call for event and tour information

Move over Astrodome, the Alamodome is here, right downtown where you can't miss it. Look for something that looks like a giant Texas armadillo on its back with its legs up. Actually, those legs are towers anchoring a unique cable-suspended roof.

It seats 65,000—but the number varies depending on the configuration of its retractable seating system (the world's largest such system). Naturally, sporting events come to mind in Domeland. It can host various sports, including football, soccer, and skating (with its ice floor), and was designed with San Antonio's basketball team, the Spurs, in mind. In 1993, shortly after an opening extravaganza, the Dome provided a key facility for the U.S. Olympic festival. It also has hosted the NBA All-Star Game. It has 100 luxury suites, a private club, and food court areas (known elsewhere as concession stands). The Dome, part of the city's convention complex, is used for conventions, trade shows, conferences, and entertainment. Whether it's the rocking religious right or real rockers, the Dome plays host. Public tours are given for a fee. Parking can be a problem, and even taxis have had trouble getting near an entrance. For a major event, look into any of the numerous VIA bus lines that converge at the Dome.

The Alamodome has already held significance for San Antonio beyond its role as a sports and entertainment venue. City voters approved a special sales tax to finance it, with the result that it is one of very few such facilities built entirely debt free. The public interest in the Dome—which stems from the days when Henry Cisneros, as mayor, boosted the idea of a Dome—has played a significant role in San Antonio's recent rise in visibility.

Oh yes—one more point. Given its architecture, the facility is hardly a dome.

THE ARGYLE
934 Patterson at Argyle • Northeast • 824-1496

This nonprofit club and its member sponsors provide financial support to the Southwest Foundation for Biomedical Research (see **Education**). Located in a delightful, old three-story mansion in Alamo Heights overlooking Olmos Dam, the Argyle has a long pedigree. It was built in 1859 as headquarters of a 1,400-acre horse ranch by Charles Anderson, who was a friend of Sam Houston and was said to have had Robert E. Lee as one of his guests. Anderson was an avid Unionist, and around the Civil War, he reportedly had to hightail it out of town, disguised in women's clothes, because of his views. Some later owner named the place after his native Argyllshire, Scotland. From a ranch, it became a stagecoach inn, and then a hotel known for its food. In 1955, it was turned into a private club, and its association with the Southwest Foundation began. Don't hold your breath waiting for an invitation to join the Argyle. The best way to see it as a nonmember is to go as the guest of a friend or attend a function held there. Otherwise the club is not open to the public.

BEXAR COUNTY COURTHOUSE
Main Plaza • Central • 220-2011 • W

Fortunately, this marvelous architectural oddity hasn't been modernized excessively, at least on the outside. It lends a unique personality to the city, as do many turn-of-the-century county courthouses. Big Red, as it was called, was designed by Alfred Giles in the Romanesque Revival style and built in 1895 of Texas pink granite and sandstone. Although the building's interior has been somewhat renovated, some of the courtrooms still retain their beautiful woodwork. It's well worth the visit to drop by one day and see the cogs of justice work.

BOOTS SCULPTURE
North Star Mall, Loop 410 and San Pedro • North

These giant brown-and-white boots loom over Loop 410 from the north parking lot of North Star Mall. Some people think them gross, but I happen to like them. After all, what other kind of sculpture would you expect in Texas? Boots are so, er, fitting. Called "Justin Boots" by sculptor Robert Wade, each boot weighs in at five tons. Wade is the same fellow who did the iguana sculpture on top of the Lone Star Cafe in New York City. The boots have become a sort of landmark.

THE BRIGHT SHAWL
819 Augusta at McCullough • Central • 225-6366
Hours vary day to day—call ahead

Headquarters of the Junior League, this home is a pleasant place to visit, with comfortable antique surroundings and is also an art gallery. The house, a Texas historic landmark, was designed by Alfred Giles for the C. E. R. King family, with its nine children. The stone had to be hauled by ox cart from nearby rock quarries.

BUCKHORN SALOON AND MUSEUM
318 E. Houston • Central • 247-4000

Buckhorn Saloon lives again. Belly up to the old wooden bar and ogle the animal trophies in a new attractive location.

HEMISFAIR PARK
Bounded by Alamo Street, I-37, Durango, and Market
Central • 207-8522 • W

This ninety-two-acre plaza in downtown San Antonio provided the site for the World's Fair in 1968, when the city celebrated its 250th anniversary. In the urban renewal process to construct the fair, some delightful old homes and historic buildings were retained. Today, HemisFair Park consists of several landscaped park areas, the landmark Tower of the Americas, a museum, a branch of the National University of Mexico, restaurants, amusements, art galleries, a theater, and a convention center. The highly acclaimed Institute of Texan Cultures is located here (see **Museums** for details, as well as the Tower of the Americas listing in this section).

This whole park makes for a good stroll for the family. The water park area has stunning ponds and falls, and little kids love the children's playground, full of natural-wood climbing structures and swings.

IMAX THEATRE
Rivercenter, Bonham at Crockett • Central • 225-4629 • Open daily
Adults $6.95, children $4.75 for Alamo movie alone

The IMAX theater, located in the Rivercenter Mall downtown believes in BIG-screen movies. A movie about the battle of the Alamo is shown on a giant screen, about six stories high, in a 430-seat theater. Jim Bowie and Davy Crockett are indeed larger-than-life heroes. This movie, *The Alamo . . . the Price of Freedom* was specially made for this theater, just a cannon shot from the Alamo itself. The theater also shows other movies, in alternation with the Alamo film.

LA VILLITA

South Alamo at Nueva • Central • 207-8610 • Open daily

This quaint, historic area of restored buildings is perfect for strolling, and many entertainment events are held here annually. It harbors shops and artisans selling their wares, along with some restaurants. (See **Historical Places** for details.)

PEARL BREWERY

312 Pearl Pkwy. at Avenue A • Near North • 226-0231
Not open to public except during special events

While driving on I-37 just north of the downtown area, you may notice a delightful cream-and-yellow Victorian structure looming to the west. This is Pearl Brewery, established in 1886. San Antonio has always been a good beer town, what with its German contingent. A replica of Judge Roy Bean's old saloon and courthouse stands there. Judge Bean was enamored of the English actress Lillie Langtry and named his West Texas town Langtry and his saloon The Jersey Lilly (misspelling it) in the late 1800s. Bean lived in San Antonio at one time. He had a dairy on what is now Glenn Avenue. When customers found minnows in the milk, he supposedly explained that the cows had lapped them up from the river!

PLAZA THEATRE OF WAX & RIPLEY'S BELIEVE IT OR NOT

301 Alamo Plaza at Houston • Central • 224-9299 • Open daily
9–10 during summertime; slightly shorter hours in winter • Adults
$11.95, children $7.95

If you enjoy wax museums, look for this one across from the Alamo. The likes of Charlton Heston, Michael Jackson, Frankenstein, Joan Crawford, Dracula, and Davy Crockett can be seen waxing eloquently. The collection includes Hollywood, historic, and horror film celebs. Ripley's, with 500 really weird items, shares the same building.

SAN ANTONIO CONVENTION CENTER

In HemisFair Park at Market and Alamo Street • Central
207-8500

Conventioneers love to come to San Antonio because the convention complex stands right in the middle of downtown, near all those places tourists want to visit—the Alamo, River Walk, and Market

Square. No need to take a cab; just walk or catch a trolley. San Antonio is known for being a fun city, and who wants a dull convention? The large convention complex includes exhibition and banquet halls and a theater. Of course, the huge Alamodome sits a couple of blocks away, with its allied facilities for conferences, meetings, trade shows, and conventions. The convention complex is within easy walking distance of most downtown hotels.

SOUTHWEST CRAFT CENTER

300 Augusta at Navarro • Central • 224-1848
Monday through Saturday 10–5 • Free • W

This center for creative artisans and the teaching of handicrafts offers a pleasant downtown oasis. It's also another example of how the city has made use of its unique historical structures. These quaint buildings, reflecting French architecture with their mustard-and-blue trim and red tin roofs, used to be Ursuline Academy (see **Historical Places**), a Catholic girls' school. They now house a gallery, a restaurant, a private club, and classrooms for teaching everything from weaving and painting to sculpture and photography. The first girls' school in town, the Ursuline Sisters started Ursuline Academy in 1851 on ten acres of land on the San Antonio River. Since San Antonio was full of immigrants, they had to teach separate groups in German, French, Spanish, and English. The San Antonio Conservation Society saved these marvelous old structures from demolition after the sisters moved the school to a new location. The society bought the property in 1965 and worked with the nonprofit Southwest Craft Center to find funding for restoration and eventual ownership. The Craft Center offers courses for all ages. But even if you don't wish to enroll, this is a good place to browse around. The old buildings are captivating, with wooden floors and pews and artwork on the walls. The Copper Kitchen lunchroom (open Monday through Friday for lunch only) serves informal, inexpensive soups and sandwiches in a comfortable, historical setting. Serve yourself cafeteria-style and eat in the old dormitory hall. Or bring a sack lunch and enjoy the shady courtyard and gazebo on the river. Also, a gallery with exhibits and artists' wares for sale graces the premises. Be sure to see the picturesque chapel, built in the 1860s, with its lovely stained glass. Call to arrange group tours.

TOWER OF THE AMERICAS

HemisFair Park near Bowie and Market • Central • 207-8615
Observation deck open Sunday through Thursday
9 a.m.–10 p.m.; Friday through Saturday 9 a.m.–11 p.m.
Adults $3, children $1 • W

The most obvious landmark at HemisFair Park is the 622-foot (750 including antenna) tower that soars abruptly into the San Antonio skyline. A starkly modern structure, it has a revolving restaurant at the top, where you can view the whole 360° panorama of the city and its surrounding hills and brush country. It takes about an hour of breaking bread to make one revolution. Daytime viewing is good, but the city's night lights provide a romantic backdrop. For the most spectacular views, try to time your visit and choose your table so you will face the west as the sun sets. If you've got a weak stomach for heights, avoid the glass elevator or at least be prepared to face the rear of the car; it zips up in fifty-two seconds to the top, where an observation deck awaits your arrival.

UNION STOCKYARDS

1716 S. San Marcos at Pendleton • South • 223-6331
Open daily • Free

Now if you want to see what real cowmen look like, head out for Union Stockyards. You'll also get the real scent of the cattle business. Started in 1889, it's the oldest market south of Kansas City. See the weather-beaten pens and the auction center where ranchers and buyers get together to buy and sell meat on the hoof. The cattle auctions are held Monday and Wednesday mornings. You may not be able to catch the auctioneer's words, however. To give you some idea of how fast they talk, they sometimes auction an average of 225 to 325 head of cattle an hour. The Exchange Building across from the yards houses not only administrative offices but also a cafe.

UNITED SERVICES AUTOMOBILE ASSOCIATION (USAA) BUILDING

9800 Fredericksburg Rd. near Huebner • Northwest
498-2211 • W+

This is one of the office wonders of the world. Indeed, the USAA headquarters building is the nation's second largest office building of its kind. And seeing *is* believing. Surprisingly, this edifice is architecturally interesting. When the insurance company built its offices on these 286 rolling acres between Fredericksburg Road and I-10, it retained the oaks and included courtyards for its employees. The building is six stories high, although only three office levels appear above ground, with about four million square feet of space. It has a company store, library, post office, physical fitness center, and cafeterias. The courtyards are landscaped with casual eating areas and exhibits. Call about special civic or school tours. USAA offers no tours for the general public, but one can drive around the main building.

HISTORIC PLACES

Much of San Antonio's history remains obvious. Historical sites, buildings, and markers flood San Antonio more than anywhere else in the state. Some are unmistakable and easy to find, while others take a little searching out and are perhaps the more interesting. A walk through downtown San Antonio and La Villita will give you a sense of the city's age, something absent from other Texas cities.

Best known among San Antonio's rich and rewarding historical sites is the Alamo—originally known as Mission San Antonio de Valero—an attraction for Texans and out-of-state visitors alike. Equally impressive are the city's other four missions. The Spanish Governors' Palace downtown also reflects the spirit of San Antonio's Spanish heritage.

The role of Spanish influence in shaping the American West goes far beyond the language spoken by half the area's inhabitants and beyond the religious traditions. It even includes the agricultural life associated with the Southwest. The word *ranch* comes from the Spanish *rancho* and indicates a way of profiting from the land that was well established in Spanish and New Spanish agricultural areas long before the Anglos moved into the Southwest.

Many of the historical sites commemorate the Spanish and Mexican past of San Antonio. La Villita and the Spanish Governors' Palace represent contrasting extremes of simplicity and elegance in Spanish and Mexican experience in San Antonio.

THE ALAMO

Alamo Plaza at Alamo Street and Houston • Central
225-1391 • Monday through Saturday 9–5:30, Sunday 10–5:30
('til 6:30 daily in summer) • Free • W

The remains of the Alamo (in downtown San Antonio) can now scarcely do more than suggest the dimensions of the fort that approximately 189 defenders (numbers on both sides are still debated) held from February 23 to March 6, 1836, against a Mexican army estimated to number 1,500 to 2,500 (see **History**). What remains is the chapel of the Alamo; the entire stronghold was far larger—probably twice the size of what is now called Alamo Plaza. Past construction in Alamo Plaza, directly across from the Alamo, has revealed traces of the wall that enclosed the compound. Inside the Alamo, the Daughters of the Republic of Texas have established both a shrine and a number of exhibits of objects relevant to the defenders. The shrine is neither chauvinistic nor gaudy. In contrast to some of the rhetoric about the Alamo, it is a dignified, moving, and evocative tribute to the fallen. Texas may claim all those brave defenders who died as being among the state's first heroes, but the exhibits show that they came from many states and countries. The exhibits emphasize the history of the Alamo in 1836, plus its earlier life as a mission. In fact, the Alamo was the first mission established in San Antonio, in 1718, and was called Mission San Antonio de Valero.

OTHER MISSIONS

Between 1691, when the first Spanish trod the area that would become San Antonio, and 1718, when the first mission (the Alamo) was established, San Antonio existed as a named place, not a settlement with a European presence. Beginning in 1718, not one, but five missions were established inside what is now the city of San Antonio.

Amazingly, all five of those missions still exist. Most are not in their original forms; they have been reconstructed to a greater or lesser extent at one time or another, and they have all been closed or secularized from time to time. A visitor to the historical sites of San Antonio can visit all five and so absorb some of the atmosphere that was San Antonio's during the eighteenth century.

Excluding the Alamo downtown, the other four missions comprise the San Antonio Missions National Historical Park in the south part of the city. Actually, the park isn't all in one place but occupies four different locations along the San Antonio River, where the missions were built to take advantage of the water resource. This particular park doesn't have camping facilities like some, but some of the sites are pastoral due to their vast acreages and sparse populations. The National Park Service runs this park in conjunction with the Catholic Church because some missions still operate as parish churches. Our Lady of the Lake University has many mission documents in its library, the primary repository of source documents for the history of the missions.

Of the five missions, the Alamo has become the least evocative of its original purpose. The battle at the Alamo in 1836 occurred well after the mission had been abandoned as a place of worship, and hence the historical significance of the site overshadows its religious importance.

Missions were much more than churches. They were used to expand the frontiers of Spain and of the church and, at least in Texas, to contest the influence of the French, who were spreading into Texas from the east, just as the Spanish were from the south.

A mission brought an entirely new way of life to the Indians already living in Texas. The process did not simply attempt to spread Catholic religious beliefs to Indians and leave their lives otherwise untouched. Rather, Indians of the missions learned a new system of living—agriculturally, politically, economically, and spiritually. They even had to learn a new language and were given Spanish names. Much of an Indian's time in a mission, when not devoted to productive labor (mostly agricultural), was spent learning. Missions also taught building techniques, crafts, farming and ranching methods, and of course religion.

As one might imagine, the Indians weren't entirely enthused about being force-fed this new culture and frequently came and went from the missions. Evidently, when the Indians returned to the missions, they did not always do so wholly voluntarily. The early accounts repeatedly mention the padres' having to go out and convince them to return. Sometimes soldiers assisted in the process. Ironically, the missions offered the Indians relative safety from the raids of rival tribes, which occasionally swept through the San Antonio area.

For more background information and detailed maps on the Alamo and other San Antonio missions, see *Texas Missions, a Lone Star Guidebook.*

SAN ANTONIO MISSIONS NATIONAL HISTORICAL PARK

In four locations along the San Antonio River, beginning with Mission Concepcion at 807 Mission Rd. at Felisa • South 534-8833 (park headquarters) • Open daily 9–5 • Free

This national park (not a camping one) includes four Spanish missions at different locations along the San Antonio River as it meanders in south San Antonio. You can do a quick tour of the missions in a half day, but it makes more sense to take a picnic lunch and make a day of it. (Missions are listed in geographical order from downtown San Antonio.)

MISSION CONCEPCION

807 Mission Rd. at Felisa • South • 534-1540 • W with assistance

All that remains of many missions, in San Antonio and elsewhere, are the church buildings. And of the church buildings in San Antonio, that of Mission Concepcion, or Mission Nuestra Senora de La Purisima Concepcion de Acuna, is one of the most graceful and handsome— even without substantial reconstruction or restoration. Indeed, Mission Concepcion is one of the oldest unrestored stone church buildings in the country. The mission was first founded in East Texas in 1716 but did not flourish, in part because of the hardships of poor crops and illness and in part because of conflict between Spain and France. After two or three false starts, Mission Concepcion reopened in San Antonio in 1731 on the same date as the founding of Mission San Francisco de la Espada and Mission San Juan Capistrano and only days before the Canary Islanders arrived in San Antonio. The present church building was dedicated in 1755. Mission Concepcion became part of Mission San Jose in 1794 and in 1813 ceased to be a place of religious services; shortly afterward, all inhabitants abandoned it. Of the full mission compound, only the church itself and a few closely associated buildings still stand. Be sure to pick up a copy of the brochure about the missions. Many features warrant mentioning; for example, even the decorative arts in the mission are originals, not restorations.

MISSION SAN JOSE

3200 block of Roosevelt at Napier • South • 932-1001
W variable

Here, more than at any of the other missions, you can grasp a sense of what daily life must have been like for the Indians and missionaries. Mission San Jose gives an impression of the extent to which mission life embodied an entire way of life. Founded in 1720, San Jose was the second of five local missions to open its doors, although it was not moved to its present site until years later. The present church building's construction began about 1768. During its early days, Mission San Jose was highly successful both in recruiting Indians to mission life and in developing its agricultural program. The mission contained a granary, a blacksmith shop, a carpenter shop, and a sugar mill, as well as other workshops necessary to agricultural enterprise. The work of the mission continued until 1794, when it was partially secularized. Then, in 1824, it was abandoned. Most of the mission compound was restored and reconstructed in the late 1930s through the combined efforts of the Catholic Church, the San Antonio Conservation Society, the WPA, and Bexar County. The facade and much of the outside of Mission San Jose's church are original. The intricate stone carving of the window on the south side of the church, the legendary rose window, is one of the most celebrated in San Antonio.

MISSION SAN JUAN CAPISTRANO

9100 block of Graf at Ashley • South • 534-0749

Mission San Juan Capistrano, like Mission Espada, had its origins in East Texas and was moved to San Antonio in hopes of finding more fertile fields for missionary success. The ancient Payaya village named Yanaguana ("refreshing waters") probably stood close to the site of the mission. The village was the place first named San Antonio in 1691 when the first Spaniards passed through the area. Here one can feel in touch with the aspects of San Antonio that the Spaniards described almost 300 years ago. That feeling of peace, emphasized by the mission's setting in a bosky area that seems many miles from central San Antonio, still prevails. Today, the chapel at the mission is very much in use and serves as the parish church.

MISSION SAN FRANCISCO DE LA ESPADA
10040 Espada Rd. • South • 627-2021

The smallest, most isolated, and perhaps most charming of the missions, Espada retains the air of an outpost in the wilderness. Although Mission Espada was established in San Antonio in 1731, the same year and even the same day as Mission Concepcion and Mission San Juan Capistrano, and thirteen years after Mission San Antonio de Valero (the Alamo), it has a longer history than any of the other four missions in San Antonio. First started in East Texas in 1690, it failed to thrive, was closed though not disbanded, and eventually was resettled at or near its present location. Like the rest of the missions, Espada had its hard times, aggravated by friction between its missionary and the governor. At times of danger from hostile Apaches, the governor often recalled the mission's soldiers to the city, leaving the mission without a trained protector. In 1745, only six years after a disastrous smallpox epidemic, the mission's Indian population was 204, and the mission's cattle herd numbered 1,150, plus goats, sheep, and horses. Such animal husbandry was carried on in addition to raising crops in irrigated fields. Clearly, the administration and management of even a small mission, such as Espada, involved a major undertaking.

ESPADA AQUEDUCT
9044 Espada • South

Massive but graceful, this masterpiece of hydrological engineering has survived almost two and a half centuries and testifies to the skill and determination of the Spanish missionaries. To ensure good crops, the padres used the rivers to irrigate their fields. The old *acequias*, or irrigation ditches, remain in a few places, and this watercourse is the most dramatic. Arches span Piedras Creek, carrying the water impounded in the dam, equally ancient, about a kilometer or so away on the San Antonio River. The aqueduct irrigated 2,000 to 3,000 acres, or close to four square miles.

OTHER HISTORIC SITES

CASA NAVARRO STATE HISTORICAL PARK
228 S. Laredo at Nueva • Central • 226-4801 • Wednesday through Sunday 10–4 • Adults $2, children $1 • W

One of the few remaining historically significant structures in San Antonio that suggest an accurate picture of life during the last century is the Navarro Historical Park, nestling now in the shadow of the old Bexar County Jail and once the residence of a prominent citizen and statesman. Jose Antonio Navarro was one of only two signers of the

Texas Declaration of Independence who were native Texans. He was a lawyer, the mayor of San Antonio at the time of Mexican independence from Spain, a representative to the legislature of the Mexican state that included San Antonio, a prisoner of Mexico for playing a part in the Texans' struggle for independence, and a senator in the Texas legislature. Navarro was also the only native-born Texan at Washington-on-the-Brazos when the constitution of the new state of Texas was drafted. The site consists of the kitchen, the office, and the house. The buildings are constructed of a combination of adobe and native limestone, or *caliche*. The furnishings are typical of Navarro's period. The Navarro Historical Park is a popular place for schoolchildren to visit, and special tours can be arranged. In the large yard of the compound, you'll find demonstrations of adobe making from time to time.

KING WILLIAM HISTORIC DISTRICT

King William Street and surrounding area • Central
W variable

In the last half of the nineteenth century, the German element of San Antonio's population had much of the social, economic, and political power in San Antonio. One of their number, Ernst Altgelt, laid out King William Street, planned it as the most exclusive address in town, and named it after Kaiser Wilhelm. Impressive though the street is, it was to have been even longer and grander, but a mill on the river at the end of the street put a stop to further expansion. Now, a century later, the street is one of the most captivating in Texas. It marks the center of one of the city's most desirable and handsome neighborhoods. In fact, the King William Historic District was the first historic district to be so designated in the state. Although you can see it from a car, the area is small enough for touring by foot. Most of the houses are private residences not open to the public (except on special occasions), but you can tour the Steves Homestead (see below), and the San Antonio Conservation Society has offices at 107 King William Street. The Guenther House (205 E. Guenther, 227-1061), built in 1860 by the Pioneer Mills founder, is also open, and its small restaurant is a cheery spot to lunch.

LA VILLITA

Bounded by Nueva, S. Alamo, S. Presa, and the river
Central • 207-8610 • Open at all times

La Villita has undergone one of those peculiarly American treatments—it has been spruced up and renovated to make it more authentic. From San Antonio's earliest days, a settlement has existed in La Villita. General Cos surrendered his Mexican troops to Texas revolutionaries at a house that still stands on Villita Street. Although La Villita is associated primarily with the Mexican population of San Antonio, during the last half of the nineteenth century as many European immigrants called it home as native San Antonians. By the 1930s, La Villita had become a blighted area, and San Antonio Mayor Maverick helped organize and support an effort to clean up the area and save its picturesque aspects. Today, La Villita is the home of shops, artists, and many small businesses. And every spring during Fiesta, La Villita is the scene of A Night in Old San Antonio, an event that fills the area with thousands of celebrants. La Villita is an ideal spot for a stroll (see **Tours**).

MAIN PLAZA AND MILITARY PLAZA

Between Commerce and Dolorosa, from Cameron to Soledad
Central • Open at all times • W

The bulk of the city's commercial activities has drifted away from the two plazas that used to be the heart of the city. When the first civil colonizers of San Antonio arrived from the Canary Islands, they set up La Plaza de las Islas (now Main Plaza) and called their settlement San Fernando. Just to the west, the military presidio had its own plaza, called La Plaza de las Armas (now called Military Plaza). The two plazas have continued to form the administrative and legal centers of Bexar County, with both the Bexar County Courthouse and City Hall located here. San Fernando Cathedral (see below) stretches from the east side of Military Plaza to the west side of Main Plaza. Main Plaza, shaded by old trees and decorated by a fountain, helps give San Antonio its atmosphere of antiquity. Just to the west lies Military Plaza, equally historical but less a public gathering place in early San Antonio than a military parade ground, barracks area, and headquarters. Today, the plaza is dominated by City Hall, a massive but pleasingly ornate building placed squarely in the center of the plaza. Look at one corner of City Hall for a bust of Franklin D. Roosevelt; diagonally across the plaza you'll find a grand statue of Moses Austin by Waldine Tauch, a native San Antonian. On the northwest corner of Military Plaza sits the well-restored Spanish Governors' Palace (see below).

SAN FERNANDO CATHEDRAL

115 Main Plaza between Commerce and Dolorosa • Central
227-1297 • Open daily 6–6 • W

In 1731, when the Canary Islanders established their new settlement of San Fernando, they had no satisfactory place of worship and immediately sought to establish their own church. Approval from the governor came seven years after their arrival, in 1738. A special fund raised from local purses started the building, but not until 1749, with assistance from the king of Spain, was the church completed. The mission baptismal and other records were sent to the church at San Fernando when the missions relinquished their religious roles. The old church's bells were used for warning of approaching Indians as well as for celebration. James Bowie married Ursula Veramendi in the San Fernando church, and during the siege of the Alamo, Santa Anna used it as an observation post. The present structure, San Fernando Cathedral, incorporates some of the original church's construction and is of more interest for its historical significance than as an exemplar of cathedral architecture. One of the historical sidelights of the cathedral is that in 1936 the remains of human bones were discovered beneath it. They were thought to be remains of the defenders of the Alamo, but scholars have disputed such a claim.

SOUTHERN PACIFIC RAILROAD DEPOT

1174 E. Commerce at Hoefgen • Central • W

The old Southern Pacific Depot is notable both for the role it has played in San Antonio's transportation and for its splendid design. Fortunately, it has been restored and thus will not take its place among other architectural gems of American railroading as a mere memory. Stop in for a look at the ornate interior when you visit St. Paul's Square. It's been recently restored and turned into an entertainment complex.

SPANISH GOVERNORS' PALACE

105 Military Plaza • Central • 224-0601 • Monday through Saturday 9–5, Sunday 10–5 • Adults $1, children 50¢ • W with assistance

Of all the historical sites in San Antonio, this one gives the best impression of the way a culture of Spanish traditions dominated early San Antonio. To visit the Governors' Palace is to be whisked back through two centuries to the days when a succession of captains, mayors, and governors lived here. Certainly the residence did not always equal the splendor to which the San Antonio Conservation Society has now restored the structure and its garden, but a tradition of high officials has lived there. The building has also seen less noble uses, serving variously as a store, a school, a restaurant, and a bar. Today, the Governors' Palace offers an oasis away from San Antonio's traffic, noise, and heat. A visit impresses one with that part of the Spanish character that sought order, beauty, and tranquility, even in the midst of an often inhospitable frontier. The garden in back of the house makes a good place to sit for a while to absorb the atmosphere of Spain in the middle of San Antonio.

STEVES HOMESTEAD

509 King William St. at Johnson • Central • 225-5924
Open daily 10–4:15 • Adults $2, children under 12 free

The San Antonio Conservation Society now owns and operates the Steves Homestead, built in 1876 by Eduard Steves. Located in the heart of the King William Historic District, it is the only one of the mansions on King William Street regularly open for display and tours. It gives a good view of what life must have been like a century ago in San Antonio's fanciest area. The furnishings and kitchen equipment hail from the same period as the house. One especially interesting item is an inlaid table, which could easily be a museum piece. The River Haus, on the rear of the property, harbored the city's first indoor swimming pool. Members of the Conservation Society conduct tours of the Steves Homestead and include informative comments about the King William area. Most of the other houses in the neighborhood have been restored to their original states and are still in use—revealing San Antonians' taste for antiquity.

URSULINE ACADEMY

300 Augusta at Navarro • Central • 224-1848 • Monday through Saturday 10–5 • W with assistance

The Ursuline Academy originally occupied this location, which is now a crafts school and gallery owned by the Southwest Craft Center (see **Points of Interest**). The buildings date to the middle of last century—a Frenchman built the oldest as a private dwelling, but unforeseen domestic differences (his wife apparently did not appreciate the chance to live on the American frontier and declined to leave France) led him to sell it to Ursuline nuns, who started the first school for girls in San Antonio. One can see the cultural diversity of San Antonio, even in those days, through the polyglot nature of the instruction—classes were taught in English, French, Spanish, and German. The grounds and buildings are very much worth a visit, especially to see the simple but well-proportioned chapel and the clock tower with faces on only three sides (the population to the north was apparently too sparse to warrant a clock face on that side). People routinely rent the chapel for parties and receptions—it is one of the grandest and most historically interesting places in town to have a party. The Conservation Society owned the buildings from the time the school moved until the 1970s, when the Crafts Center bought the property. Ursuline provides a perfect place to stroll and have a light lunch at the pleasant lunchroom.

YTURRI-EDMUNDS HOUSE AND MILL

257 Yellowstone at Mission Road • South • 534-8237 or 224-6163 Days and hours may vary, call ahead • Admission

The Yturri-Edmunds site lies a bit off the beaten path, but if you are visiting the nearby missions, then a stop may be in order. The adobe house dates from the nineteenth century and is almost the only house of such age open to the public. In good condition, the house has hosted inhabitants until recently and is furnished with period furniture. One interesting peculiarity involves the *acequia,* which goes under the house to the mill. This was a lateral of the water ditch built for Mission Concepcion's fields. The mill, now electrically driven, still operates, at least for demonstrations. Well-informed docents act as guides to explain the history of the house, including its last owner, a legendary San Antonio teacher who spent almost a half-century in the public schools.

HISTORY

What makes San Antonio stand out from its Texas urban siblings? For one thing, it's a maverick kind of town that has kept in touch with its hard-earned past. And it has used that past to good advantage, preserving historical sites and making them both accessible and interesting (and, serendipitously, a magnet to the travel industry).

San Antonio has always attracted unfettered types, such as the Alamo's Jim Bowie and Davy Crockett. Even the word *maverick* comes from a local—old Sam Maverick, who let his cattle run about unbranded so often in the mid-1800s that folks took to calling them mavericks.

One can observe this same unbranded quality in modern-day San Antonio, where people still have a don't-push-us attitude about change simply for change's sake. That's why, unlike many other cities that have bulldozed everything in the name of progress, San Antonio still retains many of its older, unique buildings and a downtown with warmth and character that tourists flock to. The plucky San Antonio Conservation Society can take credit for much of this. It has fought cornice and nail with commercial interests over retaining many a historic site or building and so has preserved much of San Antonio's unique historical patina.

So what *is* the history of San Antonio?

It's a long one, beginning in the late 1690s, when enterprising Spaniards first camped along the San Antonio River. This later led to the establishment of five Spanish missions, including the Alamo, in San Antonio in the early 1700s. Today, San Antonio is the only city in the United States to have so many missions in its confines.

This mission period was the first of a chain of watershed events in the city's history. After the decline of the missions, the siege and fall of the Alamo was a watershed event of much more than local significance, for it was a prelude to the turning point in the history of Texas and the whole of what is now the American Southwest. The next watershed event involved the arrival of a stream of European, primarily German, immigrants to San Antonio. With the coming of the railroads, another watershed, the city changed overnight from an isolated outpost to part of a network of interconnected cities. When the railroad reached San Antonio, the city entered the modern age. The final event was more diffuse—the government's string of decisions that resulted in San Antonio's becoming the home city for the United States Air Force. Thus, the military became a dominant employer and economic force in San Antonio. Each of those events colored an era, and each influenced the city's direction.

The early history of San Antonio was the history of Indian tribes and events. But no written records, other than the observations of passing explorers, survive. When Europeans first officially visited San Antonio in 1691, in the persons of Domingo Teran de los Rios—by then the governor of Texas—and Father Damian Massanet, they found a Payaya tribe, whom they described as friendly, camped on the river bank. Because the date was June 13, a saint's day commemorating Saint Anthony of Padua, his name was given to the spot, which was probably somewhere near the present Mission San Juan.

FOUNDING OF THE ALAMO AND OTHER MISSIONS

The giving of a name during the course of a brief stop is hardly the equivalent of founding a settlement. In spite of the favorable reports of the area by Teran and Massanet, the early visit went largely unnoted, and in 1709, another party of Spaniards, seeking a site for a new mission, again came upon the area. Unaware that it had been named previously, they also called the river San Antonio de Padua. One of those in the party, Father Antonio Olivares, was a missionary in South Texas whose mission was not prospering and who was determined to try again elsewhere. In 1718, he returned in concert with Governor Martin de Alarcon to found Mission San Antonio de Valero and Villa de Bexar, the military and civil outpost associated with the mission and with the governance of the Texas province.

That mission, in due course, became the best known of all the Spanish missions in the American Southwest, not under its original name, but under its nickname, the Alamo. In all, five missions were founded around San Antonio (it is debatable whether another aborted settlement was ever a full mission or not) and prospered to a greater or lesser extent. Mission San Jose was founded two years after the founding of the Alamo. Eleven years later, in 1731, the other three missions opened (the section **Historical Places** covers their histories briefly). In the same year, a little band of fifty-five Canary Islands settlers arrived as a token civilian population sent optimistically by Spain to promote the settlement of Texas.

During the ensuing century, the missions proved unequal to the task of converting and retaining large numbers of Indians. The missions survived but did not thrive; they failed to become a continuing force advancing Spanish influence. Much of the credit for their survival must go to the energy and determination of the padres, who lived in difficult circumstances and some of whom died martyrs. The reasons given for the ultimate failure of the missions vary—they include the epidemics that ravaged the missions periodically; an overly rigid social structure, both at the missions and in the town, which allowed no dynamic society to form; feuding and quarreling among the various Spanish groups; and repeated raids by the Apache and Comanche Indians, the two tribes the missionaries never persuaded to join the missions. Even the Canary Islands settlers, long without professional people or even a school, lurched along from feud to crisis and did not develop a strong presence.

The missions were partially secularized a process of removing the property from church control, toward the end of the eighteenth century, and all were completely secularized by 1824. In 1793, Mission San Antonio was the first of the five to be secularized. Eight years after the church left, the military moved in, and a cavalry detachment romantically known as the Second Flying Company of San Carlos del Alamo de Parras occupied the structure. The company had been sent from the northern Mexican town of Pueblo de San Carlos del Alamo de Parras. The shortened name, the Alamo, stuck, not only to the company but also to the former mission building it occupied in San Antonio.

UNDER MEXICAN RULE

Today, more than a century and a half after the siege and fall of the Alamo in 1836, historians still debate the motivations, the characters, and even the actions of the defenders. The roots of the conflict that led to the events at the Alamo are complex. General Antonio Lopez de Santa Anna was not only the general of the Mexican Army; he was also the autocratic president of Mexico, independent since 1821. He did not react tolerantly to the idea of a revolt in Texas; he and his army were in Texas to keep Texas in the Mexican camp.

As a part of Mexico, Texas had always been a bit different—it had never been part of the Aztec Empire, which Spain had conquered, but rather had been settled as much to keep the French at their distance as to extend the frontier of New Spain.

During and following the close of the missions, which had produced reliable crops thanks to a well-tended irrigation system, the town declined in agricultural production and prosperity. The years between the Alamo's secularization and its use as a fortress against Santa Anna saw the mission compound used mainly as a military post, although the chapel apparently continued to serve for religious services. Those years were hard for San Antonio. Between the start of the Mexican Revolution in 1810 and the independence of Mexico in 1821, San Antonio suffered for its sympathy to the cause of Mexican independence.

Repeated battles raged in and near San Antonio between forces loyal to the king of Spain and forces dedicated to an independent Mexico. In the bloodiest of these, General Joaquin de Arredondo, in 1813, defeated the revolutionaries at the Battle of the Medina, where he virtually eliminated the so-called Army of the North, a force of about 3,000. The savagery of the conflict is attested to by Arredondo's having executed, without trial, 300 prisoners taken at the battle. Santa Anna, a lieutenant in Arredondo's forces, would return to San Antonio, to the Alamo, twenty-three years later as autocrat of an independent Mexico, again fighting rebels in the north.

After the Battle of the Medina, San Antonio could do little more than aim for survival and await better times. Those better times appeared to be at hand in 1821, when Mexico attained its independence from Spain. But at the same time, another event of deep significance was taking place. Moses Austin, father of Stephen F. Austin, had arrived in San Antonio in 1820 with a request for permission from the Spanish governor to settle 300 families in Texas.

Those 300 were to consist of Anglos, not Spaniards, and settlers, not explorers or adventurers. For the first time, residents of the young nation of the United States would come to live and establish families in Texas. Spanish resentment of Anglos, whom the Spaniards considered largely responsible for the revolutionary spirit threatening Spanish rule, prompted the governor to turn Austin down. As Austin was leaving, however, he encountered an old friend, the baron of Bastrop, to whom he explained his mission. The baron sympathized with Austin's goals and eventually persuaded Arredondo to grant the permission. The way was open for the first elements of what became a flood of Anglo immigration into Texas and the American West.

Moses Austin died before seeing the families arrive in Texas, but Stephen F. Austin fulfilled his father's dream and brought numerous families to settle along the Brazos River. The story of those settlements lies beyond the history of San Antonio, although it remains a vital chapter in the history of Texas. The families that came as a result of Austin's efforts made up the first large body of Texas settlers with ties neither to Spain nor to Mexico.

Texas, in the meantime, thrived as part of an independent Mexico. As a condition of settlement in Texas, Austin's settlers had to become Catholic and to accept Mexican citizenship. The settlers agreed to both these conditions on paper, but their commitment was based on convenience, not conviction. The new Texans, including those in and around San Antonio, were not dedicated to the Mexican state.

When the heady idea of independence and establishment of a republic began to circulate in Texas, Santa Anna sent General Martin Perfecto de Cos to San Antonio to put an immediate stop to any such foolishness. Cos occupied San Antonio, but a force of Texans and a mixed crowd of American frontiersmen, drawn to Texas for a variety of reasons, recaptured the city and accepted Cos's surrender in the Cos House, still standing, in La Villita. Colonel Ben Milam led the forces that recaptured the city, but he also fell in the fighting. Milam Square, just north of Market Square, is named in his honor.

BATTLE OF THE ALAMO

Had the victorious troops stayed in San Antonio, the course of Texas history might have been very different. But they left, leaving only a handful behind to defend the city and the Alamo. A scant ten weeks later, Mexican troops returned to San Antonio, not only to quell a nascent revolt but also to avenge a defeat. This time they were led not by General Cos, but by his brother-in-law, Santa Anna himself, and this time the Mexican troops won a victory, which in the end led to their defeat.

On February 23, 1836, the advance units of Santa Anna's troops swirled into San Antonio and made the Yturri House on Main Plaza their headquarters. William B. Travis, James Bowie, and their irregulars, soon to be joined by David Crockett and his followers, withdrew to the Alamo. The day after the Mexicans' arrival, Travis wrote the document that stands as the most famous in Texas history:

> Commandancy of the Alamo
> Bexar, Feby. 24th, 1836

To the People of Texas and All Americans in the World

Fellow Citizens and Compatriots:

I am besieged with a thousand or more of the Mexicans under Santa Anna. I have sustained a continual Bombardment & cannonade for 24 hours & have not lost a man. The enemy has demanded surrender at discretion, otherwise, the garrison is to be put to the sword, if the fort is taken. I have answered the demand with a cannon shot, & our flag still waves proudly from the walls. *I shall never surrender or retreat.* Then, I call upon you in the name of Liberty, of patriotism, & everything dear to the American character, to come to our aid with all dispatch. The enemy is receiving reinforcements daily & will no doubt increase to three or four thousand in four or five days. If this call is neglected, I am determined to sustain myself as long as possible & die like a soldier who never forgets what is due his honor & that of his country.

VICTORY or DEATH.

> William Barret Travis
> Lt. Col. Comdt.

P.S. The Lord is on our side. When the enemy appeared in sight, we had not three bushels of corn. We have since found in deserted houses 80 or 90 bushels and got into the walls 20 or 30 head of Beeves.

> Travis

As is well known, no one heeded the call except a band of thirty-two from Gonzales, Texas, who joined the defenders. The Alamo stood until March 6—thirteen days. When Santa Anna's army finally breached the walls and took the fort, with staggering losses, he kept his word. As his first act after arriving in San Antonio, Santa Anna raised a red flag over San Fernando Church, indicating no quarter for the enemy. The few surviving defenders were shot. The odds of defenders versus attackers were horrendous. Historians debate the numbers, but an estimated 189 Alamo defenders died fighting several thousand Mexican Troops.

Not only had no reinforcements come; communications had not been effective. The defenders did not know that, while they held the Alamo, Texans declared their independence from Mexico. The two weeks that the defenders held the Alamo against Santa Anna's onslaughts provided the brief breathing spell the Texans needed to prepare resistance to Santa Anna farther east in Texas. Without the respite bought at the Alamo and without the huge losses and seriously weakened condition of Santa Anna's troops, the Battle of San Jacinto, in which the Texans finally defeated Santa Anna and secured their independence from Mexico, might well have turned out differently.

The forty years after the fall of the Alamo were momentous ones for Texas—first independence, then statehood, then the Civil War, with Texas as part of the Confederacy, and then reconstruction. During all this time, however, San Antonio went its own way in many things. The independence of Texas did not mean the end of struggle with Mexico—further battles and further uncertain days came and went before Texas became the twenty-eighth state at the end of 1845. Before Texas' statehood, San Antonio grew only slowly and retained its almost totally Spanish and Mexican character. With the influx of German stock into the population, San Antonio became more and more of a German town. Between 1845 and 1860, the population increased from about 800 to about 8,000, thanks in large part to European immigration to San Antonio.

During the 1860s, San Antonio had to fight epidemics and reestablish the area's economy. Ranching in the surrounding area proved lucrative, especially now that the U.S. Army was at hand to help defend against the Indians. In spite of the difficulty of life in a city as isolated as San Antonio, some aspects of the city blossomed during this period. The splendid Menger Hotel, for years claimed to be the grandest in the Southwest, opened in 1859, and in 1868, St. Joseph's Church, still standing and in use, was begun. King William Street and its mansions also date from the period between statehood and the coming of the railroad.

The railroads generated a number of western cities and ensured the survival of others. San Antonio was different; the city was already prosperous, though in some ways still wild and wide open, when the Iron Horse arrived in 1877. The trains made a difference not by creating or spurring the growth of a city but rather by linking the city with others to the east, north, and west. Suddenly, in the space of a day, San Antonio was no longer isolated. In short order followed gas lighting, telephones, and even electricity, which became available by 1887.

For all its progress, San Antonio remained part of the Wild West. History books overflow with stories of killings, lynchings, and various acts of depravity at all periods of the city's life. Plenty of rough-and-ready characters still lived in and around San Antonio, so Theodore Roosevelt had little trouble filling the ranks of his Rough Riders when, in 1898, he arrived to serve under Colonel Leonard Wood in the training and drilling of the troops. Whether he actually recruited at the Menger Bar isn't confirmed, but that story has passed into the folklore of San Antonio.

And so San Antonio entered the twentieth century, and history begins to shade into living memory and even into the present. Despite all its modernization, growth, and urbanity, San Antonio has retained a spirit that speaks of the diversity of its past—a diversity of cultures and historical periods. The periods have left their marks on the attitudes and outlooks of the people, and the groups are represented still. Even now, people proudly identify themselves as descendents of the original Canary Islanders, and the prevalence of German names in the city is still notable. As for the Mexican influence, it would be misleading to say it is an important part of the city, for in some ways, it *is* the city. Large areas of the city are Mexican or Mexican-American in background, and few areas of life exist in San Antonio where you cannot feel the influence of the city's Mexican and Indian heritage.

Nothing can diminish San Antonio's long and dramatic history, but innumerable forces can diminish the surviving evidence of that history. The ravages of time, weather, neglect, and indifference chip away at the traces of history that remain. More recently, the physically significant historical sites and artifacts have faced a new foe, the pressure of redevelopment and urbanization. Historical treasures and sites often stand in the way of major rebuilding projects, and those who plan and direct the projects usually have priorities that are not particularly sympathetic to historical preservation.

San Antonio answered the threat of the loss of historically significant sites with the San Antonio Conservation Society. For years, the Conservation Society has had a hand in the recognition, preservation, and protection of almost every historically significant structure in the city. The members of the Conservation Society (once, but no longer, all women) perform a service entirely out of proportion to their numbers. Their recommendations for historic preservation often arouse spirited and vigorous opposition, but clearly, if such opposition did not exist the city would have no need for the Conservation Society.

REFERENCES

Numerous books about San Antonio's history have been published. Unfortunately, many are now out of print, forcing readers to scour used bookstores to find them. The list of more readable works that follows is not intended to be exhaustive—rather, it indicates the range of books and booklets available. Those interested in research would probably find a visit to the Daughters of the Republic of Texas Library at the Alamo a worthwhile trip.

American Guide Series. *Texas.* New York: Hastings House, 1940.

American Guide Series and San Antonio Conservation Society. *San Antonio: An Authoritative Guide to the City and Its Environs.* San Antonio: Clegg, 1938.

Buck, S. M. *Yanaguana's Successors.* San Antonio: R. M. Benavides, 1980. The story of the Canary Islands settlers and their descendents.

Chabot, F. C. *San Antonio and Its Beginnings.* San Antonio: F. C. Chabot, 1936.

Daughters of the Republic of Texas, ed. *The Alamo Long Barrack Museum.* Dallas: Taylor Publishing, 1986.

Fehrenbach, T. R. *Lone Star.* New York: Collier, 1968. This book is required reading for students of Texas history. Although it offers far more than a history of San Antonio, it makes clear the significance of happenings in San Antonio to the broader story of the history of Texas.

Fehrenbach, T. R., et al. *The San Antonio Story.* San Antonio: Continental Heritage Press, 1978.

Foster, Nancy Haston. *Texas Missions, a Lone Star Guidebook.* Houston: Gulf Publishing, 1995. While a travel guide, it has abundant background historical information.

Habig, Marion. *The Alamo Chain of Missions,* rev. ed. Chicago: Franciscan Herald Press, 1976.

Lanier, Sidney. *San Antonio de Bexar.* 1872, reprinted 1980, With notes by Mary Ann Noonan Guerra. Accurate Litho, 1980.

Long, Jeff. *Duel of Eagles.* New York: Quill, William Morrow, 1990. A more recent historical perspective and a more complete account than that offered by Lord (below), this book has particularly good information about the background events leading up to the siege of the Alamo. It focuses on the characters of Santa Anna and Sam Houston in its explanations of the events.

Lord, Walter. *A Time to Stand*. New York: Harper and Brothers, 1961. Lincoln: University of Nebraska Press, 1978. Of the numerous books about the Alamo, this one readably combines careful scholarship and good writing.

Michener, James. *Texas*. New York: Random House, 1985. While a novel, not a history book, Michener's epic compresses into a mere thousand pages a lot of the historical, mythical, and cultural background that native Texans naturally acquire as they grow up. For newcomers who want to see how Texas developed and old-timers who want to see how the state appears to a remarkably perceptive outsider, this book can be a useful, if somewhat ponderous, read.

Newcomb, Pearson. *The Alamo City*. San Antonio: Pearson Newcomb, 1926.

Noonan Guerra, Mary Ann. *An Alamo Album*, rev. ed. San Antonio: Noonan Guerra, 1981.

Noonan Guerra, Mary Ann. *San Fernando, Heart of Bexar*. Published by Francis J. Furey, archbishop of San Antonio, 1977, in connection with the restoration of the cathedral. *San Fernando*, with a large format and plenty of illustrations, tells the story of San Fernando, once the parish church of the first Canary Islands settlers and now the cathedral of the archdiocese of San Antonio. The historical sections of the book emphasize the church/cathedral and the life of its parishioners, but numerous pictures of nineteenth-century San Antonio make this an interesting read for anyone who wants to poke through a bit of the city's past.

Ramsdell, Charles. *San Antonio: A Historical and Pictorial Guide*, rev. ed. Austin and London: University of Texas Press, 1976.

Ryder-Taylor, Henry. *Visitors Guide and History of San Antonio, Texas*. San Antonio: Tengg, 1908.

Torres, Louis. *San Antonio Missions*. Tucson: Southwest Parks and Monuments Association, 1993.

TOURS

Fidgety to get out there and tour the city for yourself? Love to walk? Or hate the thought of walking and consider exercise the devil's work? Well, this chapter on tours suggests some options.

Whether you're after downtown walking or driving tours that you meander on your own, or organized tours that you join and they drive you, see below. By foot or by carriage or boat, you're bound to cotton to one of these many unusual ways to view San Antonio.

A DOWNTOWN WALKING TOUR

American cities, especially western ones, have become more and more oriented toward the automobile, making pedestrians something of an anachronism. San Antonio's rapidly developing north side fits into that pattern; there, a person virtually must have a car to get around efficiently. In contrast, the downtown area maintains the streets, the flavor, and even many of the buildings that were there long before the flowering of America's love affair with the car. Many people still get around the downtown area on foot, and a walking tour is the best way to capture its special flavor.

Allow two to three hours for this tour, although you can cover any part of the tour in the time you have available. Parts of the tour, such as La Villita, the River Walk, and Market Square, are easily worth an hour each. The tour winds in and around the heart of the oldest part of San Antonio. A map would help in following the walking tour; either use the downtown one in the front of this book or ask for a more detailed downtown map at the Visitor Information Center. Because of the changing levels and numerous steps along the River Walk, those in wheelchairs should not attempt the walking tour.

The tour starts and ends just out of the centermost area of downtown, near good parking facilities, near the River Walk, and at the edge of La Villita. Start at the corner of Presa and Villita streets. Stroll up the continuation of Villita Street, called Paseo de la Villita, which is closed to most traffic, into La Villita (see **Historical Places**). Historic buildings line both sides of the street, most notably the Cos House (see **History**) on the left. Pass to the left of the Cos House to visit the Arneson River Theater, the site of many spring and summer performances, then return to Villita Street. On the right is the original site of St. Philip's College, still functioning elsewhere in town, which began its life as St. Philip's Saturday Evening Sewing Class for Black Girls. Also on the right is La Villita Church. Pass the church and enter into La Villita proper, an area that combines an air of genuine antiquity with the clearly evident effects of a recent refurbishing. Originally the home of many soldiers in the Spanish army, La Villita had crumbled almost into ruins by the 1930s; today, thanks not only to recent efforts but also to the original rehabilitation program organized by a former San Antonio mayor, this popular site attracts tourists and natives as well, especially during Fiesta, when it becomes the setting for A Night in Old San Antonio.

La Villita is the essential wandering ground of San Antonio—take some time to poke around and visit the buildings. Many of the shops offer arts, crafts, and Mexican goods that in one way or another typify San Antonio. Fountains and Spanish-style architecture mix with the influence of the German population in La Villita—the area reflects the cultural diversity of San Antonio's history, although it emphasizes the Mexican-Spanish aspect of that history.

Leave La Villita on Villita Street and continue a very short block west (away from Alamo Street) to Navarro Street, where a right turn and a half block will lead you to the San Antonio River. Cross the river and take the stairs down to the River Walk. The walking tour now heads toward downtown (equivalent to a right turn from Navarro Street onto the River Walk), as it follows the river for much of its loop through downtown. Cross back and forth on the many bridges and return to street level to check the surrounding city; as long as you return to the river and keep going in the same direction, you won't stray from the tour route.

A marker at Mill Crossing, where the tour descends to the river, identifies the location believed to be the place where horses drank from and forded the river. The River Walk widens here—this popular place attracts many summer picnics at the lunch hour, thanks to the concrete benches and the little island in the river. This part of the River Walk, away from the more commercial center of the downtown area, is an especially agreeable meeting of urban San Antonio and the River Walk's quiet seclusion.

Pass under Presa Street, go on past a cascade of water coming in from the left, watch the squirrels gambol in the trees, and continue under the spreading trees, past gardens and rock walls, to the Arneson River Theater and its footbridge over the river. Cross to the side that has the seats of the Arneson River Theater. Continue in the same direction, toward the center of the River Walk, pausing to read the historical marker about the river and how the city nearly lost it to a paved street. Pass the Little Rhein Restaurant and continue into the area of the River Walk where shops, hotels, and businesses become the dominant features. The Hilton's guests can have breakfast right on the River Walk; other restaurants are inside the hotel. Just across the river from the Hilton is the starting point for river barge tour trips.

Continue along either side of the River Walk, but don't turn down the spur to the right unless you are heading for the Marriott Hotels, the Convention Center, or the Rivercenter Mall. On the left side of the river at this point is the Casa Rio Restaurant, which probably serves up kazillions of plates of Mexican food. It can be a good place to stop for a snack. Continue under Commerce Street, unless you're hungry for lunch, in which case think of climbing to Commerce Street and visiting Schilo's for a good German delicatessen meal and a wide selection of different beers.

Back on the River Walk, continue in the same direction but on the left side of the river. Here beats the very heart of the River Walk's most commercial area. Clubs and bars, galleries, shops, and restaurants line both sides of the river. The short stretch between Market and Crockett streets could easily consume an hour if your plan includes shopping.

Pass under Crockett Street and walk to the Hyatt Regency, one of the River Walk hotels. (A walkway leads through the Hyatt up eastward) into Alamo Plaza, making a side trip to the Alamo convenient at this point. Or continue on past the Hyatt, where you can browse in a number of shops on the river level, and then on past Presa Street (here you can cut back to the starting point of the tour if time runs short), past Navarro Street and La Mansion del Rio Hotel, and so to North St. Mary's Street, where the tour leaves the river and returns to street level. The River Walk continues for some distance, but at this point the walking tour diverges from it.

Cross to the other side of St. Mary's Street and walk down it on the left a block and a half to Market Street. Turn right onto Market Street, cross the main channel of the San Antonio River, and continue half a block into Main Plaza, just across from the imposing facade of the Bexar County Courthouse. From the center of the plaza, you can admire the front of San Fernando Cathedral. Then pass to its left down Dolorosa Street to Military Plaza, formerly the center of the Spanish military presence and now dominated by City Hall.

A bust of Franklin D. Roosevelt, dedicated by a Hispanic civic association to his memory and to the memory of others who died for the cause of freedom, stands in front of City Hall. A historical marker summarizes the history of the plaza both as a military center and, later, as a commercial center of the city. When City Hall was built around 1890, the market area moved from Military Plaza a few blocks west to what is now Market Square. A small cenotaph in front of City Hall pays tribute to the role that Mexico and Mexicans have played in the development of Texas. In the northwest corner of the plaza you'll find a statue of Moses Austin by noted local sculptor Waldine Tauch. Austin visited San Antonio in 1820 to obtain permission for Anglo immigration into Texas. Although he did not live to see that happen, his son Stephen F. Austin fulfilled his father's dream of bringing settlers from the United States to Texas.

Across from the statue, on the corner of Camaron and Commerce streets, stands the Spanish Governors' Palace, San Antonio's best place to visit for a sense of the extent of Spanish influence in early San Antonio. Continue west on Commerce Street, through an area where businesses are somewhat declining, to Santa Rosa Street. Cross Santa Rosa Street and visit Market Square. After a block, turn left onto Dolorosa Street and walk a block to the corner of North Laredo Street. Continue south along Laredo Street to the Navarro House. Turn left on Nueva and go a block to South Flores Street, where a left turn leads back to Military Plaza.

Return to Main Plaza by turning right on Dolorosa Street where South Flores meets it, and then turn right on Dwyer and almost immediately left on Villita.

Continue on Villita Street, stepping into the lobby of the Tower Life Building for a look at the arched cathedral-style ceiling. This dramatic building has had many names, owners, and tenants, including, in 1941, General Dwight D. Eisenhower, of the Third U.S. Army. Two more blocks along Villita Street to the east returns the tour to its starting point at the corner of Presa Street.

DRIVING TOURS

The time spent driving around San Antonio is a good time to let the city's charm and diversity soak in. For a more concentrated dose of San Antonio's flavor, a special driving tour might be in order. Here are two tours, one south of downtown and one north, designed to give the visitor a quick look at the city's high spots.

Although I have tried to give explicit directions, be sure to take a map, both for getting back on the track if you get off it and for seeing where you are in relation to the city as a whole. Some parts of the tours lead into places where the streets are hard to follow, thanks in part to the city's cavalier attitude toward such details as street signs. A map also helps because of the frequency with which city streets are closed for repair or rerouted for new construction. Both tours will not only reveal some of the city's more interesting and attractive sights but also introduce visitors to the general geography of the city.

Both tours start in the heart of downtown, at the corner of Alamo and Commerce streets. Allow several hours for each tour, without stops, in medium traffic. Naturally, stops, side trips, traffic conditions, and your own pace will influence the amount of time each trip will take. The high spots on the trip south of downtown are the historical missions; the main attractions north of downtown are Brackenridge Park and the museums.

SOUTH

Starting at the intersection of Alamo and Commerce streets, head west on Commerce into the downtown area. Commerce is one of the main commercial streets of the city. After leaving Alamo Street and crossing Losoya, Commerce Street crosses over the San Antonio River, the first of many crossings that these driving tours make. Crossing the river here brings you into the loop of the San Antonio River, which for centuries has enclosed and protected central San Antonio. After a few blocks, first Main Plaza and then Military Plaza appear on the left. The Spanish Governors' Palace at the corner of Camaron is a good place to stop and have a look around. Continue west on Commerce three more blocks to Santa Rosa and turn left. Market Square and El Mercado are located here. Continue two blocks to Nueva, turn left again, and continue east over the San Antonio River. Very shortly after crossing the river, turn right onto St. Mary's Street.

A long block or two leads to the intersection of Durango Street; immediately after crossing it, turn right onto King William Street. Plan to spend some time meandering through King William area and along King William Street, often cited as one of the loveliest historical districts in Texas. Certainly you won't find the combination of old architecture, trees, and lawns in many parts of Texas. Return to St. Mary's Street and again head south. (Or you might want to detour again by taking a right, southwest, onto South Alamo Street. This commercial area of Southtown is known for its funky coffeehouses and galleries, particularly the contemporary Blue Star Arts Complex.)

St. Mary's Street passes through a mixture of residential and commercial areas, then dips and passes under a railroad line. Almost immediately after the underpass, turn right into Roosevelt Park and onto Mission Road, which will lead into the most richly historic parts of San Antonio. Continue south on Mission Road. At Grove Street, just before leaving the park, look to the left for the Yturri-Edmunds Historic Site. If it is open, it makes a quiet and relaxing place to stop and pick up a bit of local history (see the description under **Historical Places**).

Mission Road crosses under I-10 and shortly comes to Mission Concepcion, one of San Antonio's four missions that make up the San Antonio Missions National Park. Each of the missions has its strong points. Mission Concepcion is very photogenic, Mission San Jose is the most beautiful and extensive, Mission San Juan Capistrano has a fine small museum, and Mission San Francisco de la Espada appears least affected by the impact of time and tourism. It also creates the most convincing impression of functioning antiquity.

Leaving Mission Concepcion, continue south on Mission Road, past Riverside Park golf course and over the San Antonio River, often swelled at this point by the waters of San Pedro Creek, and on to Roosevelt Avenue. Mission San Jose is at the intersection of Roosevelt and Mission Road; a stroll through the grounds and buildings could be the high spot of the tour. Mission Road takes a jog at Roosevelt—turn right on Roosevelt from Mission Road, then left again onto the entrance street into Mission San Jose. From there, Mission Road turns right (south) shortly after leaving Roosevelt.

Mission Road continues on and crosses Military Drive where Mission Road takes a decided jog to the left. The driving route continues south on Mission Road, along which the scenery changes from urban to more nearly rural. Continue between two cemeteries, past Stinson Airport to where, at the end of the airport property, Mission Road ends and runs into Ashley Road, which continues straight and then turns right. Turn right, follow the border of the airport a few hundred yards to its junction with Espada Road. Turn left on Espada and continue to where the road bends sharply to the right. At this point, the Espada Aqueduct, a few yards to the left, is one of the high points of the trip— a 250-year-old structure that combines beauty and function. Espada Road to the south (i.e., do not turn back toward Ashley) continues on to Mission de la Espada.

Warning: Get a map when driving the area just mentioned, or you'll get lost! (You can get one from the Missions National Park.) Street signs are often missing, and to make matters worse, the streets do not always agree with those shown on some maps. Fortunately, signs for the Missions Historical Park will help you reach the missions and the aqueduct. After a visit to Mission Espada, head back north on Espada Road back to Ashley (at the corner of the airport), turning right there and again at the end of the airport. Shortly thereafter Ashley intersects with Graf, where a right turn brings you into Mission San Juan Capistrano or a left turn on Graf leads to Presa, one of San Antonio's main north-south streets, on which you turn left, or north, for the trip back to town.

Continue north for more than a mile on Presa, then turn right on Military Drive, and you'll pass by Brooks Air Force Base on your right. Soon you'll see the big intersection with I-37. Go north on I-37 to head back toward downtown. When you approach downtown, you can't miss the Alamodome sticking out on your right. Take the Durango exit. (You might want to tour the Alamodome.) Turn right on Durango, then soon left (north) on Cherry Street. Go a few blocks and take a left (west) on Commerce Street. There on Commerce Street is the old Southern Pacific Railway depot, now well restored and a reminder of the days when by train was the only way to travel and, frequently, the occasion for considerable luxury. Commerce Street leads through St. Paul's Square, an area of restored buildings of historical and architectural significance, and back to the tour's starting point.

NORTH

This trip also starts at Commerce and Alamo but heads north along Alamo Street. The Alamo itself stands on the right after two blocks. As a visit to the Alamo makes clear, the remaining chapel is only a small part of the whole mission compound—the original walls probably stretched for a block to the north and west. Turn left on Travis Street then, after two blocks, right onto Jefferson. Look for Travis Park on the left; here the city often holds musical entertainment events.

Jefferson Street ends at Auditorium Circle and Municipal Auditorium. Near it stands the Vietnam Veterans Memorial. Swing once around to the right of the auditorium, then turn right onto Fourth Street (a very short jog via Avenue A leads to Fourth) and follow it two blocks to Broadway. Turn left on Broadway. After seven blocks, turn left onto Jones.

Jones crosses the San Antonio River. Then on the right stands the San Antonio Museum of Art, a splendidly successful conversion of an old brewery to a museum. A block or so after the museum, turn left onto Camden, which joins at a five-way intersection. The other street at the intersection is St. Mary's Street; follow along Camden for five blocks and turn right onto McCullough.

The tour now generally follows or parallels McCullough, a main north-south street, for several miles. After a mile or so, McCullough leads through the Monte Vista area, one of San Antonio's most staid and desirable older neighborhoods. Turn left on Woodlawn, then right (north) after two blocks onto Howard. Howard passes through an attractive part of Monte Vista and leads after a dozen or so blocks to Hildebrand, a narrow but major east-west street. Turn right on Hildebrand, return to McCullough, and turn left. At the intersection of Hildebrand and McCullough is a drugstore with an old-fashioned soda fountain—if the tour falls on a hot day, then one of the fountain's genuine ice cream sodas can offer a welcome reason for a stop. The next few blocks of McCullough lead into Olmos Park, one of the most fashionable older areas of the city.

Olmos Park merits a look, so the route of this tour makes a series of concentric circles through it. Turn right off McCullough onto Hermosa (if you reach the railroad tracks on McCullough, you've gone too far; Hermosa is two blocks before the tracks). Hermosa leads to the heart of Olmos Park, Alameda Circle. Swing counterclockwise around the circle once or twice, admiring the scenery, then turn right back onto Hermosa, the same street that led in from McCullough. A right on Hillside followed by a right on Mandalay leads around the next ring out from Alameda Circle. Turn left on Broadmoor, bear left, then turn left on Paseo Encinal. Follow this, the next ring, to Hillside, and turn right.

Turn right again onto Contour, then immediately left at the next street, which will be Dick Friedrich Road, which leads out of Olmos Park and into Alamo Heights after passing under the McAllister Freeway and across the upper reaches of the San Antonio River.

Alamo Heights, although more subdued and less grand than Olmos Park, is equally prized as an older residential address. Turn left on Devine Road, then right onto Alamo Heights Boulevard. Another right onto Corona will lead to Broadway, but a few side excursions into Alamo Heights will give you a better sense of the character of the area. At Broadway and Corona, turn left (north) on Broadway, then right onto Bluebonnet. Continue to New Braunfels Avenue. The McNay Art Museum sits at the intersection of Bluebonnet and New Braunfels. Of all the places where one might break this drive, the McNay may be the most rewarding. Even if only for a stroll around the museum's grounds, the McNay looks extraordinarily attractive. Leaving the McNay, head south on New Braunfels, then go right on Austin Highway and follow it back to Broadway. At this point turn left (south).

After Broadway crosses Hildebrand, Brackenridge Park lies just out of sight to the right. Enter the park on Tuleta, which intersects just after the Witte Memorial Museum. Tuleta leads through the heart of the park to the zoo, aerial tramway, miniature railroad, and the Japanese Tea Gardens. Tuleta continues through the park and under McAllister Freeway to Stadium Drive, which borders Trinity University.

Turn left on Stadium Drive, then right into Trinity University at the main gate, which has a fountain just inside. A walk or a drive through the campus will show why so many San Antonians prize the contributions San Antonio's master architect, O'Neil Ford, has made to Trinity's campus and thus to the city's architectural heritage. Leaving Trinity, return to Stadium Drive and continue south, turning right after leaving the entrance near the fountain. Just as Stadium Drive appears about to enter the freeway, North St. Mary's Street crosses obliquely and branches off to the right. Follow St. Mary's Street south.

St. Mary's Street winds its way toward the downtown area, passing through commercial areas and leading eventually to the corner of Navarro Street, where you'll find the Southwest Crafts Center located on the grounds of the old Ursuline Academy. Another eight blocks along St. Mary's leads to Market Street, where a left turn and five more blocks will take you back to Alamo Street, a block from the tour's starting point.

SIGHTSEEING TOURS

Want to sit back and leave the driving to *them?* Here's where to look for sightseeing tours. San Antonio offers plenty of choices in transportation—trolley, bus, river barge—about everything except skate-board. Most leave from near the Alamo.

ALAMO VISITOR CENTER

216 Alamo Plaza at Crockett • Central • 225-8587
Open daily 8:30–5

This privately owned visitor center near the Alamo provides a central place to buy tickets for various city tours; it also sells tickets to numerous local attractions—tickets cost the same here as at the various attractions, but buying them here may save time you would have spent in ticket lines.

GRAY LINE BUS TOURS

Leave from Alamo Plaza (tickets at 217 Alamo Plaza) • 226-1706
Open daily • Adults $20 (regular tour)

You can buy tickets for these large, air-conditioned bus tours just before departure. But get there about fifteen minutes ahead of time.

Currently Gray Line offers two tour options plus a combination tour of the first two. The regular tours last about three and one-half hours in both the morning and afternoon, with the combo lasting longer. Tours usually leave around 9 a.m. and 1:30 p.m., but check ahead because over the years the times may vary. The tour sites include the missions, La Villita, San Fernando Cathedral, Institute of Texan Cultures, King William District, El Mercado, Brackenridge Park, Fort Sam Houston, and Lone Star Brewery.

HORSE 'N' CARRIAGE RIDES

Alamo Plaza • Central • Open daily, roughly 10–6 in winter, longer hours in summer • About $10 minimum, more for longer rides

Let the gas guzzlers pass you by while you see the city the slow, nostalgic way—in a horse-and-carriage. Several companies offer this service, and you can usually find at least one of their buggies waiting near the Alamo. It's not inexpensive, however; most charge about $10 per person per ride of thirty minutes or so. A longer tour to the King William area costs more. Rides are also available in the evening, from the Alamo, but hours vary with the season and weather, so if you don't want to trust your luck, call beforehand. Two companies offering the services are Yellow Rose (225-6490) and Lone Star (656-7527).

TROLLEY, VAN, & MINI-BUS TOURS

Leave from near Alamo • Central • Open daily • Fees vary

Aside from the established Gray Line Bus tours, other outfits usually operate city sightseeing tours in smaller buses, trolleys, and vans. These depart from the vicinity of the Alamo in the morning and afternoon.

YANAGUANA RIVER CRUISES

Leave from Market Street bridge near Hilton Palacio del Rio Hotel; also from Rivercenter • Central • 244-5700 Open daily 9–10, but varies in winter • Adults $4, children 5 and under $1

Venice this isn't, but every tourist ought to take this merry barge trip on the tiny San Antonio River as it winds through the landscaped River Walk of shops, cafes, and hotels. Tour barges leave at ten- or fifteen-minute intervals. But during wintertime and bad weather, the hours may vary. The trip goes one and one-half miles up the river and lasts about forty-five minutes. Group meals on barges are also available through several River Walk restaurants.

GROUP SPECIAL INTEREST TOURS

Various sites, centers, and manufacturing plants about town offer guided tours for groups. But call ahead to make arrangements; you can't just drop by. Many cost nothing, but some charge a fee. Although these certainly aren't all the entities offering such group tours, here are some of the more publicized ones.

Alamodome (207-3652)
Baptist Memorial Healthcare System (302-3006)
Bexar County Courthouse (students only) (220-2011)
Brooks Air Force Base, School of Aerospace Medicine (536-3234)
H.E.B. Grocery Company (246-8000)
Lackland Air Force Base (671-1110)
Methodist Hospital (692-4000)
Randolph Air Force Base (652-1110)
San Antonio Shoe (924-6562)
San Antonio Zoo (kids) (734-7183)
Southwest Craft Center (224-1848)
University of Texas Health Science Center (567-7000)
USAA Building (498-0929)
WOAI Radio (736-9700)

ANNUAL EVENTS

San Antonio offers a legion of annual events, both cultural and recreational. Many of the city's festivals have ethnic accents, frequently Mexican. Here are some of the more prominent happenings for the various months. Specific dates aren't usually given because they vary from year to year. Check with the Visitor Information Center (see **For Your Information Chapter**) or individual event sponsors for exact dates.

JANUARY

LOS PASTORES
Various Catholic churches • December 24 through February 2 • Free • W variable

Start off the year with an old Hispanic Catholic custom, Los Pastores. This colorful Christmas pageant about the shepherds' journey to see the infant Jesus is performed several times between December 24 and February 2 at various Catholic churches around town. Some of the most popular performances include those at the beautiful San Jose mission, usually on the first Saturday and Sunday evenings after Christmas (see December listing).

GREAT COUNTRY RIVER FESTIVAL (CURRENTLY IN SEPTEMBER)
Arneson River Theater and River Walk • Central • 227-4262 Free • W

Here's your chance to hear nonstop country and western music and to sit jean-to-jean beside the river. Every urban cowboy and cowgirl around shows up for this three-day music bash, so go early if you want a grassy seat. Country music recording artists perform on the stage, while local favorites serenade from barges on the river. (Warning: Event dates have changed over the years.) In the past, such artists as Darrell

McCall, Larry Gatlin, and Frenchie Burke have performed. Beer and food booths.

SPORT AND BOAT SHOW

Convention Center, S. Alamo and Market • Central • 207-8500 One week in January • Admission • W

Display of the latest in boats, campers, and recreational vehicles.

MARTIN LUTHER KING, JR., MARCH

Various locations • 207-7080 • One day in January on holiday around MLK's birthday • Free

A large march of people honors Martin Luther King, Jr., on the MLK holiday, plus many related activities around town.

COWBOY BREAKFAST

Central Park Mall parking lot • Near North • 344-4848 • One day in late January or prior to Stock Show and Rodeo • Free

Hey guys, where else can you get a free breakfast and free entertainment? and because it's free, thousands of city slickers crowd here for the coffee, tacos, and biscuits. Course, it's usually cold and rainy (and outside), so wear your long johns. A kickoff event of the upcoming Stock Show and Rodeo.

FEBRUARY

SAN ANTONIO STOCK SHOW AND RODEO

Freeman Coliseum, Houston Street and Coliseum Road, and other locations • East • 225-5851 • Two weeks in early February • $5 grounds admission or $12–$17 for rodeo (includes grounds admission) • W

This two-week shindig of rodeo performances, country and western stars, animal judging, and auctions starts off with a parade downtown. It begins even sooner for the hardy souls who saddle up in the trail-ride caravans that converge on the city for the show. There's an event to please everyone—bareback bronco and wild bull riding, calf roping, goat milking contests, a children's barnyard, and even a highly respected western art show. Western music stars such as Michael Martin Murphy, Clint Black, and Reba McEntire sing at the rodeo, but it would be a mistake to consider this just an entertainment event. To those who use ranching as a livelihood and way of life, the Stock Show and Rodeo provides an annual opportunity to get together with like-minded others, to catch up on advances in animal science and husbandry, and to give themselves and their children a chance to enter livestock in serious competition for excellence.

RIVER WALK MARDI GRAS

River Walk • Central • 227-4262 • Several days in February
Free • W

If you love music and crowds, then this is your kind of event—a pre-Lenten bash with a Mardi Gras celebration. People consume beer in large quantities, while legions fill the riverbanks to listen to music groups play everything from conjunto to jazz. Music performances occur at different staging areas on the river, so stroll along to sample it. Also arts and crafts show.

MARCH

ANNUAL TEJANO MUSIC AWARDS

Alamodome • Central • 222-8862 • Usually one day in March

This is such a big event for fans and artists of Tejano music that it takes the Alamodome to hold them.

ST. PATRICK'S DAY FESTIVITIES

River Walk • Central • 227-4262
Weekend nearest March 17 Free • W

The river is usually a drab color, but for St. Patrick's Day, it's dyed green for all good Irishmen! This weekend of Irish fun features a parade, festival, music, dancing, and green beer.

APRIL

STARVING ARTIST SHOW

River Walk and La Villita • Central • 226-3593
First weekend in April • W

Artwork and crafts by local and national artists are displayed along the river, at HemisFair Park, and along La Villita. Moderate prices with some good bargains, some white elephants.

FIESTA

Various locations • 227-5191 • Ten days around April 21 • Many events free • W variable

The biggest festival celebration in town. See the **Fiesta** chapter.

MAY

CINCO DE MAYO

Market Square, 514 W. Commerce • Central • 207-8600
Weekend nearest May 5 • Free • W

This is one of two Mexican holidays celebrated in San Antonio with weekend festivities. Mexico won an important victory over occupying French troops on May 5, 1862. Go to Market Square and get in on the celebration. Mariachi, conjunto, salsa . . . there's music in the air, food booths, and a parade. Share the celebration of an event that changed Mexican—and so, Texas—history.

BEETHOVEN MAENNERCHOR CONCERTS AND DANCES

Beethoven Home, 422 Pereida at S. Alamo • Central • 222-1521
Every third Friday, May through September • Admission • W
outdoors

These open-air German band concerts and dances are held at this old home, which is now a beer garden. The event is ideal for family fun— all ages can get in on the dancing. German food booths can satisfy one's nonmusical appetites.

BROWN BAG DAYS

Various downtown parks and Farmers Market • 207-3131
Selected days, usually in May, June, and July but varies • Free

This event provides free entertainment in downtown parks and at Farmers Market at lunchtime (about 11:45–1:15). So take, what else, your brown bag lunch.

ARMED FORCES WEEK

Various locations • Mid-May • Free • W variable

With five military bases in town, it's no surprise that San Antonio celebrates the Armed Forces with a whole week instead of the usual Armed Forces Day. Most bases hold special activities and open houses during this week. Events range from sports to band concerts. Throw in numerous community speeches, luncheons, and seminars, and you have Armed Forces Week. An especially popular attraction is a visit by the Air Force's precision flying team, the Thunderbirds.

TEJANO CONJUNTO FESTIVAL

Rosedale Park • 271-3151 • One week in May • Admission

Conjunto music performers come from all over to join in this festival, which stages performances in a southside park. Go to the park and make a day of it, listening to continual performances of this lively music, which combines the accordion and guitar. Conjunto blends the musical traditions of Mexico with the instrument of German immigrants, making it a truly international musical idiom.

JUNE

ENTERTAINMENT ON RIVER WALK AT ARNESON RIVER THEATER

During the summer, always look for some local Hispanic entertainment each evening on the River Walk at the outdoor Arneson River Theater. It starts at 8:30 p.m. and includes Fiesta Noche del Rio, Fiesta Flamenca, and Fandango (all listed below), plus various other shows.

FIESTA NOCHE DEL RIO

**Arneson River Theater, River Walk • Central • 226-4651
June through August • Admission • W**

Entertainment takes the stage every Thursday, Friday, and Saturday evening at 8:30 p.m. at the open-air Arneson River Theater during the summer months. Mexican and Spanish folk dances and flamenco guitar are featured. Sponsored by the Alamo Kiwanis Club.

FIESTA FLAMENCA

**Arneson River Theater, River Walk • Central • 927-3389
June through August • Admission • W**

A fast-paced musical show with colorful costumes takes place every Sunday night during the summer months at the Arneson River Theater. Performances feature Spanish and Mexican dances and flamenco guitar.

FANDANGO

**Arneson River Theater, River Walk • Central • 207-3133
June through August • Admission • W**

The Parks and Recreation Department sponsors this musical review every Wednesday evening during the summer. Mexican folkloric dance, Spanish music, and mariachis make up many of the presentations.

MARKET SQUARE ENTERTAINMENT

Market Square, 514 W. Commerce • Central • 207-8600 • Various days from June through August • Free • W

During the summer, musical and dance groups perform, frequently on weekends, at Market Square in Mariachi Plaza. You're also especially likely to find them there during special fiestas.

BROWN BAG DAYS
(See May listing.)

JULY

FOURTH OF JULY CELEBRATIONS
Various locations • Free • W variable

These festivities occur at different places around town and vary from year to year, so check the newspapers. There's usually a fiesta at Market Square. Some of the military bases also have fireworks displays. Check local neighborhood associations like Alamo Heights, Monte Vista, and King William for informal parades, entertainment, and food.

BROWN BAG DAYS (See May listing.)

MARKET SQUARE ENTERTAINMENT (See June listing.)

FIESTA NOCHE DEL RIO (See June listing.)

FIESTA FLAMENCA (See June listing.)

FANDANGO (See June listing.)

AUGUST

TEXAS FOLKLIFE FESTIVAL
Institute of Texan Cultures, HemisFair Park, Bowie and Durango • Central • 458-2300 • Four days in early August
Admission • W outdoors

You can never tell when you might need to know how to pluck a goose, spit watermelon seeds, or build a log cabin. You'll encounter such useful information and much more at Texas' biggest block party and country fair rolled into one. Held on the fifteen-acre grounds of the Institute of Texan Cultures, the festival is one big ethnic reunion. Every ethnic group imaginable comes here for this hectic, four-day festival to set up food booths, to dance, or to demonstrate nearly forgotten crafts. The institute teaches us the state's cultural heritage, and this seems as painless a way to do it as I know. Eat Greek baklava, Jewish bagels, Chinese egg rolls, German apple strudel, Japanese teriyaki, Cajun gumbo, or soul food. Watch Czech, Polish, Spanish flamenco, or tribal Indian dances. Listen to gospel singers, fiddlers, and Scottish pipers. Name it and it's here, if you have the stamina to see it all.

Admission fee doesn't include food. Look for large crowds due to its popularity. And the dog days of summer can get plenty hot here, so if the heat bothers you, try early evening. Also, take care to park in official parking lots and not tow-away zones.

FIESTA NOCHE DEL RIO (see June listing.)

FIESTA FLAMENCA (see June listing.)

FANDANGO (see June listing.)

MARKET SQUARE ENTERTAINMENT (see January listing.)

SEPTEMBER

GREAT COUNTRY RIVER FESTIVAL (see January listing.)

JAZZ'SALIVE

Travis Park, at Travis and Navarro • Central • 207-8478
One weekend in September • Free

Jazz is alive and well in San Antonio and always has been. Spread a blanket and picnic on the ground at this comfortable, old downtown park while taking in this jazz festival featuring New Orleans and San Antonio jazz bands. Those not inclined to take a picnic can take advantage of the food booths.

DIEZ Y SEIS DE SEPTIEMBRE

Various locations • One weekend around September 16
Most events free • W variable

The sixteenth of September marks Mexico's Independence Day. So naturally, San Antonio celebrates it with a big bang. Speeches, concerts, and fiestas usually stretch into a long weekend. Check the newspaper for a schedule to see what suits your fancy, but take in something during Diez y Seis to get the flavor of the city's Mexican heritage. Look for *charreadas* (Mexican rodeos) and the fiesta at Market Square, with free music, lively entertainment, and food booths. If you keep hearing about El Grito, that refers to the call for revolution in 1810 that eventually won Mexico its independence from Spain. Also tied in with Diez y Seis is La Feria del Rio, held at La Villita and the Arneson River Theater. It's another entertainment and food festival. Admission free.

TEXAS OPEN

La Cantera Golf Club, 16401 La Cantera Pkwy. • Northwest
341-0823 • One week, usually in September or October but may vary each year • Admission

One of the oldest PGA golf tournaments around, the Texas Open in San Antonio has been traditionally played in October, but now television and national tour constraints may change it to different months in various years. So you just have to check the calendar and sports pages for the current date. The golf club site may also change from time to time.

OCTOBER

ZONTA ANTIQUE SHOW

Live Oak Civic Center, 8101 Pat Booker Road • Northeast
653-9494 • One weekend in October • Admission • W

A weekend show with dealers from all over the country displaying collectibles.

RIVER ART SHOW

River Walk • Central • 226-8752
First weekend in October • Free • W

Major Texas artists display and sell their wares along the River Walk on a Saturday and Sunday. A pleasant way to spend a fall afternoon, enjoying arts and the Paseo del Rio.

OKTOBERFEST

Beethoven Home, 422 Pereida at S. Alamo • Central • 222-1521
Admission • Two weekends in October • W outdoors

Bring on the good old German oom-pah-pah music and food. There's nothing like a polka to cheer the soul. This two-day festival with singing and dancing is held at the beer garden of Beethoven Home, headquarters for the Maennerchor and Damenchor, venerable German singing societies.

ALZAFAR SHRINE CIRCUS

Freeman Coliseum, Houston Street and Coliseum Road • East
496-1625 • One weekend in October • Admission • W

Performances for big and little kids who delight in the circus.

GREEK FUNSTIVAL

St. Sophia Greek Orthodox Church, 2504 North St. Mary's Street
Near North • 735-5051 • One weekend in October
Admission • W

These Greeks bear a few entertainment gifts at their weekend festival. The Funstival features authentic Greek folk dancing in colorful costumes, along with special food, from souvlaki to baklava. In addition, look for a bazaar, imported foods, Greek wines, and coffee.

TEXAS OPEN (See September listing.)

NOVEMBER

WURSTFEST

Landa Park, New Braunfels, about thirty miles from San Antonio (210) 625-9167 • Ten days in early November
Admission • W variable

This annual ten-day fest, starting on the Friday before the first Monday in November, is full of German food and music. Eat some *dummaburd* (sausage on a stick, dipped in jalapeño cheese!) or *pute bein* (charbroiled turkey leg). Mix with folk songs, costumes, accordion music, singalongs, and lots of people, and you've got Wurstfest. The fest also features a melodrama, art show, sailboat regatta, and walkfest. From San Antonio, take I-35 north thirty miles to New Braunfels. Go west on TX 46 to the park entrance on Landa.

HOLIDAY RIVER PARADE AND LIGHTING CEREMONY

River Walk and Alamo Plaza • Central • 227-4262 • Friday after Thanksgiving • Free

Just as at the department stores, Christmas comes early to the river, but the big difference is that the River Walk display is a more welcome sight. This nighttime Christmas River Parade has become one of the most popular events in the city. The 70,000 lights in the trees and on bridges are turned on, to be left on until January 1, and the result is delightful. Hang over the bridges or in a friend's downtown apartment and watch the festivities as Santa arrives by barge sans reindeer. All kinds of music trumpets forth from the other barges. Or saunter to Alamo Plaza for the official lighting of the tree there. Forget the car—many thousands will be fighting for the same parking spaces. Instead, think of taking the park-and-ride buses from the suburbs.

DECEMBER

KING WILLIAM HOLIDAY HOME TOUR

King William Historic District (see Historical Places chapter)
Central • 227-8786 • First Saturday in December • Admission

If you admire older homes, take in this tour of several in King William when they are all done up for the holidays.

RIVERCENTER CHRISTMAS PAGEANT

Rivercenter Mall • Central • 225-0000 • Several weekends in December • Free

Traditional Christmas story, with accompanying holiday music, is performed on barges and the entertainment island in the arm of the San Antonio River that snakes into Rivercenter Mall.

FIESTA NAVIDENAS IN EL MERCADO

Market Square, 514 W. Commerce • Central • 207-8600 Weekends in December • Free • W

Christmas merriment at the Market but with a Mexican flair. During the week, the Market offers mariachi music, folk dances, choirs, and traditional Mexican holiday foods, such as *pan dulces* (sweet pastries and bread). For the children, piñata parties and blessing of the pets. And Pancho Claus comes to visit.

FIESTA DE LAS LUMINARIAS

River Walk • Central • 227-4262 • Several weekends in December • Free • W

This phrase means "festival of lights" and offers a beautiful way to see the River Walk at Christmastime. All along its length, the River Walk glows with candles in paper sacks and strings of lights in the overhanging trees. Everyone should see this scene at least once; most people go back for more. Las Luminarias symbolizes lighting the way for the Holy Family. Local choirs sing Christmas carols.

LAS POSADAS

River Walk • Central • 224-6163 • One Sunday evening in mid-December • Free • W

Posadas means "shelters," and this ceremony reenacts the Holy Family's search for an inn. Candle-bearing singers wind their way from place to place on the River Walk, begging for shelter, ending up at La Villita. A piñata party for children follows. Sponsored by the San Antonio Conservation Society.

LOS PASTORES

Mission San Jose, 3200 Roosevelt at Napier • South • 224-6163 First or second weekend after Christmas • Free • W

This colorful Hispanic Christmas pageant is presented between December 24 and February 2 at various local Catholic churches. Usually on the first weekend after Christmas, the pageant is presented in the evening at beautiful Mission San Jose. Free performances, with Mexican food booths and choirs. (Be sure to try some *buñuelos*—light crisp pastry.) The players wear colorful costumes that reflect native traditions in this ancient play about the shepherds' journey to see the infant Jesus. The San Antonio Conservation Society sponsors the pageant.

ALAMO BOWL

Alamodome, 100 Montana • Central • 207-3600 • Day late in December • Admission

You know what football fanatics live in Texas, so naturally we have to have an Alamo Bowl game along with all the other bowls around the nation. On a day near to New Year's Day, the Alamodome starts jumping with major college football, featuring teams from the Big Twelve and Big Ten conferences.

FIESTA

Various locations throughout the city • For general information contact Fiesta San Antonio Commission, 122 Heiman, 78205 • Central • 227-5191 • Ten days in April
Many activities free

This is *the* major annual event in San Antonio and practically takes over the city during the ten days that surround April 21. If you want to visit San Antonio at this time, make hotel reservations early. If you're a resident who doesn't like fun and crowds, hibernate for the duration. What does Fiesta entail? Parades, food, fairs, ethnic festivals, art shows, concerts, mariachi music, fireworks, running races, and Mexican rodeos, to mention a few. Even royalty and pomp. For while Fiesta is certainly for the general public, at this time many private parties and other social functions abound. This ten-day festival always begins on a Friday and ends on the second Sunday.

You can blame all this frivolity on President Benjamin Harrison. He was to visit San Antonio on April 20, 1891, and the city wanted to put on a bit of fanfare. Who really started Fiesta is hard to say. A man by the name of Ballard supposedly suggested that because 1891 was San Antonio's 200th anniversary, a bicentennial celebration would be in order. Harrison's visit conveniently fell around the anniversary of the Battle of San Jacinto, April 21, when Texas won its independence from Mexico in 1836. The *San Antonio Express* ran a story on the matter, which included a description of a flower carnival in Mexico City. Some of the town's prominent ladies then mapped out plans for a similar parade, since one of them had seen the "flower battle" in Mexico. It rained on their parade, and they had to postpone it until April 24. So Harrison never got to see it. But the parade was evidently a grand spectacle. It contained carriages decorated with real flowers, floats drawn by horses, and mounted cavalry. And the participants ended up at Alamo Plaza, parading around and throwing flowers at each other. Thus, the origin of the Battle of Flowers Association and parade. Later on, the Order of the Alamo and the Texas Cavaliers started the custom of choosing a queen and king each year to reign over the festivities. These organizations are composed of men from San Antonio's prominent families. And King Antonio and the queen somehow tend to turn up from these same families, too. A number of the private parties held during Fiesta honor the king and queen.

Over the years, Fiesta grew. Events and parades were added, and even another king, El Rey Feo ("the Ugly King"). Now it lasts for ten days, with pre-Fiesta celebrations tacked on besides. Far too many events occur to list them all, so I've included the more traditional and obvious ones, arranged roughly in sequence. Since times and locations may vary from year to year, see the special Fiesta sections in the daily newspapers for details. Or call the Fiesta Commission (227-5191).

ONGOING ACTIVITIES THAT SPAN ENTIRE FIESTA

FIESTA DEL MERCADO
El Mercado, 514 W. Commerce • Central • Daily, various times • Free

Colorfully dressed Mexican singing and dance groups are featured, along with bands and food booths.

FIESTA EN LA VILLA DE SAN FERNANDO
San Fernando Cathedral, 115 Main Plaza • Central • Daily, times vary • Free

This historic cathedral church provides the backdrop for food, dancing, and music on the equally historic downtown plaza.

FIESTA CARNIVAL
Downtown • Central • Daily • Times vary

Rides, concessions, and a midway make up the attractions of this pedestrian, but popular, carnival.

CALENDAR OF FIESTA EVENTS IN SEQUENCE

A TASTE OF NEW ORLEANS
Sunken Garden Theater • Northeast • Saturday and Sunday afternoons • Admission

An outdoor fair, heavy on Cajun food, with all sorts of entertainment, including jazz.

ARTS FAIR

Southwest Craft Center, 300 Augusta • Central • Saturday and Sunday afternoons • Admission • W

Arts and crafts for sale in this genteel, historic setting. Food booths. Artists attend from much of the Southwest and often display unusual and unique art forms.

OYSTER BAKE

St. Mary's University, One Camino Santa Maria • Northwest Saturday afternoon and evening • Admission • W

Get a bucket of oysters or shrimp and eat to your heart's (or stomach's) content. Devotees carry their own oyster shell openers. This giant picnic also features music (mostly rock), game booths, and other food besides fish.

EL REY FEO RECEPTION

Location downtown • Central • Saturday evening • Admission

Reception for El Rey Feo, the "Ugly King," with food and entertainment.

CORONATION OF KING ANTONIO

Alamo Plaza, downtown • Central • Saturday evening Free • W

King Antonio is crowned in this spectacular event staged in front of the Alamo against a backdrop of burning torches.

A DAY IN OLD MEXICO AND CHARREADA

San Antonio Charro Ranch, 6126 Padre • South • Sunday afternoon Admission

See *charros* in colorful riding attire competing in typical Mexican horsemanship events. Mexican food and entertainment.

BAND CONCERT AND FIREWORKS DISPLAY

Fort Sam Houston, N. New Braunfels and Grayson • Northeast Sunday afternoon and evening • Free • W

The Fifth Army Band and the Fife and Drum Corps provide some musical fireworks, along with the real thing.

PILGRIMAGE TO THE ALAMO

Alamo Plaza, downtown • Central • Monday afternoon Free • W

A solemn processional to the Alamo, where floral offerings commemorate Texas heroes.

RIVER PARADE

River Walk, downtown • Central • Monday evening • Free • W

This is one of the better parades, with night lights and a festive atmosphere on the river. The boat floats have to be small enough to negotiate the narrow river, and part of the fun is watching them maneuver to make the turns. Somehow, the River Parade seems more informal and intimate than others. Natives frequently throw parties in hotel rooms or at restaurants, offices, or apartments along the parade route. Seats are available for a price, but the bargain way is simply to hang over a bridge. Sponsored by the Texas Cavaliers.

RIVER ART SHOW

River Walk • Central • Tuesday through Thursday
No admission fee

Local artists display their works and wares along the River Walk.

A NIGHT IN OLD SAN ANTONIO

La Villita, Villita and S. Presa • Central • Tuesday through Friday
5:30–10:30 • Admission

Probably the most popular event during Fiesta, A Night in Old San Antonio is a glorified block party thrown on four evenings in the heart of downtown at historic La Villita. The San Antonio Conservation Society sponsors the affair. If you don't like crowds, this won't be your cup of sangria. With wall-to-wall people pushing from one food and dance area to another, it's sometimes an endurance test. But it's so pleasant in the evening with the lights as a backdrop to the old village that everyone keeps going back year after year, sometimes 35,000 nightly! Get there when it opens, because the crowds usually haven't arrived yet. If an ethnic group doesn't have a food booth here, I don't know about it. Freshly made tortillas in the Mexican area with conjunto music. Delicious hot pastry doughnuts that only the French Quarter can serve. German bands and polkas to mix with sausage. Country and western entertainers in the western area, with barbecue and fried mountain oysters to choose from. Start off with Chinese egg rolls and finish up the international repast with Irish coffee. Many visitors take in a lot of *cerveza* (beer) along the way—late in the evening it begins to show. The quality of the food is surprisingly good at most of the booths, although one can't count on high standards everywhere. Parking can present a problem unless you arrive early, and even then, it will cost you. However, buses with park-and-ride services will take you from various suburban malls to La Villita.

MARIACHI FESTIVAL

River Walk • Central • Tuesday through Friday • Free

Lively mariachi bands serenade from floating barges.

CORONATION OF THE QUEEN OF THE ORDER OF THE ALAMO

Municipal Auditorium, downtown • Central • Wednesday evening Admission

Sponsored by the Order of the Alamo, the coronation reveals the identity of the queen and shows off a lot of elaborate, expensive, long-trained gowns worn by young women in her court. Open to the public, though at rather stiff prices, this event gives you a chance to see San Antonio's society taking itself seriously while having a good time doing it.

CORNYATION

Beethoven Hall, HemisFair Park • Central • Tuesday, Wednesday, and Thursday nights • Admission

These performances parody the real Fiesta queen's coronation and take aim with a general satire of the city.

FIESTA GARTEN KONZERT AND DANCE

Beethoven Home, 422 Pereida at S. Alamo • Central Wednesday, Thursday, and Friday evening • Admission

If you prefer a smaller crowd, take in this German music and food festival at the Beethoven Home. The program includes choir singing, a band concert, and dancing.

BAND FESTIVAL

Alamo Stadium, 110 Tuleta at Hildebrand • Near North Thursday evening • Admission

March over to Alamo Stadium and hear high-school marching bands compete.

BATTLE OF FLOWERS PARADE

Downtown • Central • Friday afternoon • Free

Here's the event that started it all. The parade comfortably combines attractive floats, covered with plastic or paper flowers, marching bands, military drill teams, and mounted horse units. Look for the parade route in local papers. It generally starts on Broadway (at Grayson), marches by the Alamo, and then goes down Commerce, ending near Santa Rosa. San Antonians watch it in various ways. Some take their folding chairs and cold drinks and homestead early on vacant sidewalks. Others buy tickets for reserved seats. The party people rent hotel rooms with views along the route, a painless way to watch the parade, which lasts several hours. But you miss the feel of the crowds and getting soda pop dripped on you.

KING WILLIAM FAIR

King William Park, King William Street • Central • Saturday
Free

This event is for the history buff who prefers fine old neighborhoods. It also shows much of the neighborly enthusiasm typical of San Antonio. The King William Fair is not only a neighborhood fair with a parade, ethnic foods, bands, and art displays in King William Park—it's also an open house of Texas' first historic district. Located just south of downtown, the King William Historic District overflows with fascinating old homes built from 1850 to 1920. Each year at Fiesta time, several homes open for a tour sponsored by the King William Association. Some are huge Victorian mansions, and others are smaller Greek Revival or Texas farmhouse types.

FIESTA FLAMBEAU PARADE

Downtown • Central • Saturday evening • Free

Floats, bands, and more bands, with torches, electrical lights, and luminous glow-sticks lighting the way.

A DAY IN OLD MEXICO AND CHARREADA

San Antonio Charro Ranch, 6126 Padre • South • Sunday afternoon
Admission

A repeat of the festivities offered the previous Sunday. Colorful Mexican horse riding.

ISRAELI FESTIVAL

Agudas Achim, 1201 Donaldson at St. Cloud • Northwest • Sunday
Admission • W

Look for this one-day festival on Sunday. Israeli dancers, with accordion, guitar, and flute music. Jewish food and gift boutique.

BOWIE STREET BLUES FESTIVAL

Institute of Texan Cultures, HemisFair Park • Central
Sunday • Free

Blues musicians play.

ST. LUKE'S FIESTA FINALE

St. Luke's Catholic Church, 4603 Manitou at Callaghan • Northwest
Sunday evening • Free

Fiesta winds down with a street dance, food, and games.

SAN ANTONIO NEIGHBORHOODS

Like any city, San Antonio is a conglomerate of suburbs and neighborhoods. Some are old, with fine-honed character; others, modern, concrete urbania. Here we'll look briefly at a few of the more established incorporated suburbs, plus some older recognizable neighborhoods with less formal structure. Space limits this guide from touching on them all, for enumerable neighborhoods exist in a growing city of one million.

ALAMO HEIGHTS

Bounded by Incarnate Word College, Olmos Basin, and Tuxedo, Nacogdoches, and New Braunfels streets • Northeast

Alamo Heights is the grande dame of San Antonio's suburbs, dating back to 1890. The area wasn't officially incorporated until 1922, however, and some of its homes date back even further. The Argyle, for instance, was built in 1859 by Charles Anderson as headquarters for a 1,400-acre ranch, much of which is now Alamo Heights. At various times a stagecoach inn, a hotel, and now an exclusive dinner club, this fine old southern mansion stands in the heart of old-line Alamo Heights.

The suburb's name comes from the name of George Brackenridge's estate, the same Brackenridge House located on the campus of Incarnate Word College on the southern edge of present-day Alamo Heights. Brackenridge also owned what is now Fort Sam Houston and Brackenridge Park.

Alamo Heights is a jumble of older homes ranging from prairie-style cottages to southern mansions, dating from the 1900s on up to the present day. You'll find the older southern veranda homes near Cambridge Circle and Patterson. While much of the suburb is made up of affluent families and yuppies who have renovated homes, it still has a homey nature and many small, modest homes (though the prices may not always be modest).

It's not just a bedroom community, either. Alamo Heights has a healthy, restored business district, centered along Broadway, which is dotted with small shops, some elegant, some nondescript. There is a neighborhood cohesiveness, punctuated with spirited politics aimed at keeping Alamo Heights as it is. Many parents think so highly of the Alamo Heights School District, which extends beyond the city limits, that they move into the neighborhood to enable their offspring to attend its schools.

CASTLE HILLS
Bounded by Jackson-Keller, Blanco, Lockhill-Selma, and Wedgewood • North

Castle Hills, located around Loop 410 and NW Military Highway, is a fairly upscale neighborhood of traditional and modern homes built mainly in the 1950s and 1960s. Incorporated in 1951, the suburb consists of 2.46 square miles, and many doctors, lawyers, and retired military live there. Much of Castle Hills used to be the Prinz family dairy farm prior to the city's northward drift. Now shopping centers and commercial establishments almost surround the once-peaceful bedroom community. Central Park and North Star malls lie only a credit card's throw away. Castle Hills has its own police and fire departments.

KING WILLIAM
Roughly bounded by Durango, St. Mary's, Adams, and the San Antonio River • Central

This restored old neighborhood just south of downtown has become an "in" address for old-line families, the nouveau riche, and young professional couples who love to spend their money and sweat on rejuvenating sagging houses. The area roughly encompasses the King William Historic District, about a twenty-five block area of once fashionable homes that came upon hard times and, in recent years, were renewed because of their architectural character and convenience to downtown. In the late 1800s, this largely German residential area was the most elegant in the city, and its main street, King William, was named after the Prussian Kaiser Wilhelm I (see **Historical Places**). Today, some of these fine old Victorian homes (actually, they date from the 1850s to the 1920s) look just as elegant as ever. Others on the fringe are smaller, sometimes with paint peeling or in the process of being renovated. The San Antonio Conservation Society has its handsomely restored headquarters on King William Street, and many festive social events occur in the neighborhood, which has a convivial and politically vocal neighborhood association. (The King William Fair is a popular event during Fiesta; see the Fiesta section under **Annual Events**.) Some definitely casual restaurants on the fringe of King William, such as Rosario's and El Mirador, are favorite haunts of KW natives.

MONTE VISTA

Roughly bounded by Hildebrand, Shook, Ashby, and San Pedro Near North

Another historic residential district, though not as old as King William, Monte Vista has been architecturally born again. Some resplendent Victorian mansions date back to the 1890s, but many of these are from the 1920s Spanish colonial revival style. In the heart of Monte Vista, most houses are impeccably maintained; on the fringes, they may be run down and rentals. Monte Vista is not an incorporated city but strictly a neighborhood—and a vocal one when nearby businesses and churches try to encroach. Politicos, civic leaders, and numerous professionals call this area home. Nearby dining spots range from the haute Chez Ardid to the no-frills Olmos Pharmacy.

NORTH MAIN AVENUE

Along Main from Mulberry to Poplar • Near North

There's everything in this area, from gay clubs and billiard parlors to art galleries and a junior college. Just north of downtown, this amorphous, eclectic old neighborhood clings around its namesake, North Main, roughly from Mulberry to Poplar streets.

At the northern edge, the houses are Victorian and prairie style, many in the rejuvenation stage. The Mexican restaurant La Fonda is popular. Farther south, you encounter bars, girlie shows, offices, cafes such as Luther's, and run-down, older two-story houses with rooms for rent. San Antonio College and Trinity University are nearby, so a large student population lives in the area.

OLMOS PARK

Bounded by McCullough and Contour streets, and Olmos Basin • North

This affluent suburb, presumably, got its name from nearby Olmos Creek and the flood basin. Originally a real estate development called Olmos Park Estates, the area lies slightly north of downtown, just north of Hildebrand.

One of the better-heeled incorporated neighborhoods, Olmos Park has as homeowners the likes of former state governor Dolph Briscoe, who has a home here as well as his Uvalde ranch. Houses range from small bungalows to big estates built roughly between the 1920s and 1940s, some with Spanish-style architecture. A row of small, assorted stores on McCullough provides its only association with commercialism.

Nearby Olmos Dam was constructed after the terrible flood of 1921, which killed fifty people. During the flood, thirteen inches of rain caused water downtown to rise almost to the mezzanine of the Gunter Hotel. Since the *San Antonio Light*'s presses were submerged, the newspaper had to print a special flood edition on the menu press of the St. Anthony Hotel. The Olmos Basin, emptying into the San Antonio River, was the chief culprit of the disaster and became a target for flood control. Olmos Dam was finished in 1926.

SOUTHTOWN

Area roughly around S. Alamo Street and south of downtown
Central

This older, amorphous area just south of downtown has become popularly known as Southtown, with its more recent commercial resurgence. With no set boundaries, Southtown is primarily commercial, with some workingclass residences (largely Hispanic) sprinkled in. Many of the businesses, whether funky or simple restaurants, cluster on South Alamo and South St. Mary's streets. Southtown has also become known for its art complexes and galleries, mainly contemporary and Mexican; the large Blue Star Arts Complex in old warehouses on South Alamo provides a prime example. The more ritzy historic neighborhood of King William borders this area.

TERRELL HILLS

Bounded by N. New Braunfels, Burr, and Rittiman streets and Fort
Sam Houston • Northeast

Architect Alfred Giles got around with his pencil and paper. Along with many other local homes, he designed one for the Dr. Frederick Terrell family in 1912, and the Terrell farm is what later became Terrell Hills. Still sparsely settled in the 1930s, Terrell Hills grew more in the 1940s and 1950s.

This is definitely a bedroom community, with large bedrooms. The San Antonio Country Club (the city's oldest and most prestigious) abuts Terrell Hills by no accident. Part of the incorporated suburb is made up of long blocks with immense lots and mansions, with appropriately manicured lawns or estates. Many of San Antonio's oldest families live here. This is one bastion of the city's economic and social structure. Not all of Terrell Hills is large scale, however; a cross section of moderate homes does exist here.

MEXICO IN SAN ANTONIO

San Antonio, more than any other Texas city, has long been a meeting ground for diverse cultures—Spanish, Native American, Anglo, German, African-American, and Polish are only the most obvious. The city's two dominant cultures today are Anglo and Mexican. Those two cultures have a complex history, not always peaceful, of sharing the land and opportunities of South Texas. This section points up some of the more typically Mexican aspects, establishments, and customs (including events, cooking, cultural activities, and shopping) of San Antonio, with the aim of revealing some of the pleasures and excitements that suggest the city's rich Mexican heritage. However, this chapter does not include restaurants and historical places, which are covered elsewhere in this book.

This chapter touches on only a few of the high spots of Mexico in San Antonio. Any drive or walk around sections of San Antonio will reveal many more. In fact, any time you hear Mexican music, hear the Spanish language, or see the art of Mexico, you have found a piece of Mexico in San Antonio.

EVENTS

FIESTA

Various locations • 227-5191 • Ten days around April 21
Many events free • W variable

See the separate section on Fiesta (in the **Annual Events** chapter) for details about San Antonio's biggest festival event of the year. Many of the festival events have a distinctly Mexican flavor.

CINCO DE MAYO

Market Square, 514 W. Commerce • Central • 207-8600
Weekend nearest May 5 • Free

Cinco de Mayo celebrates a military victory by the Mexican Army over French troops in 1862, when Napoleon III was trying to gain a foothold in North America via the Mexican route. Although the French were not finally driven out until 1867, the victory proved psychologically important, because until then, the young nation's troops had not been proven in battle against hardened European troops, such as those of the French. The victory gave Mexico a new sense of confidence and national competence. The event is commemorated with special festivities around town, especially at Market Square, including Mexican music and food.

FIESTA NOCHE DEL RIO

Arneson River Theater, River Walk • Central • 226-4651 • Thursday, Friday, and Saturday evenings June through August • Admission • W

The musical presentations usually emphasize the multicultural and, therefore, Mexican and Spanish aspects of San Antonio's history. Expect a different show every summer, but all tend to focus on San Antonio's past. The shows include both song and dance, featuring professional performers from the San Antonio area.

DIEZ Y SEIS DE SEPTIEMBRE

**Various locations • One week around September 16
Most events free • W variable**

The sixteenth of September celebrates the anniversary of the beginning of Mexico's struggle for independence in 1810. On this day the revolutionary priest Miguel Hidalgo y Costilla issued his courageous *grito*, or "cry," for freedom and sparked the eleven-year revolt that ended with Mexico's independence.

CULTURAL ACTIVITIES

INSTITUTE OF TEXAN CULTURES

**HemisFair Park, Bowie and Durango • Central • 458-2300
Free • W**

This grand favorite museum in San Antonio highlights the different cultural groups, including Mexicans, that have contributed to the present diversity of Texas. For more information, see the listing in **Museums**.

INSTITUTO CULTURAL MEXICANO

Plaza Mexico, 600 HemisFair Park • Central • 227-0123 • W

For the Mexicophile, this is one of the city's top spots. Basically, it is a gallery with changing exhibits, but it seems much more. The exhibits are chosen and mounted with such care that the institute is becoming an excellent general art museum even though it addresses only one culture. The exhibits change often and feature many varied media.

While traveling shows and temporary exhibits provide its staple fare, the institute also presents movies, conferences, and even occasional performances of drama or music. The newspapers usually announce its shows—check the weekend entertainment supplements. Call before going to make sure it's open.

SAN ANTONIO CHARRO ASSOCIATION
6126 Padre • 532-0693

Charreada, the art or sport (it has elements of both) of skilled riding, is known as the national sport of Mexico. It combines some elements of the rodeo with elements of competitive riding. The association is dedicated to keeping the skills of the early Hispanic and Mexican charros alive. Ranching, after all, was an important Spanish activity. Hence the association preserves very old traditions and skills that developed as a consequence of a way of life in which the horse played a major part. The association sponsors a number of events, including Mexican rodeos, each year. The city's annual Fiesta festival always features charreadas. Practice sessions are often held on Saturday and Sunday afternoons at the practice field on Padre Drive, adjacent to Mission County Park. Anyone is welcome to stop by and watch.

EDUCATIONAL OPPORTUNITIES

All of the local colleges and universities offer opportunities to study Spanish, and some offer courses in Mexican archaeology, history, culture, and folklore. Check the **Education** chapter for details.

UNIVERSIDAD NACIONAL AUTONOMA DE MEXICO
600 HemisFair Park • Central • 222-8626 • W

Here, amid several other Mexican attractions, you'll find a branch of the University of Mexico. While it does not offer a full degree program, it does present an opportunity to learn Spanish at any of four levels and to study various aspects of Latin American art, history, and anthropology. The instructors hail from Mexico, so if you want to study Spanish for a trip to Mexico, this might be a good place to start. Most courses run for a full university semester and may be taken for credit or not. Other courses are shorter, and some are offered on Saturdays. Occasional special programs may particularly interest students of Mexican topics. For example, in the past, the university has held a special series of lectures about the history of Mexican art. There is also a small university library.

MEXICAN COOKING AND PRODUCTS

While Mexican restaurants can give a visitor (or native) an excellent introduction to Mexican food, some people prefer making the food themselves. Those would-be Mexican chefs have a lot of help in San Antonio. Not only do most markets carry prepared Mexican food products of varying merit available, San Antonio also offers some fine Mexican specialty food stores. If you wish to cook Mexican food at home, hunt up a copy of one of Diana Kennedy's Mexican cookbooks. Her best-known book is probably her first, *The Cuisines of Mexico*. Critics have gone so far as to call it one of the ten best cookbooks ever written. She discusses ingredients and techniques, as well as regional differences in Mexican cooking styles. With her book and the shopping resources of San Antonio, you can hardly go wrong. When you cannot find ingredients for Mexican dishes at the local supermarket, try one of the food stores listed below.

A visit to a Mexican bakery is an eye-opening and mouth-watering experience. Both bread and pastries (*pan dulce*, or "sweet bread") differ quite a lot in Mexican bakeries from the corresponding articles in supermarkets. The bread is crustier and fresher and, for some uses, altogether much better. Mexican bakers tend to make it with less fat, however, so it becomes stale sooner than other bread and you should not buy it with the idea of keeping it for more than a day or so. *Bolillos*, Mexican dinner rolls, are special treats, with their crusty outsides and (if really authentic) faint hint of unsweetened cinnamon. Many Mexican bakers still bake pastries with lard, the traditional shortening in Mexican kitchens, which results in a superb texture but a heavier final product than many gringos are accustomed to.

The bakeries listed below carry a variety of breads and pan dulce, as do many other local bakeries. If part of your itinerary in San Antonio includes sampling things Mexican, one of these belongs on your schedule. For some reason, a little knowledge of Spanish will more likely help you in bakeries than in other businesses. But if you don't speak Spanish, don't worry. In a bakery, you can get by with pointing, indicating numbers with your fingers, and lots of smiles.

An essential of Mexican cuisine is the tortilla, a Mexican staple food similar to bread and flatter than a pancake. Two kinds, flour and corn, are common. Corn tortillas are more typical of the interior of Mexico; you'll find flour tortillas more often in northern Mexico. The two are not interchangeable in Mexican cooking, although you can serve either as a bread at a Mexican meal. A few Mexican families make their own tortillas, but the practice is probably about as common as making bread at home. Fortunately, you can purchase tortillas that taste almost as good as the ones you might make at home.

Tortillas are not made in bakeries but in tortilla factories, and some of the better-known *tortillerias* are listed here. Most of these tortillerias also sell *masa,* the dough from which tortillas are made. If you plan to do much Mexican cooking, you will certainly need masa from time to time, and real masa from a tortilleria tastes far better than that from a powdered mix. Many of the tortilla factories sell masa only before a certain hour of the day (before they have used it all up making tortillas) or when arrangements have been made the day before.

ADELANTE MEXICAN FOOD

21 Brees at New Braunfels • Northeast • 822-7681

While this is primarily a restaurant (see **Restaurant** chapter), Adelante does a lot of carryout business. This place is a good source for Mexican food for parties, especially tamales, of which Adelante has many varieties and sells them singly or by the dozen.

ALBERTO'S MEXICAN FOOD PRODUCTS INC.

2015 Nogalitos at Thompson • South • 532-4176

Although Alberto's sells tortillas, it is much more than a tortilleria. A variety of Mexican foods fills the shop—sauces, tostadas, tamales, canned goods, spices, and peppers, in addition to the usual tortillas and masa. Tamales, incidentally, are made from a kind of masa different from that used for making tortillas. If you plan to try your hand at turning out tamales, be sure to ask, here or elsewhere, for tamale masa.

BUÑUELOS INC.

108 Auditorium Circle (and 5917 San Pedro) • Central
223-3424 • Call ahead about hours

A *buñuelo* is a crisp, fried sweet bread that in Mexico plays about the same role that doughnuts play in this country; it can serve as a dessert, snack, or something to have with morning coffee. Buñuelos Inc. makes them right on the premises. The buñuelo shop is just the kind of small operation that is so common in Mexico, and the aroma of cinnamon and fresh dough in such a small space will almost overpower you when you walk in.

JJ TAMALE FACTORY

1611 Culebra at Goodrich • Northwest • 733-9822

Tamales, like tortillas, are seldom made at home. Instead, people buy them at a factory while they are fresh and hot and then rush home or to a party. It seems everyone has a favorite source for tamales, and JJ Tamale Factory is one of ours. The corn flavor in the masa seems fresher here, and the meat filling usually has just enough spices. Whether you want two tamales or a few hundred, JJ can take care of you. For a larger order, as for a big party, call in advance so JJ can save as many as you need, all hot and packaged.

MEXICAN BAKERIES

You'll notice many bakeries in town. Here are three that have proven dependable for fresh-baked goods:

LA POBLANITA BAKERY
2411 N. Zarzamora at Woodlawn • Northwest • 732-1554 • W

LOS COCOS BAKERY
3309 West Ave. • North • 349-3373

MI TIERRA CAFE AND BAKERY
Market Square, 218 Produce Row • Central • 225-1262 • W

SEGOVIA MEXICAN CANDY MANUFACTURER
1837 Guadalupe • South • 225-2102 • W

Pralines, divinity, *leche quemada*, etc.

TAXCO FOODS INC.
402 Culebra at Brazos • West • 735-1045

Tortillas and tamales are made here and sold in great numbers.

SHOPPING

EL MERCADO
Market Square, 514 W. Commerce • Central • 207-8600

El Mercado is the most thoroughly Mexican spot in San Antonio's commercial world. Here, in the fashion of markets all over Mexico, stalls crowd close to one another offering all varieties of (mostly) Mexican goods. The gamut runs from kitchen tools, clothes, and leather products to paintings and decorative art. Each of the separate shops or stalls is an independent business; each has its own peculiarities, stock, and prices. Many of the merchants import their goods directly from Mexico. Markets such as this in Mexico differ primarily in that they often have food stalls mixed in with the others. In addition, some Mexican customs, such as vigorous bargaining for the merchandise, are not often followed, but neither is Spanish spoken, so from an Anglophone's point of view, El Mercado both suffers and benefits in comparison with its counterparts across the border. Nevertheless, a visit closely approaches the experience of shopping in Mexico. Be sure to bargain snoop around; the very same item may cost less down the hall.

LA HACIENDA TILE

444 Fredericksburg Road at Colorado • Near North • 735-4457

La Hacienda provides and installs Mexican tiles, especially floor tiles, and a few other decorative Mexican items. Unfortunately, it does not have the colored ceramic tiles that are so popular for the kitchens in some parts of the Southwest, but it does have the deep, dusky red floor tiles of Saltillo.

MARKET SQUARE

Bounded by I-35, Santa Rosa, W. Commerce, and Dolorosa • Central • W

Much of the Mexican life accessible to visitors takes place here, either in the open area or in adjacent businesses. Many Saturdays and Sundays, the central courtyard of Market Square is given over to a celebration, commemoration, or other fiesta. On those days, it is filled with music (from Mexican and Latin to rock) and with small stalls selling various kinds of food. The food booths serve tamales, guacamole, fajitas, beer, and other food and drink. *Fajitas,* a popular feature of San Antonio's Mexican cuisine, are strips of skirt steak—marinated, grilled over charcoal, and then swaddled in a hot, fresh flour tortilla. A master fajita chef once confided to me that his secret cooking method included placing whole raw onions among the coals used for cooking. The burning onions give off a scent that perfumes the meat and makes it especially flavorful. When covered with guacamole and perhaps a little *pico de gallo*—a Mexican condiment of chopped, seasoned raw onions, peppers, and other vegetables—fajitas can be a memorable eating experience of San Antonio. Many shops, restaurants, and galleries with a definite Mexican flavor fill up Market Square. This place is for browsing and strolling rather than just a brief stop on a walking tour. You'll find El Mercado, the Mexican market, here also.

MATERIALS MARKETING CORPORATION

120 W. Josephine • Near North • 731-8453

Materials Marketing has a wide range of items in stock—this place is for finding such things as tile and carved stone garden ornaments, as well as a variety of imports from much of Europe. A walk through the outdoor garden decorations may inspire you to relandscape your backyard.

MAYAN TEJIDOS DE GUATEMALA

520 River Walk • Central • 226-7665

Mixed in with the Guatemalan merchandise, one can find bits of Mexican pottery and Oaxacan dresses. The store definitely rates a visit. The colorful beauty of the Central American themes in clothes, placemats, fabrics, and miscellaneous handmade goods makes this a fine store for those who have come to San Antonio to shop.

KIDS' STUFF

Children enjoy many of the attractions listed elsewhere in this book, such as the Alamo, Sea World, Six Flags Fiesta Texas, Cascade Caverns, the Quadrangle at Fort Sam Houston, the Hertzberg Circus Museum, the Institute of Texan Cultures, Market Square, Mexican rodeos, the River Walk, the San Antonio Zoo, the Tower of the Americas, and many others. Below are some additional suggestions for entertaining and educating children.

BOOKS AND MAGAZINES

OUR KIDS—SAN ANTONIO

8400 Blanco • North • 349-6667

This monthly magazine fills a real need in San Antonio by giving parents ideas not only of what to do with kids but also of what to do for them, about them, and to them. The widely varied contents range from a calendar of events of interest to kids, through medically and psychologically oriented articles, to product and service reviews.

THE RED BALLOON

5009 Broadway • North • 826-5087

Children's books, mostly, fill the space here, but the care that has gone into the books' selection is a special feature. A few toys and games fill out the store, but The Red Balloon is mostly a bookstore and an unusually fine one.

ACTIVITIES

ALAMO HEIGHTS NATURE TRAIL
227 Greely at Viesca • Northeast • 822-6433 • Open by special arrangement by calling Alamo Heights Police Department

San Antonians enjoy pointing out that San Antonio is one of the largest cities in the country. Yet within this big city exist areas in which urban life seems far away. The Alamo Heights Nature Trail is one such area. This trail through a wooded area gives the impression of being miles from any city. The area is popular with local birdwatchers—the Audubon Society meets nearby. If you visit after a rain, stay on the trails; the mud there is the heavy, sticky variety.

AMF COUNTRY LANES
13307 San Pedro • North • 496-3811 • Open daily

Bowling and electronic games, a popular mix locally, provide the drawing power here. Teenagers find the spot especially attractive.

BRACKENRIDGE PARK MINIATURE RAILROAD
**Brackenridge Park, 3910 North St. Mary's • Near North
736-9534 • Open daily • Adults $2.25, children $1.75**

One good way to take in vast Brackenridge Park is to ride through it on the park's miniature railroad that follows a twenty-minute circuit around the park. The train glides through the woods and past the stables, stops at the Witte Memorial Museum, then passes through a short tunnel, and finally ends up where it started. The pace is usually slow (joggers often catch the train and pass it by) but fun, at least on most of the trips. A few years ago, the train slipped into a replay of Texas history when bandits stopped it in the woods and held it up.

BRAUNIG LAKE PARK
**Dunop Road, off I-37, four miles south of Loop 410 • South
635-8289 • Open at all times except December and January**

Although the huge power plant on this dammed-up lake removes this spot from the category of wilderness, Braunig is one of the closest lakes where youngsters can try their luck at fishing. Boating and fishing are the attractions, and amenities are few.

CRYSTAL ICE PALACE
I-10 at DeZavala • Northwest • 696-0006 • Open daily, but call ahead; hours vary

Texas on ice? Well almost. This is one place where kids don't need sunblock during the summertime. Though not too many Texans know the ways of ice skating, here's where you can take lessons or skate.

DISCOVERY ZONE

5751 NW Loop 410 • Northwest • 681-3232

Designed for younger children, Discovery Zone is full of climbing and crawling spaces, bouncing rooms, special slides, and games of skill for little hands.

MALIBU CASTLE GOLF AND GAMES

3330 Cherry Ridge at Loop 410 & I-10 North • 341-6663
Open daily, hours vary

Miniature golf courses, bumper boats, go-carts, and video games.

MALIBU GRAND PRIX

7702 Briaridge near Loop 410 and I-10 • Northwest • 341-2643
Open daily, hours vary

You can drive pint-sized autos around a facsimile of a racing course.

SAN ANTONIO'S CHILDREN'S MUSEUM (See Museums)

SCIENCE TREEHOUSE

Witte Museum, 3801 Broadway at Brackenridge Park
Northeast • 357-1900 • Open daily

At the Witte Museum (see **Museums** for more details), this recent four-level addition of a Science Treehouse has all sorts of hands-on activities that kids enjoy.

SKYRIDE AT BRACKENRIDGE PARK

3910 North St. Mary's at Tuleta • North • 736-9534
Open daily • Adults $2.25, children $1.75 • W

Take the cable cars in Brackenridge Park for a panoramic view of the park's grounds and the San Antonio skyline.

SPLASH TOWN (See Parks)

NOTE that some of the stores in the Shopping section are especially suitable for shopping for children—see, for example, A Brighter Child and Kids Junction Resale.

PARKS AND OUTDOORS

With a climate that ranges from balmy at its coolest to, let's face it, sometimes downright hot, the city is outdoors-oriented. Folks just naturally gravitate to the great outdoors and acres of parkland and recreational areas. And like most Americans, they like to sweat and play away their free time, so listed below are the major parks, gardens, and zoo. Like any good-sized city, San Antonio has its share of citizens who enjoy doing as much as they can outdoors. San Antonio has enthusiastic nature lovers in the local Sierra Club and Audubon Society chapters and legions of joggers and runners. The local chapter of the Sierra Club even wrote and published a book about outdoor activities in the local area, *Outdoor San Antonio and Vicinity*. The edition is well worth digging for in the city's used bookstores.

BRACKENRIDGE PARK

3800 Broadway • Northeast • 207-3000 • Open daily
Free • W variable

This big daddy of the parks is a fine, aged one with character. Brackenridge has been around since 1899, when the Water Works Company, under president George Brackenridge, deeded it to the city. Besides its many trees, Brackenridge Park has quaint rock buildings and old-fashioned metal bridges spanning the San Antonio River as it winds its way through the park. Bridle paths and hiking trails, a golf course, a miniature railroad, an aerial skyride (see **Kids' Stuff** and **Sports**), the Witte Memorial Museum (see **Museums**), and the San Antonio Zoo (see entry in this chapter) round out the offerings of the 343-acre park. It's a pleasant place for a family day outing or a weekday picnic lunch at the stone tables along the river. But watch out for the bumper-to-bumper traffic on some weekends.

CITY PARKS AND RECREATION DEPARTMENT

950 E. Hildebrand (main office) • Northeast • 207-3000
Monday through Friday • Many activities free • W variable

San Antonio sports about 150 parks and plazas, with around 6,000 acres of parkland and recreational areas, including about 24 year-round community centers. Activities offered by the Parks and Recreation Department range from Brown Bag Days (free park concerts) and dances to craft lessons and senior-citizen domino tournaments, plus a large sports program. Call the central office for details about these manifold public programs (many are free) and the community center nearest you.

FRIEDRICH WILDERNESS PARK

Milsa Road • *Take I-10 north, past Loop 1604, and exit at Camp Bullis; go west under freeway and take a right on access road; continue one mile, turn left on Oak Road, then right on Milsa* • **Approximately twelve miles from Loop 410 Northwest** • **698-1057** • **Wednesday through Sunday 8–5 in winter, 8–8 summer** • **Free** • **W**

This unspoiled wilderness park of about 280 acres of Hill Country provides a sanctuary for wildlife and plants . . . and the urban species who wants to view the vanishing breed. Seven nature trails wind through the park, varying in hiking difficulty and distance. The Forest Range Trail, near the entrance, takes about thirty minutes of easy strolling on paved trails. And it has hand ropes for the blind and mobility-impaired. The Main Loop Trail (which offers access to the other trails), on the other hand, is more rugged and requires an hour of walking. The Water Trail is easy walking along a creek. Norma Friedrich Ward donated the bulk of this acreage to the city in honor of her parents. Open year-round. Inquire about special programs and guided monthly tours.

JAPANESE TEA GARDENS

3800 North St. Mary's at Tuleta • **Northeast** • **207-3000**
Open daily, dawn to dusk • **Free** • **W variable**

The Japanese Tea Gardens were originally a limestone rock quarry and cement plant, established in 1880. Its limestone was used to build the state capitol building. The gardens were first called the Japanese Gardens, but World War II led to a name change to Chinese Gardens. Later the name became the Sunken Gardens, and now it's back again to Japanese. Walkways, rock bridges, and ponds with goldfish are interspersed with lush, colorful semitropical flowers.

McALLISTER PARK

Jones-Maltsberger and Buckhorn • **Northeast** • **207-3000**
Open daily • **Free** • **W**

This large northside park of 856 acres is suitable for jogging and cycling. Located just northeast of the airport, it has several picnic pavilions and an overnight tent camping area (by reservation only). It also has soccer fields—much in demand by local leagues—little league diamonds, and extensive picnic areas. Although the city is building right up to the edge of the park, in the park's remote areas you'll find it easy to feel many miles away from San Antonio—visitors even spot deer here from time to time.

NATURAL BRIDGE WILDLIFE RANCH

About seventeen miles northeast of San Antonio • *Take I-35 north, then turn left onto Natural Bridge Caverns Road (TX 3009) and follow the Natural Bridge Caverns signs* • **(210) 438-7400** • **Open daily, 9–6:30 summer, 9–5 winter** • **Adults $6.55, children $4.20**

Since the wildlife ranch is next to the Natural Bridge Caverns, just follow the caverns' signs to get here. This is, in effect, a drive-in zoo, where you drive slowly along a three and one-half mile road to spot the animals, which range from ostriches and buffalo to zebras and giraffes. Many of them come up to the car windows panhandling for food. You're not allowed to feed them, but watch it—some may not want to take no for an answer. This makes for a good outing, with some 200 acres of rugged Hill Country land on which the animals roam. Take your own lunch bag if you like—there's a picnic area. Also petting zoo.

SAN ANTONIO BOTANICAL GARDENS

555 Funston at N. New Braunfels • **Northeast** • **821-5115**
Open daily 9–6 • **Adults $3, children $1** • **W**

This lovely hideaway is a place where you can get back to nature and escape urbanitis. It also pleasantly surprises those who expect gardens to be dull. The San Antonio Botanical Gardens are a learning experience on thirty-three acres near Fort Sam Houston. Thanks to help from the San Antonio Garden Center, located next door, the city can boast of a very unusual center. It probably has the best collection of native plants in Texas. Several sections of the land are devoted to East Texas, Southwest Texas, and the Hill Country, with early Texas homes, in styles from log cabins to adobe, scattered about to give authenticity. The land and plants are purposely cultivated to look like natural rural areas, with walking trails throughout. This is a particularly good place to take children on educational hikes. The center has even created its own East Texas lake and brought in a nineteenth-century cabin. It also has the award-winning Lucille Halsell Conservatory, a huge greenhouse complex. The formal gardens exhibit herbs and biblical plants, and you'll also find a special fragrant area for the blind here. A children's garden hosts special children's classes about growing plants. Be sure to visit the gazebo high on the hill for views over much of the city. The entrance to the gardens features a restored 1896 limestone carriage house moved stone by stone from downtown San Antonio. The Carriage House Kitchen there makes a pleasant place for lunch.

SAN ANTONIO ZOOLOGICAL GARDENS AND AQUARIUM

3903 North St. Mary's at Tuleta • Northeast • 734-7183
Open daily 9–5 in winter, 9–6:30 in summer • Adults $6, children $4

Known simply as the San Antonio Zoo, this makes an entertaining and educational place to go, particularly for the kids. The San Antonio Zoo dates back to around 1910, when a few animals were kept over at San Pedro Park. Then, in 1914, George Brackenridge gave some elk and buffalo for display in Brackenridge Park, and by 1929, the San Antonio Zoological Society established the zoo at its present location. San Antonio's zoo is rated as one of the top ten zoos in the country, well known for its breeding capabilities. Apparently, not all zoos have that special knack of coaxing animals to reproduce in captivity. Outside of Africa, the San Antonio Zoo was the first to produce a white rhinoceros. It has had similar success with flamingos and whooping cranes. Despite its relatively small size (fifty acres), the San Antonio Zoo still has one of North America's biggest collections, with more than 3,400 creatures and more than 700 species.

Built in and around the bluffs and cliffs of an old rock quarry, the zoo, with its hilly terrain, rock walls, flowing streams, and attractive plants, has a comfortable, seasoned look in its natural habitats. Part of the zoo is divided into special areas where animals from the same regions share spaces—there is Amazonia (South America), Africa Rift Valley, and an Australian walkabout.

The zoo is litter free and well kept. Spend several hours there, or take a picnic lunch and make a day of it. The zoo is shady in most parts, so even on the hottest days, you can find a cool spot. Food is also sold. Don't miss the Children's Zoo. It has a tropical boat ride, an animal nursery, and a petting zoo. The zoo is particularly well known for its collection of antelopes, birds, and reptiles. Visit the reptile house and see boa constrictors, vampire bats, vipers, and huge pythons. The zoo also offers tours and special programs.

SAN PEDRO PARK

1500 San Pedro at Dewey • Near North • 207-3000
Open at all times • Free • W

The site of McFarlin Tennis Center and the San Antonio Playhouse, San Pedro Park has a colorful background. This shady old park, just north of downtown, is the oldest in the city and the second oldest municipal park in the United States. Located around San Pedro Springs, the park was born in 1852 and became a favorite resort for families. It featured a bathhouse, museum, pavilion, tropical garden, and even a zoo with a bear pit. It also proved a popular spot for political rallies, and in 1859, Sam Houston railed against secession here. In 1878, the first mule-drawn street car in San Antonio traveled the rails from Main Plaza to the springs. A nostalgic bandstand still remains as a token of the good old days.

SPLASH TOWN

I-35 at Coliseum Road • East • 227-1100 • Open daily June through August, weekends only in May and September • $17.99 for adults, $12.99 for children

You can't get away from the sun or the crowds here, particularly the teen groupies who love to splash, socialize, and pose. This park was set up from scratch with no significant natural landscape to fit into. That and its location between the Southern Pacific Railroad's main line and the freeway make it a distinctly urban park, but that doesn't cut down on the fun. You'll encounter dipping speed slides, big waves in a large pool, a kiddie swimming area, and a gently flowing tube float-along. New rides open from time to time—such as the long, completely enclosed slide that takes you from top to bottom in thirty seconds of swooping and twisting in total darkness. Sand volleyball courts, picnic areas, and food service complete a popular picture.

Sports

Hold that gut in. It's fashionable to be in shape these days, and certainly erstwhile local jocks can't resist the whistle of sports either. From San Antonio's own NBA pro basketball team, the Spurs, to golf (the city is fast becoming a destination for golfers), this chapter encompasses both spectator and participation sports. So whether you prefer sipping suds in the bleachers or getting in on the thrill of victory and the agony of defeat, there's something here for everyone.

CITY PARKS AND RECREATION DEPARTMENT
950 E. Hildebrand (main office) • 207-3000
Many activities free • W

Some twenty-four community centers around town offer many sports activities and classes. Call the main office of the Parks and Recreation Department for more information. It sponsors both community center programs and municipal leagues in all sorts of sports, including softball, basketball, flag football, and volleyball. The city also provides recreation centers and day camps for the handicapped. Naturally, the city has numerous swimming pools, golf courses, and tennis courts. For more details on these sports, see the separate headings below.

YOUNG MEN'S CHRISTIAN ASSOCIATION
903 North St. Mary's (downtown branch) • 246-9622 • Hours vary
from branch to branch • Fees vary • W some branches

The YMCA has a vast sports program, with several branches around the city. The basic membership fee entitles you to participate in the various programs and stay at YMCAs across the country that rent rooms (San Antonio's doesn't). The individual classes, activities, and leagues have their own fees. Branches have leagues, team sports, and swimming lessons, but the programs vary. Programs range from jogging and karate to soccer and football. The special adult athletic facility at the downtown branch includes a track, a sauna, whirlpools, and sophisticated bodybuilding and gymnastic equipment.

YOUNG WOMEN'S CHRISTIAN ASSOCIATION
503 Castroville at Cupples • Northwest • 433-9922 • Fees vary

The YWCA offers classes in swimming, karate, and aerobic exercise. Also some leagues in basketball and volleyball.

ARCHERY

GASSMAN'S ARCHERY AND AIR GUN HEADQUARTERS
102 Jackson-Keller at Recoleta • North • 822-7131

Indoor range.

AUTO RACING

ALAMO DRAGWAY
15030 Watson at Highway 16 • South • 923-8801

This track features quarter-mile auto drag racing on Saturdays, except during the Christmas season.

SAN ANTONIO SPEEDWAY
14901 S. Highway 16, four miles south of Loop 410
South • 628-1499

This NASCAR track has late model, super street stock, thunder, and charger car racing. The speedway is part of the Winston Racing Series and offers a variety of programs.

BALLOONING

Balloon-ride companies seem to come and go like, well, the wind. If you want to go up, up, and away, check the current listings in the Yellow Pages. Usually you'll find several listed in the area. Rides are not cheap, because of the crew needed to launch and collect the balloon and because of the cost of the balloon and its fuel. One can count on a fare of around $160 per person for a flight of a few hours.

BASEBALL

MUNICIPAL LEAGUES

The Parks and Recreation Department (207-3110) has softball leagues, as does the YMCA (246-9622).

SAN ANTONIO MISSIONS

Nelson Wolff Municipal Stadium, 5757 Highway 90 W at Callaghan Road • Northwest • 675-7275 • April through August • $4–$8

The San Antonio Missions Class AA pro team competes in the Texas League and is part of the Los Angeles Dodgers' farm system. As with any minor league team, the caliber of play varies (some players do graduate to the majors), but the fans' enthusiasm and the dedication of the players are major league. Low prices, frequent promotions, special event nights, and often good baseball all contribute to good attendance.

BASKETBALL

MUNICIPAL LEAGUES

Leagues are conducted by the Parks and Recreation Department (207-3110), the YMCA (246-9622), and the YWCA.

SAN ANTONIO SPURS

Ticket office at Alamodome, 100 Montana • Central • 554-7787 October through April • $10–$48 (higher-grade seats may range up to $120) • W

Since San Antonio has no NFL football team or major league baseball team, local fans go wild with Spurmania. This is Mr. Robinson's neighborhood in the person of All-Star center David Robinson, who sets a rare sports role model both off and on court. The Spurs currently play at the Alamodome, which has numerous seats and makes for record crowds (but many seats aren't as close-in as in an arena configuration).

BICYCLING

San Antonio's climate and the rolling terrain to the north make it a natural for bicycling. For families who like to cycle together, call the San Antonio Wheelmen, a club open to all ages who enjoy riding on rural roads nearby. To get information about the Wheelmen or about the local racing clubs, inquire at one of the local bike stores (such as Bike World, 828-5558).

BOATING AND FISHING

About fifteen lakes lie within 150 miles of San Antonio, and the Gulf Coast is only about that same distance away. Some of the closer area lakes are listed below.

CALAVERAS LAKE

Take US 181 southeast, about fifteen miles from San Antonio • **W variable**

This 3,500-acre lake has good bass and catfish fishing. It has the advantage of easy access from San Antonio.

CANYON LAKE

This 8,200-acre lake lies about forty-five miles north of San Antonio, near New Braunfels and Gruene. Of all the local lakes, Canyon Lake is probably the most scenic and most visited, and restrictions on lakeside development have kept it from appearing to be a resort. Formed by a dam in the Guadalupe River, Canyon Lake is popular with sailors, windsurfers, picnickers, and fishermen (see **Side Trips**).

LAKE McQUEENEY

Take I-10 thirty-five miles east to FM 78, turn left, and go two miles
Approximately thirty-seven miles northeast of San Antonio
W variable

This 396-acre lake is popular for waterskiing and as a site for weekend homes. Fishing, boating, and swimming facilities, with weekly ski shows during the summer.

MEDINA LAKE

This 5,570-acre lake lies about thirty miles northwest of San Antonio near Bandera (see **Side Trips**).

BOWLING

San Antonio has numerous commercial bowling alleys listed in the Yellow Pages. For information about the assorted leagues and tournaments, call University Bowl at I-10 and De Zavala (Northwest), 699-6235.

BOXING

The Parks and Recreation Department (207-3110) has a boxing program. Look for the Golden Gloves tournament around February, sponsored by Boys and Girls Clubs of San Antonio (434-4383).

CANOEING AND TUBING

Enthusiasts of these activities can find good spots around New Braunfels on the Guadalupe River. Other nearby rivers, such as the San Marcos, the Blanco, and the Medina, have their devotees as well, but the Guadalupe is the most popular. If you're a novice, inquire about the river's safer areas, and remember that there is more to canoeing than meets the eye—it's distressingly easy for a beginning (or even an experienced) canoeist to get sideways in the river and have the river wrap the canoe around a tree. Some parts of local rivers are deceptively dangerous for both canoes and tubes. Canoe and tube outfitters abound on the stretch of the Guadalupe River below Canyon Dam and above New Braunfels. Call the New Braunfels Chamber of Commerce (800-572-2626) for information.

COLLEGIATE AND HIGH SCHOOL SPORTS

Area colleges naturally have numerous sports programs (both men's and women's) to follow. Some of the more visible teams are the St. Mary's and UTSA basketball ones. And Trinity University has traditionally fielded top tennis and skeet teams.

Local high schools participate in all sorts of sports, but in keeping with Texas tradition, football inspires the most fan hysteria. The sports section of the daily newspaper covers many of these events.

FISHING

See Boating and Fishing.

FOOTBALL

MUNICIPAL LEAGUES

The Parks and Recreation Department (207-3110) has leagues.

HIGH SCHOOL AND COLLEGE FOOTBALL

As stated above, high school football attracts high-voltage loyalty among Texans in general and San Antonio parents and alumni in particular. Check the fall schedule in most daily or weekly papers for some pigskin action every weekend. Fridays are the big evenings for football locally, but games are occasionally played other days as well.

Although San Antonio has not had big-time college football teams to call its own, the advent of the Alamodome has brought NFL preseason games, occasional locally played games between major Texas college teams, and post-season action with the Alamo Bowl game around New Year's, which includes some top collegiate teams from the Big Twelve and Big Ten conferences.

PROFESSIONAL FOOTBALL

While the dream of an NFL team in San Antonio remains just a gleam in the eye of its optimistic promoters, you can see NFL pre-season games at the Alamodome. The chances for a local team ratcheted up a bit with the building of the Alamodome, but there's no telling when and if it will ever happen.

GOLF

With the mild climate that lasts so many months, teeing off is a favorite pastime in San Antonio. Besides the private country clubs, the city has six municipal golf courses and many other privately run ones that are open to the public. The city course fees are currently $14 weekdays and $16 weekends (except for Cedar Creek, which is higher). But fees at the private courses can run on up to even $90 to $100. So call ahead to verify fees.

BRACKENRIDGE GOLF COURSE

2315 Avenue B at Mill Race • Northeast • 226-5612

An oldie, opened in 1917, Brackenridge has been renovated and has a championship course of 6,185 yards. Located near the center of town in Brackenridge Park, this city-owned course was the original site of the Texas Open tournament.

CEDAR CREEK GOLF COURSE

8250 Vista Colina • Northwest • 695-5050

This municipal course in a Hill Country setting is full of valleys. The championship course is 7,150 yards.

HYATT REGENCY HILL COUNTRY RESORT GOLF CLUB

Hyatt Regency Hill Country Resort, 9800 Hyatt Resort Drive
Far Northwest • 647-1234 • $90 weekdays, $100 weekends

This course, probably the city's most glamorous, opened in 1993 as part of the Hyatt Regency Hill Country Resort (see **Accommodations**). The course completely encircles the main complex of the resort and offers excellent views of the surrounding hill country. Reservations for local players are taken forty-eight hours in advance.

LA CANTERA GOLF CLUB

16401 La Cantera Pkwy. • Northwest • 558-4653

With old limestone quarry walls and Six Flags Fiesta Texas theme park as an adjacent backdrop, this has recently been the site of the PGA's Texas Open.

MISSION DEL LAGO

1250 Mission Grande • South • 627-2522

Another city-owned course, 7,208 yards.

OLMOS BASIN GOLF COURSE

7022 N. McCullough at Basse • North • 826-4041

Opened in 1963, this well-kept, city-owned, eighteen-hole course of 6,894 yards has hosted many tournaments.

PECAN VALLEY GOLF COURSE

4700 Pecan Valley at Southcross • East • 333-9018

Pecan Valley is not city-owned, but this course is open to the public as well as members. This is another championship course, of 7,116 yards.

QUARRY GOLF CLUB

444 E. Basse • Northeast • 824-4500

Another quarry-turned-golf-course, this one is more inside the populated area and a very tony one at that. You won't find many shade trees here, but you can cool off later at the nearby upscale shopping centers.

RIVERSIDE GOLF COURSE

203 McDonald at Roosevelt • South • 533-8371

Riverside includes an eighteen-hole layout and a set of par-3 holes. This city-owned, family golf course of 6,602 yards boasts a variety of holes for all ages.

WILLOW SPRINGS GOLF COURSE

E. Houston Street at Coliseum Road • East • 226-6721

This city-owned course of 6,407 yards is convenient for those on the city's east side.

NATIONAL TOURNAMENTS

SENIORS PGA

**One Dominion Drive at Dominion Country Club • North
698-3582 • Admission**

All the big-name senior guys stop here for a PGA Seniors tournament at this private country club.

TEXAS OPEN

**16401 La Cantera Pkwy. • Northwest • 341-0823 • One week in
either September or October • Admission**

The Texas Open boasts of being the fourth oldest on the PGA tour, having begun in 1922 at Brackenridge Park with a huge purse of $5,000—which was then considered outrageous. Some skepticism that the purse could be met existed, and in fact, the hat had to be passed on the eighteenth green. Compare that sum with recent million-dollar purses. Inflation and golfers have come a long way.

HIGH SCHOOL SPORTS

See Collegiate and High School Sports.

HANDBALL

You'll find several commercial clubs in town, and the YMCA also has courts.

HIKING

Many hiking areas lurk in area parks (see **Parks and Outdoors**). Also look for occasional Volksmarches and walkfests in the city, some sponsored by the military bases or a local group of the American Volkssports Association (see Community Organizations under the **Health, Safety, and Community Services** chapter).

HORSEBACK RIDING

Unfortunately, our old standby for horseback riding in our "city slicker" setting has fallen plumb out of the saddle. Brackenridge Stables, which used to offer horseback riding at Brackenridge Park, is no longer in business. No more saddling up there pardner. You have to look mainly to outlying smaller towns, such as Seguin, Pipe Creek, Bandera, or Bulverde to find some currently listed riding services in the yellow pages.

HORSE RACING

RETAMA PARK

One Retama Parkway, on IH-35, just northeast of town
Northeast • 651-7000 • Live racing season May through
November • $2.50 general admission

Ever since pari-mutuel horse racing became legal in Texas, several race tracks have popped up around the state, and many have had financial problems keeping afloat. Retama is no exception, but it has so far survived. This class track can accommodate 20,000 fans, with air-conditioned clubhouse, bars, and restaurants. Has had quarter-horse and thoroughbred live racing during the summer and televised simulcast races from across the country year-round. General admission is low, but of course, Retama hopes you bet a lot more dinero on the nags.

ICE HOCKEY

As of this writing, San Antonio has had several ice hockey teams in professional hockey leagues. But since these teams, like lower-level professional football teams, seem to bounce around due to lack of financing or whatever, I'm not going to list any. Check the sports pages to see which one may be currently playing.

HORSE SHOWS

See Rodeos and Horse Shows.

KARATE

Try the Parks and Recreation Department, the YMCA, and the YWCA for classes in this sport. As in any city, private gymnasia and tutors also offer instruction.

PENTATHLON

UNITED STATES MODERN PENTATHLON ASSOCIATION
246-3000 • Free

The pentathlon is a competition consisting of five events: riding, fencing, shooting, a 300-meter run, and a four-kilometer cross-country race. The pentathlon center trains national and Olympic teams at various sites around the city area, since the five sports vary so much. And the competition, which may be at the national and international levels, may be held at different venues (though frequently at Fort Sam Houston). You can see the best in this sport, because many former champions live in San Antonio. Horse shows and competitions are open to the public.

POLO

San Antonio has been home to many nationally rated polo players. Call the San Antonio Polo Club (651-5217) for information on the season. It plays at the Retama Polo Center, northeast of town at 16315 Lookout Road.

RACQUETBALL

You'll find several commercial clubs in town, and the YMCA also has courts.

RAFTING

GRUENE RIVER COMPANY

In Gruene, near New Braunfels • (210) 625-2800

One safe way to take a raft down the Guadalupe River below the dam is to let experienced guides take you. The Gruene River Company in the community of Gruene, on the edge of New Braunfels, offers guided raft trips year-round. Call about trip options and cost. While customers should call ahead for reservations, some can be accommodated without advance notice.

RODEOS AND HORSE SHOWS

CHARREADAS

San Antonio Charro Association Ranch, 6126 Padre South • 532-0693 • Some events free

Charreadas are a kind of Mexican rodeo with riding and roping competitions. Rather than emphasizing the rough-and-tumble aspects of the typical north-of-the-border rodeo, the charreada concentrates on the skills and discipline of the dedicated horseman. Look for these events on special holiday weekends, such Diez y Seis (September) and Fiesta (April). The events occur on Sundays and the San Antonio Charros Association sponsors them at its ranch near Mission County Park.

SAN ANTONIO ROSE PALACE

About fifteen miles northwest of downtown San Antonio
Take I-10 to Leon Springs, and go three miles west on Boerne Stage Road
698-3300

Look for horse shows at this fancy arena but also occasional rodeos and competitive events.

SAN ANTONIO STOCK SHOW AND RODEO

Freeman Coliseum, Houston Street and Coliseum Road East • 225-5851 • Two weeks in February • $12–$17 to see the rodeo • W

Rodeo performances abound at this annual show, in addition to a complete livestock exhibition and judging as well. See **Annual Events** for more information.

ROLLER SKATING

You'll find plenty of commercial rinks in town, and instruction at all levels is available either through the rinks or from independent instructors.

RUNNING

Check the sports page of the newspaper for various benefit runs that pop up year-round. The Run-a-Way Runners Store (3428 North St. Mary's Street, 732-1332) hosts free running clinics Tuesday and Thursday evenings and Sunday mornings. People run in the annual San Antonio marathon in November, and five- and ten-kilometer races occur almost every weekend at various spots around the city. Most stores that specialize in running shoes have information and announcements about the races. Two good places to look are Run-a-Way and Roger Soler's Sports (2589 Jackson-Keller, 366-3701).

SAILING

The city's own Woodlawn Lake is small but suitable for very minimal sailing. Canyon Lake, about forty-five miles north of town, has several yacht clubs (see **Side Trips**). Some local boat dealers either offer sailing instruction or can give information about local instructors.

SKEET AND TRAP SHOOTING

A PLACE TO SHOOT
Two miles south of S. Loop 410 on Moursund Boulevard South • 628-1888

Whatever your shooting sport, you can tune your eye here. A number of ranges, from a 200-meter target range to a 25-yard pistol range, let customers take their practice. Instruction is offered.

SAN ANTONIO GUN CLUB
928 E. Contour • North • 828-9860

Open to both members and the public. Plenty of skeet fields and trap ranges offer chances to shoot.

SNORKELING AND SCUBA DIVING

The YMCA offers lessons, and several commercial dive shops in town give lessons in their own pools, rent equipment, and arrange outings at Canyon Lake and nearby rivers. The larger operators also offer frequent tours to the coast and to diving locations in Mexico and nearby islands. Check the Yellow Pages of the telephone directory under "Divers' Equipment and Supplies."

SOCCER

Local leagues abound. Call the YMCA (246-9622) or the San Antonio Soccer Association (681-5408), which can steer you to others. A number of the city parks have excellent soccer fields along with city leagues.

SWIMMING

CITY POOLS
Various locations • 207-3000 • Open daily during the summer, mostly afternoons • Small fee

The city has more than twenty pools, open daily during the summer. Swimming lessons are offered for children at some of them. It's a good idea to check a specific pool's hours—they may vary from year to year. The San Antonio Natatorium, an indoor pool, is an especially sleek facility for swimming competitions. It's open seven days year-round. The city pools are:

    Cassiano, 1400 S. Zarzamora and Cassiano Park (434-7482)
    Concepcion, 600 block E. Theo and Concepcion
      Park (532-3473)
    Cuellar, 502 SW Thirty-sixth and Cuellar Park (434-8028)
    Dellview, 500 Basswood and Dellview Park (349-0570)
    Elmendorf, 4400 W. Commerce and Elmendorf
      Park (434-7380)
    Fairchild, 1214 E. Crockett (226-6722)
    Garza, 5500 Hemphill (434-8122)
    Joe Ward, 435 E. Sunshine (732-7350)
    Kennedy, 3101 Roselawn (436-7009)
    Kingsborough, 350 Felps (924-6761)
    Lincoln, 2803 E. Commerce and Lincoln Park (224-7590)

Monterrey, 5919 W. Commerce and Monterrey Park (432-2727)
Normoyle, 700 Culberson and Normoyle Park (923-2442)
Roosevelt, 300 Roosevelt Ave. and Roosevelt Park (532-6091)
San Antonio Natatorium, 1430 W. Durango (226-8541)
San Pedro, 2200 N. Flores and San Pedro Park (732-2778)
Southcross, 819 W. Southcross Blvd. and Southcross
    Park (927-2001)
Southside Lions, 900 Hiawatha and Stringfellow (532-2027)
Sunset Hills, 103 Chesswood (435-4011)
Westwood, 7601 W. Military Dr. (673-3382)
Woodlawn, 1100 Cincinnati and Alexander (732-5789)

TRINITY UNIVERSITY and **PALO ALTO COLLEGE** both have excellent facilities for swimming competitions. The Palo Alto Natatorium, 1400 Villa Real on the Palo Alto campus (921-5234), is open to the public certain hours and days. Admission.

YMCA AND YWCA

Both the YMCA (246-9622) and YWCA (433-9922) have swimming classes and competitions.

TENNIS

The city runs two main tennis centers, Fairchild and McFarlin. Beyond these, numerous courts are scattered about the city's parks. Also, two tennis ranches have programs in the New Braunfels area: John Newcombe Tennis Ranch and T-Bar-M Tennis Ranch.

FAIRCHILD TENNIS CENTER

1214 E. Crockett at Pine • East • 226-6912 • $1.50 per hour before 5, $2.50 per hour after 5

Fairchild has fourteen lighted courts and is open daily year-round.

McFARLIN TENNIS CENTER

1503 San Pedro at Ashby • Near North • 732-1223 • $1.50 per hour before 5, $2.50 per hour after 5

These twenty-two lighted courts have been the scene of many tournaments. Make reservations (accepted one day in advance) to assure a court. Open daily year-round, except on major holidays. Lessons are given for a fee, and a pro shop sells equipment and stringing services. McFarlin also coordinates a variety of tennis leagues.

TUBING

See Canoeing and Tubing.

VOLLEYBALL

The Parks and Recreation Department and the YMCA and YWCA have leagues.

GUNN SPORTS PARK

12001 Wetmore Road • Northeast • 545-2700 • Open daily
Fees vary, call for details • W

Volleyball attracts the customers here, where twenty sand courts make it the city's premier location for that sport. Six softball diamonds, pavilions with concessions, a shop for volleyball and softball supplies, and facilities for picnics round out the picture. Groups can go for casual games or to join leagues.

WALKING

Many hiking areas lurk in area parks (see **Parks and Outdoors**). Also look for occasional Volksmarches and walkfests in the city, some sponsored by the military bases or a local group of the American Volkssports Association (see Community Organizations under the **Health, Safety, and Community Services** chapter).

SIDE TRIPS

It's nice to get away from the urban crush sometimes. Some delightful small- and medium-sized towns surround San Antonio, particularly to the north in the Hill Country. Some are even void of traffic lights and parking meters. And, by golly, strangers actually speak to you! All of these towns lie only thirty to seventy miles from San Antonio, an easy day's outing with time to spare for meandering and poking into history or sampling some country cooking.

BANDERA

From San Antonio take TX 16 north. Approximately 49 miles northwest of San Antonio.

"Mommas, don't let your babies grow up to be cowboys," warbles the country and western song. Well, the next best thing is to take them to Bandera to *play* cowboy. Bandera, northwest of San Antonio, has a population of around 900. Bandera's main industry is dude ranches, or "guest" ranches, as they are euphemistically called. Around twelve ranches in the area (the Mayan Dude Ranch is one of the largest and oldest) cater to tenderfoot visitors hankering to sample the Wild West. Things are a little tamer nowadays, however, with air-conditioned rooms, eighteen-hole golf courses, and even airstrips at some of the plusher ranches.

Yet it's still exhilarating to get out and enjoy the Hill Country scenery of the Bandera Mountains, cowboy breakfasts and meals by the campfire, and horseback rides or hayrides. And there's plenty of nightlife in Bandera with places like Silver Dollar to go western dancing and drinking. If you want to look the part, Bandera has western wear stores galore. They seem to battle the barbecue stores for prominence.

All in all, Bandera has survived its tourism fairly well. It still looks much like a country town and the county seat that it is, with its wide

Main Street and small side streets with no curbs. The courthouse gives a fine example of 1891 courthouse architecture, with its limestone facade and silver dome.

One block from the courthouse stands the small Frontier-Times Museum (506 Thirteenth St.), chock-full of some 40,000 pioneer items. It corrals a little bit of everything, from powder horns and branding irons to old farming tools and mustache cups. You'll even see an old printing press, early typewriters, and muzzle-loading rifles. (Small admission fee.)

Even the Bandera County Chamber of Commerce isn't quite sure how Bandera got its name. It might be after a Spanish general by the name of Bandera who was sent in to get rid of the Indians, or the nearby Bandera Mountains, named for the Spanish word meaning "banner" or "flag." A banner was raised in the mountain pass to remind everyone of a Spanish-Apache treaty made in 1732. This same pass was the site of many Indian skirmishes. The town was first settled around 1852, about ten years after the Texas Rangers and Comanches clashed at the pass.

For a good homestyle meal at a reasonable price, try the O.S.T. Cafe. With calico oilcloth on the tables and horns on the walls, it's a typical small-town cafe where the townsfolk meet and eat. There's a luncheon special during the week. You definitely won't come away hungry. Or for a picnic, drive down Main Street (TX 173) south to the Medina River. It's quite peaceful and pleasant, with picnic facilities just off the highway. Big cypress trees tower over the river.

You can rent canoes and tubes in town, and Medina Lake (see below) isn't far away. For information about the various dude ranches, you can stop by the Bandera County Chamber of Commerce, at 1808 Highway 16 South. Mailing address: P.O. Box 171, Bandera, Texas 78003.

GARNER STATE PARK

From Bandera, take TX 16 west to FM 470 and turn left; go west 29 miles, then take FM 187 south 2 miles to Utopia. Turn right onto FM 1050 and go west 15 miles; then take US 83 south 2 miles • **Approximately 50 miles from Bandera (830) 232-6132** • **Open daily 8–10, at all times for camping** • **$5 per person** • **W variable**

Garner, an old park and a popular one, often overflows with people in the summer. Its 1,420 acres on the Frio River offer cabins, screened shelters, campsites, a grocery store, a snack bar, and a miniature golf course. Visitors can just take it easy, fish, swim, boat, or hike. Be sure to make overnight reservations ahead of time. Mailing address: Route 70, Box 599, Concan, Texas 78838.

LOST MAPLES STATE NATURAL AREA

From Bandera, take TX 16 west 3 miles to FM 470 and turn left; go west 29 miles; then take FM 187 north, past Vanderpool, 12 miles • **Approximately 45 miles from Bandera** • **(830) 966-3413** • **Open daily 8–10, at all times for camping** • **$4 per person** • **W variable**

A colorful spot to see the autumn leaves, Lost Maples covers 2,174 acres and was the first designated as a state natural area. A stand of maples provides one of the state's few spectacles of fall foliage. Visitors can study animal and Indian lore going back 12,000 years along the Sabinal River canyon. Campsites with water are available, as are picnic sites and restrooms with showers. Mailing address: P.O. Box 156, Vanderpool, Texas 78885.

MEDINA LAKE

From Bandera, take TX 16 east 9 miles to Pipe Creek, then south 11 miles to Park Road 37; turn right and go west 11 miles • **Approximately 30 miles from Bandera** • **Open at all times** • **Free** • **W variable**

This attractive, 5,570-acre lake is surrounded by hilly terrain. Reputed to have good bass fishing, it also has water sports, marinas, rentals, RV sites, and camping facilities. While Medina attracts fewer sailboaters than Canyon Lake, perhaps because the steeper banks and more rugged topography make the winds less steady and predictable, the lake is popular with powerboaters. Also look for an area near the boat launching cove where a prevailing onshore breeze makes boardsailing or windsurfing especially safe for beginners.

BOERNE

From San Antonio take I-10 north 34 miles.

You can drive to Boerne (pronounced "Burney") in little more than the time it takes to go crosstown in San Antonio. A lunch and relaxed shopping stroll in this pleasant country town on the fringe of the Hill Country are enough to lower your blood pressure.

Boerne is a bustling small town growing bigger because of its proximity to San Antonio. It's full of quaint limestone buildings erected from 1860 to the 1900s. One landmark is the beautifully restored 1859 Kendall Inn on the square at 128 W. Blanco. Once a stagecoach stop, now houses a restaurant and bed-and-breakfast inn. Another interesting restaurant, Country Spirit (707 S. Main), is in the elegantly restored 1870s Mansion House. It also has a quiet bar area for sipping country spirits.

For an outdoor picnic, either try the picnic area just off South Main, where Cibolo Creek is dammed up, or hike the Cibolo Wilderness Trail.

The Hill Country abounds with caves, and two of them are near Boerne. The Cave Without a Name (830-537-4212) is eleven miles northwest of town on FM 474, and Cascade Caverns (210-755-8080) is about three miles south of town, just off I-10. A large underground waterfall gives Cascade its name.

Germans founded this town around 1849 and named it after Ludwig Boerne. Boerne is the county seat of Kendall County, named after one of the founders of the *New Orleans Picayune*, who took up goat and sheep ranching in the area. Robert E. Lee stopped here several times, and the tiny house where he stayed still remains.

Some events to look for in the town include the Berges Fest (a German festival with an art show and music) in June and the Kendall County Fair over the Labor Day weekend. For information, write the Boerne Chamber of Commerce, One Main Plaza, Boerne, Texas 78006.

GUADALUPE RIVER STATE PARK

From Boerne, take TX 46 east about 13 miles to Park Road 31, then north about 3 miles • **(830) 438-2656** • **Open daylight hours for day visits, at all times for camping** • **$4 per person** • **W variable**

This park's 1,900 acres stretch across part of the Guadalupe River and its rapids. Canoeing, fishing, swimming, hiking, and camping make up the most popular activities. On a hot South Texas day, just sitting in the shallows of the Guadalupe River and letting the water wash over you can be an ideal antidote for the summer blahs. Mailing address: HC 54, P.O. Box 2087, Bulverde, Texas 78163.

CASTROVILLE

From San Antonio take US 90 west 25 miles.

This little country town provides a quiet spot for ambling and antiquing, and nobody will run you down, because there's so little traffic.

Castroville is full of historic plaques, pioneer houses, French (actually Alsatian) architecture, and churches. Much of the restored architecture dates from the 1840s to the 1860s. The town's small houses, plastered white or painted in bright colors, with steep tin roofs, suggest a European village. Colonies of Alsatians settled the place in 1844, led by Henri Castro, a French banker who loaned Sam Houston capital for the new Republic of Texas. Houston returned the favor by giving Castro a grant of land west of San Antonio.

This town also provides reasonably priced historic lodging. The Landmark Inn, built in 1849, is a state historic site run by the Texas Parks and Wildlife Department, but reserve ahead of time—only a few rooms are available (830-931-2133). The inn sits just off US 90 near the Medina River. The rooms look out on peaceful grounds, with inviting rocking chairs on the veranda. Out back is an old grist mill dating from the 1850s.

Around the town square are several things worth seeing. The Alsatian, a restaurant located behind Castroville Emporium, looks cozy and inviting, with antique wooden tables and fresh flowers. Many locals also patronize either the more modern-looking Sammy's on US 90 for blue-plate specials or the restaurant at the Best Western Alsatian Inn, high on a hill overlooking the town below. And for that true, small-town flavor, drop into Dan's Meat Market on the square. Dan's also doubles as an informal bar where local farmers and ranchers shoot the breeze over a beer. Get a little cracker-barrel philosophy and some fresh sausage in one quick stop.

On the opposite side of the square stands the beautiful St. Louis Catholic Church (1868), with lovely wooden arches and pews and stained-glass windows. If it's hot outside, it's almost fifteen degrees cooler inside the church. When the bells peal, they're beautiful, too. This is a very Catholic community. The Sisters of Divine Providence established a school here in 1868 that is now a convent and retreat. You may also find the old Catholic cemeteries over on Cross Hill rather interesting.

Many of the quaint houses with historic plaques are private residences. But some are open during a fall tour. Another event to look for in this town is St. Louis Day (the Sunday nearest August 25), a homecoming fair that serves up barbecue and sausage.

Castroville is a popular place to shop for antiques and collectibles. Several old buildings appropriately house combined antique and refinishing stores. If you enjoy the outdoors, try the regional park just outside of town on the Medina River, where you'll find camping and picnicking facilities with fishing, swimming, and tennis. Medina Lake, with camping and fishing facilities, is only about twenty miles north of Castroville along the Medina River. For more information, write the Castroville Chamber of Commerce at P.O. Box 572, Castroville, Texas 78009.

COMFORT

From San Antonio take I-10 north 50 miles.

Comfort is one of the nicest little hamlets in the vicinity, yet another Hill Country village that has attracted artists, artisans, and outsiders who are renovating its old buildings. Comfort's downtown area has remained much the same as it was in the 1900s. Listed in the National Register of Historic Places, downtown is considered one of the most complete nineteenth-century business districts left standing in Texas. The general store (Peter Ingenhuett Store, 1881), Faust Hotel (1880, now the Comfort Common, a bed-and-breakfast and antique shop), and the bank (1907) are all in good condition on High Street.

No traffic lights and parking meters here. The pace is decidedly serene. Expect to find several good antique stores and gift shops, plus restaurants such as the Cafe on High Street and Arlene's Cafe. For no-frills home cooking, try the Cypress Creek Inn (TX 27 at Cypress Creek).

If you crave history, Comfort will accommodate you. Founded in 1854 by Ernst Altgelt and other German immigrants, it has nearly 100 pre-1910 buildings within walking distance of the downtown area. Other interesting structures include an 1891 blacksmith shop turned into a tiny museum, the Brinkmann Cottage (1860), Faltin General Store (1879), and Faltin Homestead (1854). Most of these buildings only open to the public during special events.

One last historic tidbit. Comfort, despite being deep in Confederate country, has a monument to Union sympathizers. The German immigrant settlers here opposed the South's secession from the Union during the Civil War, and some of the more independent of these folk attempted to flee to Mexico rather than be forced to join Confederate forces. Confederate soldiers ambushed them, which caused the loss of the lives of about forty townspeople. The monument was erected over their common grave. For more information, write the Comfort Chamber of Commerce, P.O. Box 777, Comfort, Texas 78013.

FREDERICKSBURG

From San Antonio take I-10 north 50 miles to US 87; turn right and go north 22 miles. Approximately 72 miles northwest of San Antonio.

Fredericksburg is difficult to take in during a one-day side trip. You may want to either stay overnight or come again, because you simply can't squeeze all its pleasing features and establishments into one short day.

This little town has had the good sense to hold onto its old buildings and homes. With quaint but practical nineteenth-century limestone buildings and two-story Victorian stores and homes, Fredericksburg has one of the most delightful main streets in Texas. Some buildings are freshly painted with interiors decorated to match, and others are comfortably natural and slightly run down.

Throw in a lot of antique, hardware, and general stores, plus good eating places and beer gardens, and you've got an old German town full of warmth and just enough hustle and bustle to make it alive. Fortunately, this town of around 7,800 still ambles at a comfortable country pace.

Another thing that makes this place appealing is its mixture of German old-country roots and a little uptown intellectualism. A lot of retirees or urban dropouts from some of the state's metropolitan areas have migrated here to soak up some of that Texas ruralism. But so far, the community and the Gillespie County Historical Society have guarded the town's heritage well.

One of the best times to see Fredericksburg's historic homes and buildings is at the annual Christmas Candlelight Tour in mid-December. Also take in Kristkindl Market at the same time, and shop for Christmas ornaments, imported German toys, and local handcrafted items. Other public tours are offered on Founders Day in early May. Out-of-town clubs can arrange private group tours with the Historical Society or the Chamber of Commerce.

While people know Fredericksburg for its ranching and farming (especially peaches, which you can buy by the roadside in season), another of its main attractions is antiques. It's fun to look even if you can't afford to buy much. You'll find collectibles, primitives, old quilts, crockery, advertising tins, and more.

Eating and drinking spots abound, some of whose kitchens stay in tune with the old German traditions and some of which are in interesting renovated buildings. For natural ambience and a beer, try Plateau Cafe on Main. During the wintertime, a fire in the huge rock fireplace lends a comfortable, homey feeling to the old wooden tables and chairs. There's an old bar with a brass rail to put your foot on. In the summertime, the outdoor patio is pleasant. Another beer-drinking spot, the Altdorf Biergarten, on the same street in a picturesque old home, has reasonable prices. And for a nice, cozy, tearoom-style lunch, try the Peach Tree. At dinnertime, the Gallery specializes in genteel service and local food.

Some of the same stream of Germans that colonized New Braunfels founded Fredericksburg in 1846 and named it after Prince Frederick of Prussia. Their glorious leader was Baron Ottfried Hans von Meusebach, who later wisely shortened this to John O. Meusebach. Most of these immigrants landed at the old Indianola port on the Texas coast and made the hard journey by oxcart or foot. Many died on the way, usually from cholera, and rumor has it that you could follow their trail by the graves along the road.

Want to delve a little more into the area's history? Try the Pioneer Museum at 309 W. Main. Located in an early settler's home and general store, the museum contains nineteenth-century furnishings, utensils, tools, and other items. Admission fee.

More history resides at the Vereins Kirche, an eight-sided building on Market Square that houses artifacts and information about the county's settlement. Also visit Pioneer Memorial Library in the marvelous old 1682 courthouse.

Around town are "Sunday houses," so called because, in the 1800s, farmers and ranchers had to have someplace to stay when they came into town by wagon on the weekends to shop and go to church. The houses were usually very small, with one room on top of another and an outside stairway. Nowadays, more affluent urban immigrants have bought them as weekend homes.

One building you shouldn't miss is the old Nimitz Steamboat Hotel (340 E. Main). Apropos of its name, part of the building resembles the bridge of a ship. Built by an early settler named Charles Nimitz, it slept some famous guests like Ulysses S. Grant, Robert E. Lee, and Jesse James. Nimitz was the grandfather of the town's favorite son, Fleet Admiral Chester Nimitz, who was Commander in Chief in the Pacific during World War II. The old hotel, now called the Admiral Nimitz Museum Historical Park, houses the Museum of the Pacific War, well-filled with memorabilia related to the war and, especially, to Nimitz himself. The museum's outdoor section, several blocks away, features tanks, guns, and both American and Japanese dive bombers.

Some annual events to look for in Fredericksburg include the above-mentioned Christmas Candlelight and Founders Day tours in mid-December and early May, the Fourth of July horse races, A Night in Old Fredericksburg in mid-July, and the Gillespie County Fair in August.

For more information about Fredericksburg, write the Fredericksburg Convention and Visitors Bureau, 106 North Adams, Fredericksburg, Texas 78624.

ENCHANTED ROCK STATE NATURAL AREA

Take FM 965 north 18 miles from Fredericksburg • **(915) 247-3903**
Open daily 8–10, at all times for camping • $5 per person

They say Indians feared these large outcroppings of granite and thought the rock had supernatural powers, perhaps because on moonlit nights after a rain, the minerals in the granite sometimes glisten. Now this area is not only a scenic gathering place but also one of the best rock-climbing sites within easy striking distance of San Antonio. The park offers picnicking, hiking, and camping facilities. Call ahead on weekends and holidays; the park closes when it gets too full.

LADY BIRD JOHNSON MUNICIPAL PARK

Take TX 16 south 3 miles from Fredericksburg • **(830) 997-4202**
Open daily • Free

These 190 acres with a lake include camping and trailer hookups, with facilities for picnicking, fishing, swimming, and playing golf. Variable fees for some facilities.

LYNDON B. JOHNSON STATE HISTORICAL PARK

Take US 290 east about 22 miles from Fredericksburg
(830) 644-2252 • Open daily 8:30–5 • Free

The thirty-sixth president of the United States, Lyndon B. Johnson, grew up in this area, and his ranch near Stonewall was his pride and joy. Johnson's widow, Lady Bird, still lives part time in the ranch house on the Pedernales River. It is part of the LBJ National Park. But national park bus tours ($3 per person) of the LBJ Ranch leave regularly from the state park daily. A bit confusing, but the state park is right near the national park, and that's where you board the bus. This tour also visits LBJ's school, birthplace, and grave. The adjacent state park is about 700 acres, and the visitor center has exhibits of LBJ's boyhood and his White House days. There's also an old dogtrot cabin built in the 1840s, furnished in that era, and a farmstead. This attractive park has picnicking, swimming, and hiking facilities. Lots of river frontage helps visitors realize why LBJ was so drawn to this part of the country.

KERRVILLE

From San Antonio take I-10 north 65 miles.

Too bad Kerrville had to go the way of progress and get slicked up with new buildings and shopping malls. I rather liked it better when it was smaller and less commercialized. It doesn't seem to have retained as many historic buildings as its sister Hill Country towns.

However, Kerrville remains a popular hub for surrounding summer camps and guest ranches. Youth camps and church camps abound in the Hill Country, particularly around Kerrville and on the Guadalupe River. There's exotic game viewing and hunting at several nearby ranches, such as the Y.O. Ranch (see below), and there's also a Kerrville Camera Safari at another ranch.

The town, founded in 1856, became a ranching and marketing center for wool and mohair. Although some working ranches still exist here, the biggest game seems to be tourists and the hunters themselves.

Kerrville has two parks of note: Louise Hays Park, located near the downtown area on the Guadalupe River, which offers picnicking, swimming, and paddleboats, and Kerrville-Schreiner State Park (see below).

Horseback riding offers another local recreational possibility. Try the guest ranches in the area. Some will rent horses to visitors regardless of whether they're staying at the ranch overnight.

Kerrville sports a splendid Cowboy Artists of America Museum, one any big city would love to claim. The posh museum on rustic acreage at 1550 Bandera Hwy. exhibits works of contemporary cowboy artists.

If you're a James Avery jewelry aficionado, visit the company's headquarters and showroom just north of I-10 on Harper. The handcrafted sterling and gold pieces sell at regular retail prices, however.

And in the artisan line, sample the annual Texas State Arts and Crafts Fair, held at Schreiner College. Artists and craftsmen from all over the state exhibit in this large weekend fair that includes food and entertainment. Look for it in May, which is also the time of the extensive and well-attended Kerrville Folk Festival.

After sightseeing, what are the possibilities for food? The Holiday Inn Y.O. Ranch Hotel offers elegant dining. For a casual picnic style, the barbecue at Hickory Hut Bar-B-Que can't be beat.

For further information, write the Convention and Visitors Bureau, 1700 Sidney Baker, Kerrville, Texas 78028.

KERRVILLE-SCHREINER STATE PARK

Take TX 173 south 2.5 miles to Park Road 19 • **(830) 257-5392**
Open daily 8–10, at all times for camping • Admission

This well-kept, 500-acre state park borders the Guadalupe River. It has campsites, screened shelters, and trailer sites, plus fishing piers, picnic tables, boat ramps, restrooms, and showers.

Y.O. RANCH

Take I-10 north 16 miles to Mountain Home, turn left onto TX 41, and go
15 miles to ranch entrance • **Approximately 31 miles from Kerrville**
(800) 967-2624 • Open year-round, but call ahead for reservations

Captain Charles Schreiner, a driving force in Kerrville, started the Y.O. Ranch in 1880, and it's still going strong. Consisting of 40,000 acres, and with fifty-six different species of exotic game animals, the Y.O. claims to be one of the largest private hunting areas of its type in the world. One thing is certain—this is no ordinary little spread. It's a good place to see a working ranch, and it's open to the public.

The Y.O. offers guided hunting and photo safaris, with meals and lodging in an old log cabin, schoolhouse, or Wells Fargo stage house. You even eat along with the real cowboys in the chuckwagon. Regular folks who just want to see what a ranch is like can take the two-hour lunch tour. Make reservations a couple of days ahead.

The Y.O. also sponsors a youth program where campers live in an African-style safari camp while learning about wild game, hunting, and conservation. Some of the unusual animals on the ranch include ibex, bison, giraffe, emu, ostrich, elk, and antelope. The Y.O. also houses the country's largest registered herd of Texas longhorns.

If you think the ranch is big now, just picture what it was like in its prime. When Schreiner held some 550,000 acres, his property extended about eighty miles from Kerrville to Menard. He originally moved with his family from Alsace to San Antonio and was a Texas Ranger before building his ranching and merchandising empire. Today, later generations of the Schreiner family still run the ranch. Schreiner's old Romanesque home, located in the center of Kerrville's downtown area and dating from 1879, has been restored as a museum.

LUCKENBACH

From San Antonio take I-10 north 33 miles to Boerne, then take FM 1376 north 12 miles to Sisterdale; continue 16.4 miles and turn left off the highway just past the low-water crossing. Approximately 61 miles northwest of San Antonio.

Don't blink, or you're liable to overshoot Luckenbach. For a place that has had so much publicity, it surely can be difficult to find, mainly because tourists keep stealing the highway sign marking the way to the town.

Waylon Jennings made this little hamlet famous with a country and western song some years ago. You could definitely call this funny place a one-horse town; it's just a bunch of weather-beaten, old barnlike buildings held together with tobacco juice and love.

The "town" covers only ten acres, and the population consists of a couple of families and whoever happens to be at the general store that day. There may be five playing dominoes and drinking suds or hundreds attending some special nonsensical celebration that Luckenbach is famous for.

The late Hondo Crouch, Texas raconteur, philosopher, poet, and humorist, bought the village, which dates back to 1849, and held court there while he was alive. People would come from all around to hear Crouch poke fun at society and modern-day mores. If Capistrano could celebrate its swallows returning, why not Luckenbach its mud daubers? Thus Mud Dauber Day was celebrated. And the town continued to invent such nonsense, with chili cook-offs and a Hug-In. Dances are sometimes held in the old dance hall, but these are irregular, so call the general store and inquire—(830) 997-3224.

Luckenbach looks much as it did 100 years ago. The run-down old general store, with the small sign that says Luckenbach, Texas, Closed on Wednesdays, functions as both saloon and post office. The wooden bar counter wraps around the obligatory wood stove, with beer and advertising signs all over the walls. People really do play dominoes and shell pecans at a nearby table. On weekends, you'll often hear some informal music. The general store certainly looks the part. It's musty, the wood floors creak, and old and new goods are piled around an old cash register. And the only things that suggest tourism are the Luckenbach T-shirts.

To get to the place from Fredericksburg, take US 290 east three or four miles, then turn south on FM 1376, go about 4.6 miles, and turn right just before the low-water crossing. There may be no sign. Go a couple of country blocks, and you'll almost dead-end into Luckenbach.

NEW BRAUNFELS

From San Antonio take I-35 north 30 miles.

Several thousand Germans settled this area in 1845, led by Prince Carl zu Solms-Braunfels, who named it after his old hometown. The early settlers left a strong ethnic mark on the community that still prevails, from the work ethic to biergartens, strudel, and family gatherings.

You can't really call New Braunfels a small town anymore. With around 31,000 people, it's a small city. But get off the freeway and motel strip, and you'll find the small-town atmosphere intact. The square with its old-fashioned gazebo and 1898 courthouse is typical. Nearby, on Seguin, lies the Naegelin Bakery, which has been there for years. Try some of its breads or desserts, some reminiscent of the old country.

Not too far from the square stand two interesting old hotels. Prince Solms Inn at 295 E. San Antonio (830-625-9169) goes back to the turn of the century. Built in 1900, this elegant two-story house is decorated with antiques, old pictures, and cheery period wallpaper. Only a few rooms are available. The Faust Hotel, at 240 S. Seguin, was built in 1928 and has a restaurant. Nearby are an old mansion restaurant, the Pinto Ranch Grill, and Krause's Cafe (148 S. Castell), popular for its blue-plate specials.

The main attractions of New Braunfels include its recreational facilities. Landa Park, an attractive old park, started in 1898 at the suggestion of Jay Gould's daughter Helen. Gould's railroad ran tourist excursions to this area on the Comal River, which still runs through the park's 300 tree-filled acres. The Comal, which joins the Guadalupe River just four miles down the way, is sometimes called the shortest river in the United States.

Landa has several entrances, one being off Landa Street, just a few blocks northwest of the town square. Admission is free, but you'll have to pay various small fees for some facilities. These include a golf course, spring-fed swimming pools, paddleboats, a glass-bottom boat, amusement rides, bicycles, and numerous riverside areas for picnicking. You can rent tubes to shoot the river rapids at Prince Solms Park nearby.

The city's annual blast, Wurstfest, is held at Landa Park. This sausage-and-music-and-beer festival gets larger every year, now lasting ten days (beginning the Friday before the first Monday in November). The celebration includes German food, oompah music, polka dancing, and colorful costumes, plus assorted events such as a walkfest and races.

Another annual event to look for is the Comal County Fair in September. One of the largest county fairs in Texas, this one is the second oldest. Besides the usual activities, look for horse racing.

History buffs can check out the Sophienburg Memorial Museum (401 W. Coll), which has exhibits about the lives of early German immigrants, and the Lindheimer Home (491 Comal), built in 1852 by Ferdinand Lindheimer, a pioneer botanist and editor. Lindheimer was the original guide for Prince Carl and later became editor of *Die NeuBraunfelser Zeitung* newspaper. His abode is a good example of German *fachwerk* construction. Closed some days, according to season. There is also the Hummel Museum.

What is a German town without beer? One busy, casual watering hole is the Bavarian Village Restaurant and Biergarten at 212 W. Austin. Live music, singing, and dancing are featured in the evenings.

Several cabins and camping areas are in town, plus nearby tennis ranches. For more information on these and for maps of the Guadalupe River for tubing and rafting, call the New Braunfels Chamber of Commerce (800-572-2626) or write P.O. Box 311417, New Braunfels, Texas 78131.

CANYON LAKE

From New Braunfels head north on I-35; at the edge of town exit at FM 306 and go west about 16 miles to park entrance • **Approximately 16 miles northwest of New Braunfels** • **W variable**

Seven public parks surround the 8,240-acre Canyon Lake. Facilities are available for camping, picnicking, boating, sailing, and fishing at this U.S. Corps of Engineers lake. Beach areas, lodging, yacht clubs, marinas, and restaurants all contribute to the flow of visitors. For military personnel, both the Army and Air Force have recreational complexes out here. The public parks stay open year-round. For more information, call (800) 528-2104.

GRUENE

From New Braunfels take I-35 north to Canyon Lake exit (FM 306). Continue to Gruene Road; go west to Hunter Road and turn left • **Approximately 4 miles north of New Braunfels**

Gruene (pronounced "Green") is a born-again ghost town on the northern edge of New Braunfels. Settled about the same time as New Braunfels, in the 1840s, this tiny town has had its downers. But now Gruene is on the upswing, with its old stores and buildings rejuvenated into restaurants, shops, and galleries.

High above the Guadalupe River sits the Grist Mill, (830) 625-0684, a rustic, inviting restaurant. Where the old brick walls had deteriorated, the owners have put in glass, adding wooden tables and plants.

The Gruene River Company offers raft trips down the Guadalupe River and remains open year-round, but call ahead for arrangements (see **Sports**).

Gruene Hall may be Texas' oldest dance hall. Built by one of the Gruenes in the 1880s, the hall still has dances on weekend evenings, with country and western music.

NATURAL BRIDGE CAVERNS

From New Braunfels take I-35 south 16 miles, then turn right on FM 3009 (Natural Bridge Caverns Road); continue approximately 8 miles to entrance
Approximately 24 miles from New Braunfels • 651-6101 (local call from San Antonio) • Open daily 9–4; in summer 9–6 Adults $7, children $5

Said to be Texas' largest, Natural Bridge Caverns are conveniently located about twenty miles northeast of San Antonio (take I-35 north and go west on FM 3009). Formed from limestone more than 140 million years old, these caverns are colorful and well-suited for family outings. Wear comfortable walking shoes, but don't worry about the heat. Even if it's hot outside, it remains 70 degrees in the caverns. Large enough to hold your interest but small enough so that almost anyone can make the trip, the caverns display a broad and beautiful range of cave formations.

TEXAS HILL COUNTRY

AUSTIN AND TEXAS CENTRAL RAILROAD'S HILL COUNTRY FLYER

Leaves from Cedar Park, northwest of Austin • (512) 477-8468 Reservations required • Open weekends only, closed January and February • Adults $24, children $10; prices higher for other cars

Finally, we'll encroach on the territory of our sister guidebook to Austin to include this splendid side trip for railroad buffs, children, or those who want to get a new view of the Hill Country. A gleamingly (and lovingly) rebuilt, oil-fired steam engine (Southern Pacific Mikado type) pulls a string of restored seventy-year-old coaches from Austin on a two- or three-hour trip through the gently rolling hills west of Austin to Burnet. There, one can lunch, poke around in antique shops, and generally experience an amiable Texas small town. The return trip gets you back to Austin by late afternoon. Refreshments and snacks are offered on the train, but since a number of restaurants and coffee shops dot Burnet, you'll probably do better there. Reservations are required, and allow at least two and a half hours to get from San Antonio to the station in Cedar Park. This whole enterprise, from the restoration of the locomotive to the staffing of the trains, is a labor of love by rail fans who did not want to see steam power vanish from Texas. Bravo!

RESTAURANTS

Like those in most big cities, San Antonio's restaurants run the gastronomic gamut from posh elegance to urban cafes, with a dash of the trendy thrown in. But don't overlook the holes-in-the-wall, because there you will find some of the real color of San Antonio, particularly its indigenous Mexican food. Furthermore, the Mexican spots, like other ethnic choices, provide some of the most inexpensive meals in town. On the whole, the city has very reasonably priced food compared with the rest of the United States and even Texas, for that matter.

In general, when it comes to food, San Antonio is less pretentious and more casual than the rest of the state's cities. It's simply not Dallas or Houston and doesn't particularly want to be. Even those who can afford to do otherwise often opt for smaller cafes, neighborhood Mexican spots, or funky barbecue huts.

You can find many of the more plush (and more expensive) restaurants downtown and in the hotels. San Antonio is a big convention and tourist city, and the hotel industry isn't about to pass up an opportunity to feed the masses. Several of the hotels serve up innovative or classic cuisine that's highly rated by food gurus, and in stylish settings with attentive service. But the other end of the comestible spectrum equally represents itself downtown too, particularly on the River Walk. Fast food and sidewalk cafes abound, interspersed with hotels and nightspots. Since the River Walk is so popular with visitors and natives alike for dining and entertainment, this guidebook includes a special section listing the food you will find there. Choose your River Walk restaurant carefully however; with such prime locations some restaurateurs apparently feel they don't have to go overboard in the kitchen.

Other areas to look for a casual, quick food fix include North St. Mary's Street, about a mile north of downtown where 281 intersects it, and Southtown. The St. Mary's strip is eclectic and informal, attracting collegians, yuppies, and visitors in about equal measure. If you can't get in one restaurant because of crowds, just walk to another one. Some of the places also have live music. Southtown, just south of downtown around Alamo Street, has funky cafes interspersed with art galleries.

Want some hints on where to find TLC service or fill-'er-up bargains?

For classy service and food, try Polo's, the Anaqua Grill, Las Canarias, or, Silo. For spots that are reasonably priced or give you a lot for your dollar, try El Mirador, Barn Door (for lunch), Luby's Cafeteria, or Taco Cabana. Generally in San Antonio, ethnic is economical, particularly Mexican, Chinese, and Vietnamese.

For a romantic hideaway restaurant, visit the Grey Moss Inn, about a half-hour drive to the northwest of downtown. If heights and zippy elevators don't bother you, the Tower of the Americas Restaurant can't be topped. It's the revolving restaurant at the top of the Tower of Americas in HemisFair Park. The food might be average, but the view isn't. You get a glassed-in 360° view of San Antonio and its hinterlands while you dine.

As you might expect, southwestern cuisine is also prevalent in San Antonio, with its use of regional meats, ingredients, and spices.

HOW TO READ THIS RESTAURANT LISTING

I've tried to give a variety of food and price levels in this guide to suit broad tastes and pocketbooks, but remember, too, that there's a long lead time in printing books. Chefs, prices, and even a restaurant's owner and character can change. Consequently, food quality often changes too. The restaurants are listed under various food categories, except for the River Walk section, which lumps together different types of restaurants in that one centralized downtown location.

Prices: The following symbols indicate the cost of a typical meal for one, without drinks or wine but including a first course or a dessert.

$:	under $7
$$:	$7 to $17
$$$:	$17 to $30
$$$$:	$30 and over

Credit cards: The following symbols indicate which credit cards the restaurants accept.

AE	American Express
DC	Diner's Club
DIS	Discover
MC	Master Card
V	Visa
Cr.	All major credit cards
No Cr.	No credit cards

RIVER WALK RESTAURANTS

The River Walk downtown is one of the city's most popular areas and frequented by name-tagged conventioneers and natives alike. Therefore, this guidebook treats it as a separate section. These aren't all the restaurants there by any means, but it will give you some idea of what types of food and ambience to expect. Sidewalk cafes and nightspots sit cheek to bowl with fancy hotel dining rooms. As anywhere else, sometimes the food is strictly hurried tourist fare but at others quite good quality. During peak holiday weekends and big conven-

Some River Walk Area Restaurants

Bayous, 3
Boudro's, 8
Casa Rio, 12
County Line, 4
Fig Tree, 14
Kangaroo Court, 6
Las Canarias, 2

Little Rhein, 13
Original Mexican Restaurant, 7
Paesano's River Walk, 5
Presidio, 1
Rio Rio, 10
Schilo's Deli, 11
Zuni Grill, 9

tions, look for crowds spilling over almost into the river (watch your step, or it could be a diner overboard!), with lines waiting for service. At quieter times, it's an ideal place to have a relaxed breakfast, lunch, or evening drink. (A word to the wise: don't encourage the pigeons by feeding them, or they'll nag you to death. Squadrons of them homebase on the River Walk just for that reason.)

THE BAYOUS

517 N. Presa • Central • 223-6403 • Open daily • Call ahead for preferred seating list • $$–$$$ • Cr. • W via elevator

Long before it became fashionable, owner John Cace was turning out Cajun or Creole food. By whatever name, it means lots of fresh fish on the agenda. Blackened fish and fried seafood are popular items here. The Bayous has three levels, with bar on top and River Walk tables at the bottom. The dining room has ceiling fans, and French doors, where a taste of formality blends with casual. The Cace family hails from Louisiana, so the place looks reminiscent of New Orleans. Bar.

BOUDRO'S

421 E. Commerce at Presa, also enter via the River Walk
Central • 224-8484 • Open daily • Lunch and dinner
Reservations suggested on weekends • $$$ • Cr. • W

This small, rather New Orleans—style restaurant started out with Cajun cooking but has now branched out with Southwest items. But Boudro's still has some of its specialties, such as blackened prime rib and coconut beer-battered shrimp. Maybe blackening prime rib sounds sacrilegious, but it makes it rare and tender with a flavorful crust. The coconut shrimp are tasty too. Small outdoor patio area. Other items include smoked shrimp enchiladas and grilled salmon. Bar.

CASA RIO

430 E. Commerce • Central • 225-6718 • Open daily, but closed Sundays in January • No reservations taken • $$ • Cr.
W from parking lot; call ahead

Located on prime real estate at Commerce Street and the River Walk, one can perhaps excuse Casa Rio for not putting more effort into the cooking—the customers come anyway. It's not that the food tastes bad—just other Mexican restaurants in town surpass it. None of those others, however, sits on the River Walk, so when visitors (or natives, for that matter) want a Mexican bite to eat along the River Walk, they will likely stop here. The tables are set both inside and outside; if the weather is at all good, you must eat a meal on the river—the passing crowd and waddling pigeons just add to the fun of eating there. Bar.

COUNTY LINE (See Barbecue)

THE FIG TREE

515 Paseo de la Villita at S. Alamo • Central • 224-1976
Open daily • Dinner only • Reservations usually required
$$$$ • Cr.

Caution: entering this restaurant may be hazardous to your bank
account. The Fig Tree has a standard pricey cost for all the entrees that
excludes such details as an appetizer, wine, and dessert, to say nothing
of a generous tip for the excellent service. Is it good? Yes. Is it worth
the prices? The continental food alone may not be, but for many people
the overall impression makes up for the culinary weaknesses. The china,
silver, table settings, wallpaper, and general decor make The Fig Tree
the most sybaritic restaurant in town by a large margin. If ever one
wants to cast the kind of spell created only by funds lavishly spent, that
person should come to this charming, restored old home in La Villita.
Instead of tasting great, the cooking is just solidly good, with occasional flashes of excellence. Old standbys on the dinner-only menu include
rack of lamb, chateaubriand, and beef Wellington. Bar.

KANGAROO COURT

512 River Walk at Crockett • Central • 224-6821 • Open daily
Breakfast, lunch, and dinner • $-$$ • Cr.

OK mate, here's a likely spot to put down anchor when you've got
tired peds from strolling the river. Just look for the Union Jack colored
umbrellas at this English (or maybe Aussie) style pub and restaurant.
They don't mind your just sitting and having a cool ale, where other
cafes might scowl. Some reasonably priced sandwiches on up to fresh
oysters and seafood items fill much of the menu. The shrimp is lightly
fried almost like Japanese tempura. Inside, with its wooden bar, tables,
and booths, it has the pub look, complete with a mermaid hanging from
the ceiling. Casual. Bar.

LAS CANARIAS

La Mansion del Rio Hotel, 112 College at Presa • Central
225-2581 • Lunch and dinner daily • Sunday brunch
Reservations recommended • $$$-$$$$ • Cr.

San Antonio's first civilian settlers came from the Canary Islands—
Las Canarias—and La Mansion del Rio named the hotel's premier
restaurant in their honor. The character of the restaurant is Spanish,
even down to the flamenco guitarist who performs on certain nights.

Its more classical dishes include paella and the rich red bell pepper
soup with a subtle peppery flavor. Frequent menu changes and turnover
in the kitchen makes singling out dishes difficult, but they have includ-
ed blackened redfish and grilled beef medallions. Whatever the menu
holds on a given day, the dishes will be a little unusual—not exotic, just
inventive and interesting. In short, for atmosphere, service, entertain-

ment, and cuisine, Las Canarias is a good candidate for a special evening on the River Walk. Bar.

LITTLE RHEIN

231 S. Alamo at Market • Central • 225-2111 • Open daily
Dinner only • Reservations recommended • $$$–$$$$ • Cr.

For just a plain old good steak, Little Rhein has my recommendation. Yes, it is expensive, but when isn't good food in the heart of a downtown area expensive? Little Rhein is located on the River Walk across the street from the Convention Center and adjacent to La Villita. It has assorted steaks, from ribeye to T-bone. The atmosphere and service seem to match Little Rhein's setting in a restored 1847 rock house perched above the river—everything is comfortably informal and yet in keeping with the spirit of San Antonio's wild and youthful days. When the weather suits, you can even eat outdoors on a charming terrace overlooking the River Walk. Bar.

ORIGINAL MEXICAN RESTAURANT

528 River Walk • Central • 224-9951 • Lunch and dinner daily
$–$$ • Cr.

Another Mexican food option on the River Walk. Lots of outdoor patio seating and near the Kangaroo Court in one of the busiest river sections. The menu includes chile relleno and chalupas and other standard fare. Bar.

PAESANO'S (See Italian)

PRESIDIO

245 E. Commerce • Central • 472-2265 • Open daily
Lunch and dinner • $$$ • Cr. • W+

Located near Planet Hollywood on the River Walk, this restaurant serves up Mediterranean food, which they like to call New World Med, with a touch of Mexican and southwestern thrown in. A somewhat stylish inside dining area, plus outside seating on the river. Bar.

RIO RIO

421 E. Commerce • Central • 226-8462 • Open daily
Lunch and dinner • $$ • Cr. • W

Huge plates of freshly prepared food—whether quesadillas, one of many chicken selections, or the specialty chimichanga—always seem to have tastes fresher and lighter than those usually found in Mexican restaurants. If the weather permits, opt for an outside table on the River Walk—though there's nothing wrong with the big inside dining room. Imaginative and a little trendy, Rio Rio would fit no one's stereotype of a San Antonio Mexican restaurant. Bar.

SCHILO'S DELICATESSEN

424 E. Commerce at Navarro • Central • 223-6692 • Closed
Sunday • Lunch and dinner • No reservations taken • $–$$ • Cr.

Here's a convincing German deli in the heart of downtown, just a
flight of steps up from the River Walk. Hot plates, daily specials, and
cold plates all grace the menu, but most of the lunchers who stream in
opt for one of the sandwiches. Braunschweiger, corned beef, cheese,
chicken salad, and ruben sandwiches make up just part of the menu's list
of a score or more. Imported beer is available, but many of the customers prefer Schilo's special root beer. Schilo's interior, comfortably
old-fashioned, looks as if it's been around for a while. And it has, since
1917. Crowded, noisy, and homey, businesspeople flock here for a
quick lunch. Beer and wine.

ZUNI GRILL

223 Losoya • Central • 227-0864 • Open daily • $$ • Cr. • W

Zuni offers southwestern cuisine in a setting that suggests northwestern
New Mexico. Food ranges from such typical Mexican dishes as enchiladas
and fajitas to more innovative dishes, such as duck quesadillas and scorpi-
on-shrimp with red chiles. As at many River Walk establishments, a sense
of hustle pervades the dining room, but the harried, efficient service never
really rushes the diners—it's just always on the move. Bar.

AMERICAN

ANAQUA GRILL

Plaza San Antonio Hotel, 555 S. Alamo at Arceniega • Central
229-1000 • Open daily • Breakfast, lunch, and dinner
Reservations recommended • $$$–$$$$ • Cr. • W

Anaqua Grill remains a classy, relaxed dining room overlooking a
landscaped courtyard. The Plaza San Antonio's tradition of service has
continued undiminished through name changes of both hotel and
restaurant. Listing this among the American restaurants may be a bit
misleading, since much of the menu shows Mediterranean and Oriental
influences, but much is also influenced by the American Southwest. Bar.

BIGA

This highly rated restaurant closed its Locust Street location and is
due to re-open downtown on the River Walk. Owner-chef Bruce Auden
came into town as the first local practitioner of what is loosely known

as the New American cuisine. His training is French, his imagination vast, and his inspiration eclectic. Showing a sly humor that lets him describe an appetizer as containing "expensive mushrooms," he fills his menu with dishes as varied as lemon-braised osso buco and roast Texas antelope. His menu is usually eclectic, with items that may be American, Southwestern, Asian, or South American. Also homemade breads.

CAPPY'S

5011 Broadway at Mary D. • Northeast • 828-9669 • Open daily Reservations accepted • No smoking • $$–$$$ • Cr.

Even the menus at Cappy's have a certain flair, brightly colored with original art. Owner Cappy Lawton likes being a restaurateur, and you can tell by the comfortable feel of his places—lots of wood, greenery, textures, and oddball collectibles. His oldest restaurant is in a restored lumberyard on Broadway in Alamo Heights, where he has created an air both semicasual and intimate. Food is on the Southwestern side, with items like pecan-crusted catfish and blackened redfish. I like the beer-battered fried shrimp. Burgers and sandwiches are available for those with lighter appetites. Bar.

CARRIAGE HOUSE KITCHEN

555 Funston at Botanical Gardens • Northeast • 821-6447 Lunch Tuesday through Sunday • Closed Monday • $–$$ No Cr. • W

Combine a visit to the attractive San Antonio Botanical Gardens with lunch in its restored old carriage house in the center. Stone by stone, this old house was carried to the gardens location. Enjoy soups, salads, and sandwiches among the old, polished wood from the stable. Fat-inducing desserts.

CHESTER'S HAMBURGERS

Four locations • 16609 San Pedro at Thousand Oaks (North, 494-3333) • 9980 I-10 West (Northwest, 699-1222) • 621 Pat Booker Road (Northeast, 658-3000) • 1006 NE Loop 410 (North, 805-8600) • Daily • Lunch and dinner • No reservations taken • $ • W

For a burger and beer bash, no one can top Chester's. Not only does it offer more than 200 different beers you can get many different burgers, cooked to order to the kind of near perfection that chains seldom manage. As an old hand with green chile, I favor the green chile burger, with the fresh and lively taste of strips of hot, though hardly scorching, pepper. Inside, the decor is a cluttered, rustic eclecticism, with beer ads predominating. Beer and wine.

CHRIS MADRID'S

1900 Blanco • Near North • 735-3552 • Lunch and dinner Monday through Saturday • Closed Sunday • $ • Cr.

Aspiring politicos and the real thing seem to like sipping suds at this casual burger haven. Plain and simple in a workingman's neighborhood. Homestyle burgers. Bar.

COPPER KITCHEN

300 Augusta in the Southwest Craft Center • Central • 224-0123 Closed Saturday and Sunday • Lunch only • $ • No Cr.

This is one of those sleepers you won't likely know about unless you've been in San Antonio awhile. It's a lunchroom ensconced in the midst of a historical setting on the fringe of downtown. Look for it in the Southwest Craft Center, a restored mid-1800s French building turned into an arts school. Serve yourself cafeteria style and then sit at assorted antique wooden tables. Soups, sandwiches, and a couple of entrees make up the daily menu; they may include Mexican food or fish. This casual, cheerful site in what used to be the girls' school's dormitory hall draws local businesspeople as well as community matrons. Lunch and then a tour of the landscaped grounds on the San Antonio River make a nice outing.

EARL ABEL'S

4200 Broadway at Hildebrand • Northeast • 822-3358 Open daily • Breakfast, lunch, and dinner • No reservations taken $$ • Cr. • W

When San Antonians want a late-night meal, this is likely the place for it. When they want an informal snack after the theater, they may come here. When local seniors want a bite to eat with a special break on the price, here's where they go. The cooks make straight American fare, with steaks, fried chicken, pies, mashed potatoes, and green salads. When the goal is just to have some hearty and standard fare in an old homestyle American restaurant, you need not look elsewhere. Bar.

EZ'S

Three locations • 6498 N. New Braunfels at Sunset Ridge Shopping Center (Northeast, 828-1111) • 5720 Bandera at Loop 410 (Northwest, 681-2222) • 734 Bitters at San Pedro/Highway 281 (North, 490-6666) • Open daily • $–$$ • Cr.

Cappy Lawton's venture has proved outstandingly popular, as it combines an atmosphere reminiscent of the 1950s with up-to-date food and efficient self-service. Lots of chrome, shining plastic, and neon make up the decor, while lots of noise makes up the ambience. Overriding the happy din of customers is an employee on the PA system announcing, "NUMBER SEVENTY-FIVE, YOUR ORDER'S READY!!" But whether that order is a vegetable burger, a Caesar salad, grilled chicken, or maybe a pizza, the food will be both fast and just a little (or sometimes a lot) better than fast food has any right to be. While not the place for a romantic getaway meal, the consistent excellence of the uncomplicated food will impress you. Beer & wine.

FUDDRUCKER'S

8602 Botts Lane • North • 824-6703 • Several other locations Open daily • $ • Cr.

Hold the mayo! If you have to fix your own burger, you should pay a little less, but that's the gimmick here. And people seem to like this option of putting on their own toppings, which are always fresh. Order whatever size meat, cooked however you want it, at the meat counter. The meat is worthy, and patties range up to half a pound. Also available are taco salads, hot dogs, and sandwiches. This homegrown chain first sprouted at this main store in the Tesoro area north of Loop 410. Casual with lots of seating, some on a patio. Look for other stores at Alamo Plaza and in several shopping centers. The fresh-baked cookies taste above average—take a sackful home.

THE GAZEBO

At Los Patios, 2015 NE Loop 410 near Starcrest exit • Northeast 655-6190 • Open daily • Lunch only; except Sunday, brunch only $$ • Cr. • W

At Los Patios, some very uncitylike acreage serves as a magnificent setting for shops, boutiques, and three restaurants. Rarely does one find commercial ventures in such a stunning setting—the old estate on the banks of Salado Creek is one of the most attractive places to shop in all of San Antonio (see Shopping—Specialties). Mixed in with the shops are two restaurants—the Brazier, with its broiled specialties, and the Gazebo, serving lunches that cater to the shoppers at Los Patios. Soups and salads take up much of the menu at the Gazebo, though for a "light" hot lunch, the servings are decidedly generous. On pleasant days, much of the fun of visiting the Gazebo is eating in the garden— where the view, the trees, and the breezes make an unmatched setting. All in all, Los Patios projects an elegant, gardenlike atmosphere, even if you eat indoors. Bar.

GREY MOSS INN

Grey Forest • *Take TX 16 (Bandera Road) past Helotes to Scenic Loop Road; turn right and go three miles* **• Approximately twelve miles northwest of Loop 410 Northwest • 695-8301 • Open daily • Dinner only Reservations recommended • $$$ • Cr. • W**

This stone house, dating from the century's early days, could easily pass as any other house on the fringe of the Hill Country—this one just happens to be a restaurant. Mix up a little romance, add some good hearty steaks, take some waiters and waitresses who seem concerned only with pleasing the customers, and you have Grey Moss Inn. The menu is a little limited, but when you want a steak in relaxed surroundings, look no further. The special feeling of the place is created by kerosene lamps on the patio tables, a relaxed style of service that neither hurries nor dawdles, and a romantic set that has been the scene of not only a number of proposals but even a marriage ceremony. Either informal or formal dress fits in at this country inn. Bar.

GUENTHER HOUSE

205 E. Guenther, enter parking lot from S. Alamo just past Guenther Central • 227-1061 • Breakfast and lunch daily • $–$$ • Cr.

A bright, cheerful room in the old flour mill where the San Antonio River crosses South Alamo Street makes the setting for this boutiquelike restaurant. Breakfasts and light lunches revolve around baked goods, pancakes and waffles, egg dishes, sandwiches, and a few more substantial offerings. Some of the emphasis is on dishes derived from San Antonio's German heritage, as perhaps befits a restaurant just across the river from King William Street. Service is pert and prompt.

HYATT REGENCY HILL COUNTRY RESORT

**9800 Hyatt Resort Drive • Northwest • 647-1234
Open daily, except for formal restaurant • $$–$$$$ • Cr.**

Have a latent urge to play country squire for an outing? Drive near the Sea World area and enjoy the Hyatt's sprawling Hill Country acreage views. Several hotel eating places to choose from. The more formal, upscale restaurant, Antlers, only opens for dinner. But the more casual Springhouse Cafe is open for all meals. Even more casual, the clubhouse grill.

JOSEPHINE STREET CAFE

**400 E. Josephine at Avenue A • Near North • 224-6169
Monday through Saturday, lunch and dinner • Closed Sunday
Reservations taken for six or more • $–$$ • Cr. • W**

The Josephine Street Cafe gets down to basics as it proudly announces in its front window, in neon letters a foot high, "Steaks" and "Whiskey." If you judged from the building, you might think the restaurant dates back to the fall of the Alamo. In truth, the restaurant inherited its building from Finke's Meat Market, which occupied the site for a good fifty years. Now the restaurant packs in the patrons at lunch (by noon you can hardly find a table), although the dinner crowd is usually less pressing. The customers represent every side of San Antonio—a table of symphony-going diners will likely flank a table of cowmen spending the evening in the big city. The restaurant's brand of bold and straightforward cooking appeals to everyone who likes food plain and good. To sample the best that Josephine Street has, stick to the steaks or perhaps the pork chops (well-done but not dry). The decor consists mainly of a large pecan tree trunk poking up through the center of the room. Bar.

LIBERTY BAR

328 E. Josephine and Avenue A • Near North • 227-1187 • Open daily • Lunch and dinner • Reservations recommended for groups of eight or more • $–$$ • AE, MC, V • W

Once in a while, a restaurant comes along that has so much its own style that it clearly stands out from all others. Liberty Bar, with its fresh breads, vegetable salads, hearty sandwiches, and aggressive soups, is just such a place. Yet it achieves its uniqueness without being cute or trendy; it just ignores tradition to a large extent and cooks good food. But count on such sections of the menu as the mesquite charcoal grill fare and desserts, as well as two or three daily specials.

The Liberty Bar (the bar takes up half the establishment) is in the tumbledown building that used to house Boehler's Gardens, one of the most venerable watering places in San Antonio. The interior has a more open and spacious air than it ever did as Boehler's, but the patina (or perhaps decrepitude in some places) of age shows everywhere. No affected age here; one is surrounded by the nineteenth century, albeit a cheerful and sturdy nineteenth century. Bar.

LITTLE HIPP'S

1423 McCullough at Evergreen • Near North • 222-8114 Closed Saturday and Sunday • No reservations taken • $ No Cr. • W with assistance

When downtowners want to relax after work, some of them head for Little Hipp's, named after a now departed and much lamented establishment known as Hipp's Bubble Room. Little Hipp's serves sandwiches and burgers (a little on the thin side) in a filling station left over from the Depression. The songs in the jukebox do not date back quite as far but enough to make the middle-aged crowd feel nostalgic. The perpetual Christmas lights may seem out of place on a 95-degree summer day, but that's Little Hipp's. Beer and wine.

LUTHER'S

1425 N. Main at Evergreen • Near North • 223-7727 • Closed Saturday and Sunday • No reservations taken • $ • No Cr.

The burgers may be bigger and more glamorous at Fuddrucker's, but for the good old plain American hamburger, come to this place. Chili, a few kinds of sandwiches, and french fries are also available. In fact, the fries may overwhelm you; one order is more than enough for two. Luther's, a converted filling station, is worth a visit for its unaffected 1950s atmosphere. Its location, not far from San Antonio College, ensures that the collegiate spirit prevails, but you'll see people from every group, from laborers to lawyers, at Luther's. Beer and wine.

MAMA'S

Two locations • 9907 San Pedro (North, 349-5662)
7710 I-10 W (Northwest, 349-9367) • Open daily • $–$$ • Cr.

I don't know whose mama Mama's refers to, but regardless, this trendy fern-and-wood eatery packs in lunch crowds and the after-work singles who like to flock together for drinks and burgers. The bean burgers are popular. Also steaks, chicken, etc. Need I say, casual? Just join the gang amidst the greenery and oddball collectibles.

POLO'S

401 S. Alamo at Nueva, in the Fairmount Hotel • Central
224-8800 • Monday through Saturday • Breakfast, lunch, and dinner daily, except no lunch on Saturday, and Sunday breakfast only
Reservations suggested • $$$$ • Cr. • W

You might go here for a quiet lunch or a special dinner with attentive service. No loud music here; it's sedate and civilized, which is no doubt expected in this upscale hotel in downtown. Southwestern menu with such items as grilled quail. Bar.

TOWER OF THE AMERICAS RESTAURANT

Tower of the Americas, HemisFair Park • Central • 223-3101
Open daily • Lunch and dinner • Reservations accepted
$$$ • Cr. • W

Take a spin around the city—without leaving the dinner table. Near the top of the 622-foot Tower of the Americas sits a restaurant that makes a complete revolution once every hour or so. Calvin Trillin, in one of his most-quoted gems of advice, advised against eating in a restaurant that is more than 100 feet off the ground and that won't stand still, but as long as you realize that people visit more for the view than for the dinner, you should have no problem. Over the years the kitchen has been inconsistent, but the steaks and seafood dishes have generally been reliable. The view looks equally spectacular from the bar upstairs. If you do go for a meal, think of making the evening a full-fledged tourist occasion by taking a map of San Antonio and perhaps a pair of binoculars. The view, particularly remarkable at sunset, extends down into the flat ranching country to the south and up to the Hill Country ranches to the north. Glance at the paper to find out when the sun sets, and then choose a table that will be on the west side of the tower when it goes down. Who could ask for more? Bar.

TWIN SISTERS BAKERY AND CAFE

6322 N. New Braunfels at Brees • Northeast • 822-2265
Monday through Saturday • Closed Sunday • Breakfast, lunch, and dinner • No smoking on the premises • $ • Local checks accepted

The Alamo Heights version of a cafe, twin sisters indeed started this restaurant, in the Sunset Ridge Shopping Center. Nearby businesspeople and residents crowd in here at lunchtime for the homemade soups, sandwiches, quiches, and local gossip. The simple decor features wooden tables, booths, and ceiling fans. The sandwiches are fresh and large (a half can satisfy a medium appetite), piled with sprouts, avocado, and cheese, plus the meat of your choice. Too full for dessert? Then take home some of the homestyle baked goods, such as cookies and muffins.

TYCOON FLATS

2926 North St. Mary's • Near North • 737-1929 • Open Tuesday through Sunday • Lunch and dinner • $ • Cr.

This is not exactly a Gatsby kind of place, but Tycoon Flats probably does draw in a few quasi tycoons who go in for the casual noisiness of this college/upwardly mobile hangout. This place is strictly self-serve, and don't worry about the dress code. The line starts filling up at noon when the work lunch bunch comes in. Lots of burgers, chalupas, nachos, fries, and sandwiches fill most of the menu. Tycoon Flats makes a cheap date in the evenings, with live entertainment practically every night out back on the patio with wood tables. Music ranges from blues to soft rock. Tycoon was one of the first to put anchor down in the St. Mary's strip of eating and night spots.

BARBECUE

BOB'S SMOKEHOUSE

Two locations • 5145 Fredericksburg just south of Callaghan (Northwest, 344-8401) • 3306 Roland at Rigsby (South, 333-9338) • $ • No Cr.

Barbecue aficionados agree that this is one of the first places you should consider to sample genuine long-smoked barbecued meat, yet they also agree it's one of the last places to visit if you look for elegance and the trappings of upscale establishments. Muy informal.

CLUB HOUSE PIT BAR-B-QUE

2218 Broadway • Northeast • 229-9945 • Open Monday through Saturday • Closed Sunday • Lunch and dinner • $ • Cr.

Why the name Club House? Well not because of some tony country club atmosphere, believe me. It's because it used to be closer to the nearby Brackenridge Golf Course. Simple service and daily specials at this family-run cafe. Go there for the smoked sausage.

THE COUNTY LINE

Two locations • 10101 W. I-10 (North, 641-1998) • River Walk,
111 W. Crockett (Central, 229-1941)
Open daily for dinner; lunch on Sunday • No reservations taken
$$ • Cr. • W

The County Line is a barbecue restaurant that thrives on 1950s nostalgia, freshly made ice cream, gargantuan servings, and most of all, brawny Texas barbecue. Not many barbecue places in town have waiters and waitresses who will look after you, but this one does. You'll like The County Line's inexpensive option of splitting a plate between two diners. Those who have not fasted in preparation for a visit may find that a regular serving is too much for one person to eat. In addition to ribs, beef brisket, links, and related barbecue specialties, The County Line a lightly smoked beef roast for those not in the mood for barbecue. I have found the smoked baby back ribs to taste good. The River Walk branch is located on the south bank area. Bar.

FATSO'S SPORTS GARDEN

1704 Bandera near Hillcrest • Northwest • 432-0121 • Open daily
except closed some Sundays in summer • Lunch and dinner
No reservations taken • $–$$ • Cr. • W

Something about barbecue places always makes them more atmospheric than any other kind of restaurant. In this case, though, the barbecue atmosphere extends to include the trappings of a sports bar with television. As expected, beef, sausage, and ribs make up the choices. Can get too crowded on the nights of some sports games. Bar.

HICKORY HUT

3731 Colony Drive near I-10 access Road • North • 696-9134
Open Monday through Saturday • Lunch and dinner
No reservations taken • $ • No Cr. • W

Form a line, take a tray, name your vittles. The Hickory Hut resembles a score of barbecue places in town, so what makes it special? Maybe the friendliness of the folks behind the counter, maybe the variety of innumerable items on the walls, from old newspapers to antiques, but most probably the lean barbecued beef. Chicken and ribs are available also, but I keep going back to the sliced beef with its piquant sauce and side orders of slaw.

CAFETERIAS

LUBY'S CAFETERIAS

North Star Mall and numerous locations about town • 344-2561
Open daily • Lunch and dinner • $ • No Cr. • W

Normally this guidebook wouldn't include cafeterias or chains, but this is San Antonio's homegrown chain, and *everybody* goes to Luby's because the food is consistently good homestyle vittles for reasonable prices. This large chain is headquartered in San Antonio.

COFFEE SHOPS

JIM'S

842 NW Loop 410 at Blanco • North • 341-7137 • Numerous other locations in town; see business pages • Open daily
Some open 24 hours • $–$$ • Cr.

OK, there comes a time when you just gotta have a hot fudge sundae at 3 a.m. or breakfast at 3 p.m. If you're a late-shift worker, Jim's is where to go; it serves breakfast all day. Jim's also has the usual coffee shop fare and more—sandwiches, burgers, fried onion rings, steaks, and fish. While far from Julia Child's cuisine, the food is dependable and freshly cooked. Numerous locations about town. It's hard to find a major intersection, particularly on Loop 410, without a Jim's.

CONTINENTAL/FRENCH AND FANCY

BISTRO TIME

5137 Fredericksburg Road just south of Callaghan • Northwest
344-6626 • Dinner • Closed Sunday • $$$ • Cr. • W

A couple originally from Holland, experienced restaurateurs, settled in San Antonio to give the town a Dutch treat. In this plain strip center, slightly formal Bistro Time serves up continental fare. Almost any pâté among the appetizers will likely taste excellent, and the kitchen is especially good with chicken and fish. Bistro Time is one of only three or four

San Antonio restaurants that do in fact have the atmosphere and sense of a truly European establishment, in both style and service. Beer and wine.

CASCABEL

37 NE Loop 410 at McCullough in the Doubletree Hotel
North • 366-2424 • Open daily • Breakfast, lunch, and dinner
$–$$ • Cr. • W+

As many hotels change names often, so does this menu's cuisine. Currently Cascabel serves continental food.

CRUMPETS

3920 Harry Wurzbach • Northeast • 821-5454 • Open daily
Lunch and dinner • Reservations recommended for eight or more
$$$ • Cr. • W

Crumpets picked up its Alamo Heights feet and moved a ways from a shopping center to its very own building complete with secluded landscaped acreage, next to the affluent Oakwell Farms subdivision. The pleasant scenery adds to Crumpets' menu of French and continental fare. Seafood specialties. Beef Wellington on the weekends. Fancy assortment of European dessert pastries. Live, quietly civilized music on some days; ask ahead. Bar.

LA MADELEINE FRENCH BAKERY AND CAFE

4820 Broadway • North • 829-7271 • Open daily
Breakfast, lunch, and dinner • $–$$ • Cr.

Country French food in Alamo Heights. Serve yourself tray style. From salads and sandwiches to seafood dishes and decadent desserts.

LA SCALA

2177 Military Hwy. at West Ave. • North • 366-1515 • Open daily
Lunch and dinner • Reservations recommended on weekends
$$$–$$$$ • Cr. • W+

La Scala mimics an urbane European restaurant thanks to its subdued modern decor, cat-footed and practiced waiters, and a cuisine that is just continental without being identifiable as any particular nationality (though you may notice a tilt toward Italy). Steaks, lamb, veal, and chicken all grace the menu with more-or-less sophisticated sauces. Popular enough so you may sometimes have to wait for a table. Bar.

L'ETOILE

6106 Broadway • Northeast • 826-4551 • Closed Sunday • Lunch
and dinner • $$$-$$$$ • Cr.

Light French fare is popular; informal and early bird specials.

DELIS

NADLER'S

Two locations • 7053 San Pedro at Maplewood • North
340-1021 • Closed Mondays • Lunch only • $ • MC, V • W
with assistance • 1621 Babcock at Callaghan • Northwest
340-1021 • Closed Sunday • Lunch only • $ • No Cr.

A visit to Nadler's is in order for thick deli sandwiches—everything
from lox and cream cheese to spicy pastrami. While the prices may be a
little higher than you might expect in a sandwich shop, you get what
you pay for here. And as a bonus, after the sandwiches, Nadler's offers
an array of pastries. You can have eclairs, meringue fantasies, Napoleons,
cookies, etc., for lunch or take them out. Nadler's also makes cakes to
order. Beer and wine available at the San Pedro location.

OLD WORLD DELICATESSEN

1546 Babcock just outside Loop 410 • Northwest • 366-9523
Open daily • Breakfast, lunch, and dinner; Sunday lunch only
$$ • Cr. • W+

Germany inspired this comfortable restaurantlike deli where you
order at the counter and wait for food to be brought to the tables. Hot
plates of sliced meat or almost any kind of sausage are popular, but so
are sandwiches, with a variety of meats or combinations. Regular Ger-
man entrees make up some of the dinner plates. While meals here have
the heft characteristic of German food, they are cooked to show Ger-
man food in its best light. Beer and wine.

PECAN STREET DELI

152 E. Pecan • Central • 227-3226 • Open Monday through
Saturday • Closed Sunday • $ • Cr.

Just got in from an elongated ride on the Greyhound? Then pop in
across the street at the Pecan Street Deli to cool down. A little more
gourmet than most delis, this downtown one is located across from the
Greyhound Bus Station. Soups, salads, and sandwiches. Order at the
counter and sit. Local businessfolk like this urban respite.

POORBOY PANTRY

2018 San Pedro at Woodlawn • Near North • 735-9423
Closed Sunday • Lunch and dinner • $ • MC, V, DC

Here, amid efficient, friendly servers, visitors get some fine sand-
wiches that are big—in the case of the muffuletta, big enough to feed

three or four—and sometimes even exotic. Poorboy Pantry's sandwich-making savvy combines with a tradition of Middle Eastern cooking that gives sandwiches and other foods a range that few others can match. Baklava as a dessert is one example. All of the old favorites, such as ham and cheese, roast beef, corned beef, and other cold cuts, appear on the menu, but so do unusual ones, such as the *muffuletta*, a New Orleans specialty full of meat, olive salad, and other flavorful tidbits. A genial collegiate informality characterizes this popular deli, perhaps because of nearby San Antonio College. Beer and wine.

SCHILO'S (See River Walk)

ECLECTIC, EXOTIC, AND MEDITERRANEAN

BOARDWALK BISTRO

4011 Broadway, south of Hildebrand • Near North • 824-0100 Open Monday through Saturday • $$ • Cr. • W

Whether you seek a snack or crave a full meal, the Bistro will come through with not only food but often with some live music. I have had Italian dishes, excellent Spanish tapas, salads and sandwiches at lunch, and Mediterranean dishes. Beer and wine.

CAFE CAMILLE

517 E. Woodlawn • Near North • 735-2307 • Open Tuesday through Sunday • $$–$$$ • Cr.

In the casual St. Mary's strip area, the cafe serves up more fancy food than some of its cohorts down the road. A diverse menu, from Mediterranean to Southwestern. Live jazz some nights.

CARRANZA'S

701 Austin St., north of Jones • Central • 223-0903 Closed Sunday • $$ • AE

After about seventy years as a grocery, Carranza's remodeled to add a set of dining rooms and quickly became an unusual place to get together for dinner. Climb the long flight of wooden stairs and find a table in one of the dining rooms, two of which overlook the main line of the Southern Pacific tracks. Part of the fun here is seeing and hearing the long freights rumble past during meals. The menu has Italian, Mexican, American, and barbecue sections. The age of the limestone building combines with the 1930s furnishings to suggest an authentic visit to another era. Beer and wine.

DEMO'S

Two locations • 7115 Blanco at Loop 410 (North, 342-2772)
2501 North St. Mary's (Near North, 732-7777) • Open daily
$–$$ • Cr. • W

The emphasis on sandwiches and light food makes Demo's seem more of a lunch restaurant than anything else, as does its self-serve counter. Greek food, Greek pictures on the walls, and even Greek music leave little doubt as to the orientation of Demo's. The gyros sandwich is a Greek standby but isn't everybody's cup of tea. It's pita bread stuffed with lamb, beef, onions, sauce, and tomatoes. If you care for something less exotic, you can have a Greek-burger, a hamburger topped with feta cheese and stuffed into a piece of pita bread. A dozen other choices cover a range of quick and relatively easy Greek cooking—this is not a place to look for exotic and subtle specialties. One Greek favorite is *spanakopita*, a spinach and feta pie made with filo pastry, that multilayered triumph of lightness. Among the desserts, baklava is a favorite of almost everyone who has tried it. Demo's is run by Greeks and so has the sunny optimistic exuberance that one sees so often at Greek gatherings. Demo's on St. Mary's has a patio. One final note. Long ago, the Greeks found that adding resin to wine prolonged its keeping quality. Although bottling and corking now make it possible to keep wine even longer, retsina, or wine with resin, is still served in many Greek establishments. Since retsina is available here by the glass, wine lovers might give it a try. Beer and wine.

INDIA OVEN

1031 Patricia Drive • North • 366-1030 • Open daily
Lunch and dinner • $$ • Cr. • W+

Near one of the city's multiple shopping centers at the West and Blanco intersection, you can find this Indian spiced enclave. Tandoori chicken is one standout. Casual.

OLD HEIDELBERG

6714 San Pedro • North • 822-7866 • Open Tuesday through
Saturday • Lunch and dinner • $–$$ • MC,V • W

Despite Germans having settled much of San Antonio back in the old settler days, not many German restaurants abound in San Antonio. Here's one of them though. Traditional, hearty German food.

SILO

1133 Austin Hwy. • Northeast • 824-8686 • Closed Sunday
Lunch and dinner • Cr.

Look for Silo Restaurant hiding upstairs at the Farm to Market grocery store. First it was produce, then this independent little market grew to include a currently popular restaurant that attracts both Terrell Hills and Alamo Heights clientele. Expect to find a trendy mixture of food that, among other things, includes Asian and Southwestern and specials such as chicken-fried oysters on spinach to duck spring rolls and beef tenderloin. If its popularity continues, they recommend making reservations for Friday and Saturday dinner. A high-tech look. Entrance at back of grocery.

SIMI'S INDIA CUISINE

4535 Fredericksburg Road at Hillcrest • Northwest • 737-3166 Open daily • $$ • Cr. • W

One big plus here is the variety of dishes offered; another is the astounding range of flavors, from subtle and exotic to robust and peppery. The long menu runs through breads, fish, chicken, meat, and desserts. Those liking milder specialties might try chicken tandoor or marinated baked chicken. Order the curries as fierce or as mild as you like—just let the waiter know. At lunch, expect a rich buffet of dishes, all so tempting that you may find it difficult not to overdo. Neat but informal, this shopping center restaurant is a little more imaginative than most boxy strip center restaurants. Beer and wine.

ITALIAN

ALDINO CUCINA ITALIANA

622 NW Loop 410 in Central Park Mall, upper level facing Loop 410 • North • 340-0000 • Open daily • $$ • Cr. • W

This comfortable dining room has everything from a little humor in the pseudo-ruins of its decor to a lot of excellence in its kitchen. The cuisine, mostly northern Italian, ventures into territory where local Italian restaurants seldom visit. I have had a splendid creamy-textured risotto for lunch and well-flavored meats for dinner. Vegetable lasagna and fancy pizzas also grace the menu—the former is huge and the latter can be exotic with prosciutto and spinach. Bar.

ALDO'S

Fredericksburg Road at Wurzbach • Northwest • 696-2536 Open daily • On Saturday and Sunday, dinner only • $$$ • Cr. • W

On the fringe of the Medical Center complex, this restored 100-year-old house attracts the medical staffs who want something a little more elegant than most surrounding restaurants. In the evenings, formally dressed waiters and candlelit tables give an unrushed feeling to this place, which despite its location near a busy intersection is set in a handsome grove of trees. Pasta, veal, and seafood make up much of the menu. The crab pasta salad and cannelloni provide nice choices. Bar.

BOCCONES

**17776 Blanco Road, south of Bitters Road • North • 492-2996
Open daily • $$$ • Cr. • W**

This is a big, exuberant, southern Italian/Sicilian-style restaurant. The ebullient atmosphere sometimes makes it a little too loud for intimate conversation, but the range and variety of food compensate. Beer and wine.

LITTLE ITALY DELI AND RESTAURANT

**824 Afterglow, near West and Blanco • North • 349-2060
Closed Sunday • Lunch and dinner • Reservations recommended
for six or more • $$–$$$ • Cr. • W**

Little Italy, as any New Yorker can tell you, is the name given to a section of lower Manhattan where a large proportion of Italian immigrants settled and opened their businesses, including restaurants and groceries. From that area and its air of urgency, this restaurant takes its name. Appropriate? Yes—of all Italian restaurants in San Antonio, Little Italy most accurately re-creates the high-energy exuberance of the original Little Italy. The trappings of New York Italian restaurants are here: Italian travel posters, red-checkered tablecloths, and a style of cooking that exhibits both skill and imagination—especially in Little Italy's handling of seafood.

In addition to its restaurant, Little Italy also has an Italian delicatessen—a good place to stock up on cheese and cold cuts. And behold the spectacular, dressy, showy bar imported from Italy and lovingly reassembled.

LUIGI'S

**6825 San Pedro at Oblate • North • 349-5251 • Open Monday
through Saturday • Saturday, dinner only • $$–$$$ • Cr. • W**

Like a lot of Italian restaurants, Luigi's is a family operation with gregarious service. Nothing looks fancy in this shopping-center site with a bit of motel Italian in the red drapes and red velvet seats, but you'll find white tablecloths and the busy hum of conversation in the small dining area. Many regulars come for the good seafood served with Italian sauces. Bar.

MACARONI GRILL

**24116 I-10 West; on I-10 access road, north of San Antonio in Leon
Springs at Boerne Stage Road exit • 698-0003 • Open daily • Lunch
and dinner • Cr. • W+**

Local restauranteur Phil Romano started the Macaroni Grill chain. And usually there's a gregarious sound level at this Italian cafe, with lots of pasta and pizza and daily specials. Wine is served by the jug, and they'll even sell you cheese to take home.

MASSIMO RISTORANTE ITALIANO

4263 NW Loop 410 at Babcock • Northwest • 342-8556
Open Monday through Saturday • Lunch and dinner • $$–$$$
Cr. • W+

This Italian restaurant on the northwest side has become a palate pleaser. And it's run by an Italian straight from Italy no less. Expect many varied fish items, such as grilled squid and sauteed shrimp.

PAESANO'S

Two locations • 111 Crockett, on the River Walk (Central,
227-2782) • 555 E. Basse (Northeast, 828-5191) • Open daily
$$ • W

Paesano's has been a local favorite for years and has two different locations, one on the River Walk and one in the upscale shopping area of Lincoln Heights and the Quarry. Shrimp Paesano has always been popular.

PICCOLO'S

5703 Evers Road, between Wurzbach and Loop 410
Northwest • 647-5524 • Tuesday through Saturday • Lunch and
dinner • Reservations recommended for large groups • $$–$$$
AE, MC, V • W

This Italian restaurant does not fit into any of the neat categories of Italian restaurants, except maybe the one labeled Good. Piccolo's plays home to local businesspeople at lunch and local residents of the surrounding middle-income neighborhoods in the evening. The atmosphere is just right for the clientele—neither too fancy nor too casual.

Pasta dishes predominate on the menu, with fish dishes running close behind. Many lunch-timers choose lasagna. This restaurant's manicotti, one of the city's most subtly flavored and delicate, is the favorite of many regulars. Either of those dishes, with a small salad and garlic bread, makes a hearty lunch. Beer and wine.

RAZMIKO'S

8055 West Ave., at Lockhill Selma • North • 366-0416 • Open
daily • Lunch and dinner • $$–$$$ • Cr. • W+

Razmiko's is trying its Italian hand in a location tried by many restaurants before it. In an affluent Castle Hills shopping center, it lends itself to mild formality and attentive service. The grilled pollo alla griglia tastes good, as does the shrimp Razmiko. Bar.

MEXICAN

The greatest majority of San Antonio Mexican restaurants, even the most authentic, have menus in English rather than Spanish. However, some terms either have no English equivalents or are so widely understood in the Southwest that translations are not required for locals but may be for visitors. Here, then, are the top forty or so words you will most likely find on a Mexican menu. With this guide, and perhaps a little help from the waiter, you should be able to order something to suit your taste.

How to Decode a Mexican Menu

al carbon: means charcoal-broiled, but the term is used loosely.

asada: roast.

barbacoa: not simple barbecue but rather a special dish, usually served after mass on Sunday, that's made of a calf's head. While not common on the menus of restaurants that cater to visitors, it can turn up frequently in smaller neighborhood restaurants.

buñuelo: a Mexican pastry dessert shaped flat like a tortilla but with thin, flaky, crispy crust, topped with sugar and cinnamon.

burrito: food (usually beans or meat) wrapped in a flour tortilla; eaten like a sandwich.

cabrito: kid, or young goat, usually served barbecued or broiled. Excellent when young and tender, but disappointingly strong-flavored and tough when older.

caldo: stew that's sometimes a compromise between a thin stew and a hearty soup.

carne: meat.

cerveza: beer.

ceviche: an appetizer of fresh fish (almost always uncooked) marinated in lime juice and herbs, especially cilantro.

chalupa: a crispy fried corn tortilla spread with beans, chicken, meat, or whatever and topped with lettuce, tomato, and maybe some cheese or other garnish.

chile/chili: The first term, *chile,* usually refers to the red or green peppers that are so much a part of Mexican cuisine. About a dozen different varieties are easily available in San Antonio; they range from mildly hot to scorching. *Chili,* on the other hand, has come to

indicate the Tex-Mex dish of meat, onions, herbs, and spices, flavored with one or more kinds of dried red chile peppers.

chile relleno: a stuffed chile pepper, most properly a *chile poblano* (a large,
dark green, moderately hot chile), but sometimes an Anaheim or
other chile. The stuffing may be cheese (more common) or savory
meat, perhaps with raisins.

chimichanga: a burrito (see above) fried to make it crisp and hot. Long
popular in Mexican restaurants of Arizona, chimichangas are now
beginning to infiltrate San Antonio.

chorizo: a highly spiced (but rarely hot) Mexican sausage flavored
with chile and sometimes garlic. Chorizo tastes particularly good
with cheese.

cilantro: coriander, also called Chinese parsley. It has a strong and distinctive odor and for many people is an acquired taste. It is common in seafood dishes, often flavors pico de gallo, and occasionally turns up in guacamole.

colorado: means red, usually refers to chile.

compuesto: mixed, usually referring to a combination of different tacos
or chalupas.

empanada: a turnoverlike dessert.

enchilada: a universal favorite in Mexican cuisine, the word literally
means "treated with chile" but is always understood to mean tortillas with a filling and served with a sauce containing chile. The
filling can be cheese, chicken, meat, or almost anything, while the
sauce is commonly green or red depending on whether the chiles
used to make the sauce are fresh and green or dried and red. Generally, the green ones are hotter than the red ones.

fajitas: skirt steaks that have been marinated, then cut into strips, and
broiled. Served in flour tortillas, usually with pico de gallo, guacamole, or both. They taste best fresh off the vendor's stand.

flan: Mexican custard, varying from lightly flavorful to a cloyingly
sweet and heavy version made from condensed, sweetened milk.

flautas: corn tortillas wrapped around a filling (most commonly chick-
en) and fried until crisp. Usually served with guacamole or sour
cream.

frijoles: beans, almost always pinto beans (black beans, occasionally
seen, are *frijoles negros*). They may be served in a cup with sauce
made from their own cooking juices, or they may be refried, indicating that they are mashed in a frying pan and cooked, by tradition, with lard.

guacamole: a salad made from mashed avocado, ranging from a mush
so bland as to be insufferably dull to an exciting mixture with
onions, chiles, and cilantro. The quality of the guacamole is a
good clue to the authenticity of the restaurant serving it.

huevos: eggs.

jalapeño: one of the most popular peppers—can be very hot to bite into but not hot enough to spoil the rest of the meal, unless taken in large doses. Try one slowly 'til your stomach gets acclimated.

lengua: tongue, a popular dish in many of the more authentic restaurants. Typically served with a savory sauce made from the cooking broth.

menudo: a soupy stew made from special corn and from tripe. Sometimes served at breakfast on weekends.

mole poblano: a dark, rich sauce from Puebla, traditionally served with chicken or turkey. When made in the classical manner, the sauce contains more than twenty different ingredients, mostly ground spices, herbs, and nuts. The last-minute addition of chocolate, the ingredient for which the concoction is best known, gives the sauce part of its special depth of flavor.

nachos: crisp fried tortilla chips covered with beans, cheese, and slices of jalapeño, then heated in the oven or under a broiler to melt the cheese. Nachos can be (and often are) carried to any state of complexity, even including the addition of shrimp to the topping.

pico de gallo: a condiment consisting of chopped onions, chile peppers (sometimes extremely hot), and herbs, such as cilantro.

piquante: literally, "stinging"; figuratively, "hot or even fiery with spices." If a Mexican menu uses the term *piquante,* approach the dish with caution until your tongue is suitably calloused.

pollo: chicken.

puerco: pork.

quesadilla: a corn tortilla folded in half around a filling of melted cheese. These can be extraordinarily good, especially when filled with white Mexican cheese.

queso: cheese, often a white Mexican cheese that is mildly flavorful and melts well.

sangria: a wine drink, traditionally served in the summer, made from red wine and citrus.

taco: one of the mainstays of Mexican cuisine, a taco is a corn or flour tortilla wrapped around any kind of filling, usually beef. If made with a corn tortilla, it will likely be fried crisp before being filled.

tamales: a tamale is a portion of corn dough, similar to that which tortillas are made of (called masa), spread on a corn husk, then topped with meat, rolled up, and steamed. When at their best, they are one of the great delights of Mexican cooking. Occasionally (too rarely) one sees dessert tamales—sweet and spicy morsels that ought to be more common. Equally rare are *uchepos,* or green corn tamales, which are made from fresh corn and are one of the greatest of all Mexican treats.

tortilla: tortillas serve much the same purpose that bread serves in European cooking. They are either cooked into the dish, as in enchiladas or flautas, or served with the meal in place of bread. A tortilla is a thin, flattened morsel of dough cooked on a *comal*, a griddle on top of the stove. Corn tortillas are more common in central Mexico; northern Mexico is the home of the flour tortilla. Some suggest that the influence of the German settlers in San Antonio led Mexican cooks to experiment with flour tortillas in the first place. While enchiladas made with flour tortillas are unthinkable, some dishes, such as tacos, can use either kind. For soaking up gravy or stew, most prefer the flour variety.

tostada: the triangular chips of fried tortilla, which, served with a cup of peppery red or green sauce, start off most meals in local Mexican restaurants.

verde: means "green" and usually refers to chile.

ADELANTE MEXICAN FOOD

21 Brees at New Braunfels • Northeast • 822-7681 • Closed Sunday and Monday • Breakfast, lunch, and dinner • $ • No Cr.

Adelante offers unusual Mexican food, mostly vegetarian and healthy, including a wide array of tamales. Many of the dishes seem especially freshly made—the tired steam-table syndrome is absent here. Both tables and counter service, with art, folk and otherwise, on the walls. The service is neighborhood friendly. For those who like to eat alone (or are not good company) there is even a magazine rack. Mexican folk art is sold on the side.

BLANCO CAFE

Three locations • 1720 Blanco at Elsmere (Near North, 732-6480) • 5525 Blanco (North, 344-0531) • 419 North St. Mary's (Central, 271-3300) • Hours and days open vary with cafe • $ • No Cr.; local checks • W

The original Blanco Cafe, at Elsmere, is for those who eschew the artificial, the glossy, the transitory, and the faddish. Breakfast tacos are a big seller in the morning; the rest of the day the enchiladas take over, together with a full spectrum of simple Mexican food that makes it possible to order a meal by combining three or four small orders. One could easily overlook the building—you have to know it is there to find it. Those who go there do so because the simplicity of Mexican food without any trimmings can be reward enough. As for specialties, Blanco Cafe has none, unless you can call some of the best flour tortillas in town a specialty. Blanco Cafe II is located further north on Blanco. Same menu, but it doesn't have the same nonclass of the old one.

EL BOSQUE

12656 West Ave., near North Loop • North • 494-2577 Open daily • No reservations taken • $–$$ • AE, MC, V • W

The food is distinctly Tex-Mex, with few spicy dishes. It has a good selection of Mexican beer and an atmosphere more convincingly Mexican than many another local restaurants. El Bosque is an informal, unpolished gem of a restaurant for those who like easygoing authenticity and who want a restaurant on the far north side. Bar.

EL JARRO

13421 San Pedro at Bitters • North • 494-5084 • Open daily Reservations recommended for large groups • $$ • Cr. • W

Fajitas, or "marinated skirt steaks," are a San Antonio favorite—whenever there is a fiesta at Market Square, a few booths will surely sell fajitas—but good ones are hard to find at restaurants. El Jarro makes a specialty of them—richly flavorful beef served in flour tortillas with guacamole and a side dish of pico de gallo. And you can see an expert Mexican cook patting out tortillas and cooking them on a grill, just as others have done for centuries in Mexico. Most of the menu specialties are safe bets, but the *flautas* (rolled corn tortillas stuffed with chicken and served with guacamole) are especially crisp and full. Dance band on Friday and Saturday evenings. Bar.

EL MIRADOR

722 South St. Mary's, at Madison • Central • 225-9444 • Open daily • Breakfast, lunch, and dinner, except no dinner on Sundays No reservations taken • $–$$ • MC, V

For a fast, economical lunch on the edge of downtown in Southtown, opt for El Mirador. Located near the edge of the King William District, it attracts a lunchtime crowd that includes downtown businessmen, some courthouse politicos, a few tourists, and a covey of King William residents. Enchiladas, as elsewhere, are a house specialty, but for dinner, entrees can get more sophisticated, with items such as smoked-quail chalupas. On weekends, the specialties are soups: two chicken-broth concoctions so full of chicken and vegetables that they are almost stews. Known as Xochitl and Azteca soups, they claim a following of fans who come in regularly to get big bowlfuls; the recipe for one has even appeared in the *New York Times*. El Mirador is strictly a casual restaurant and one to bear in mind when looking for a breakfast spot. The informality extends to the service.

ERNESTO'S

2559 Jackson-Keller, at Vance Jackson • Northwest • 344-1248 Open Monday through Saturday • Lunch and dinner, except dinner only on Saturday • Reservations recommended for five or more $$ • Cr. • W

Ernesto's bases its dishes on the fancier, more-evolved recipes of Mexico yet prepares them with consideration for the tenderness of many a gringo palate. The dishes resemble those a good restaurant in a Mexican coastal resort town might serve. The main courses emphasize fish and seafood, with such items as red snapper. You'll find nothing fancy, affected, or theatrical here, but Ernesto's is a seasoned San Antonio restaurant. Bar.

LA CALESA

2103 E. Hildebrand, at Broadway • Northeast • 822-4475
Open daily • Lunch and dinner • $–$$ • Cr. • W

"Authentic Mexican Cuisine" modestly announces La Calesa's business ad. It seems an understatement for a restaurant that serves a version of the characteristic dish of Yucatan, *cochinita pibil*, which is pork baked in a pit covered with earth. Well, maybe La Calesa skips the earthen pit, but it does serve a worthy replica of the dish. Other dishes tend more toward the styles of interior Mexico than to the Tex-Mex persuasion, but most are simple rather than complex. Shrimp dishes form a generous section of the menu—some piquante, others gentler.

The atmosphere of a Mexican home turned into a restaurant permeates the place, (and why not? it's actually in an old house) complete with Mexican decorations and Diego Rivera posters. Those who feel unsure of their taste for Mexican food, prefer a combination plate, or seek mild flavors might prefer other establishments, but for those who know Mexican food well, a trip to family-friendly La Calesa can be a treat. Bar.

LA FOGATA

2427 Vance Jackson, at Addax • North • 340-1337 • Daily Lunch and dinner; breakfast Friday through Sunday • $–$$ • Cr. • W

Since its opening, La Fogata ("the bonfire") has attracted crowds and has added on piecemeal additions to keep up with them. Avoid this restaurant when pressed for time. But when you can afford the luxury of a relaxed meal in busy surroundings, then head for the casual La Fogata. Simple Mexican foods—flour tacos, charro beans, grilled green onions, and a range of dishes common in Mexico yet rare in Tex-Mex restaurants—are prepared convincingly, which makes them especially rewarding. Many of the dishes are small—three or even four orders might make a meal. Try, for example, tacos al carbon, *frijoles borrachos* (literally, "drunken beans"; very flavorful beans), and maybe an order of *quesadillas* (melted cheese in corn tortillas). La Fogata recreates the best of what one might find at a small and unpretentious restaurant in the northern part of Mexico. Patrons enjoy patio dining in San Antonio's glorious spring or fall weather. Although La Fogata is often crowded, visit anyway for the authentic food. Not long ago ownership changed hands. Bar.

LA FONDA

2415 N. Main, at Woodlawn • Near North • 733-0621 • Monday through Saturday • Lunch and dinner • $–$$ • Cr. • W

For those leery of Mexican food but wanting to try a safe meal (one that will leave the palate utterly unscorched and the senses intact), try La Fonda, which old-line northsiders have frequented since the 1930s. La Fonda, long a fixture on North Main, caters to those who want their Mexican food toned down but still made with the best ingredients. The restaurant's colorfully gay Mexican decor, reminiscent of the crafts sold at a street market in the San Angel area of Mexico City, brightens up the clean and graceful interior. The theme for the food is delicacy not robustness. Even the size of the servings matches the presumed appetites of the largely feminine lunch clientele. The old standby menu has been innovated a bit under new ownership.

LA FONDA

Sunset Ridge Shopping Center at 6300 block of N. New Braunfels Northeast • 824-4231 • Open daily • Lunch and dinner, but no lunch on Saturdays • $$ • Cr.

This Fonda, no longer affiliated with the Main Avenue restaurant, is a favorite of many a northeastsider. The menu runs the gamut of Tex-Mex fare, and dishes are served with a generous hand.

LA MARGARITA

Market Square, 120 Produce Row • Central • 227-7140 Open daily • $$ • Cr. • W

About the time that Mi Tierra (see below) got so popular that lines of would-be customers snaked through the waiting area and out the door, the owners decided to open a second establishment just a few doors down at Market Square. But the second restaurant turned out even better than the original. Now lines of people wait to get into La Margarita. Visit La Margarita for the food, not to have a tête-à-tête or to thrash out a business deal over dinner—the din can almost overpower you at busy times. La Margarita's specialty is one of San Antonio's native delicacies, *fajitas*, or "marinated skirt steaks." Another specialty, seafood (including an oyster bar), is a holdover from the previous occupant of La Margarita's quarters. Popular with tourists, La Margarita also attracts its share of San Antonians. With its prominent location on Market Square, people sometimes dismiss the restaurant as less substantial than it is. If it's cool enough, sit outside on the patio and sip a cool margarita (what else?) while people-watching. Bar.

LOS BARRIOS

4223 Blanco, at San Angelo • North • 732-6017 • Open daily Late breakfast, lunch, and dinner • $–$$ • Cr. • W

Los Barrios has for years been a place to get the blatantly flavorful food served throughout Mexico and a few South American dishes as well. With the green enchiladas, the taste of real *tomatillos* (small, green tomatolike vegetables with papery husks) comes through in the sauce. Visit casual, no-frills Los Barrios for tacos, enchiladas, chalupas, and flautas served in the plain and solid style of much of Mexico. As a bonus, a special section offers "continental cuisine," though we have never been able to figure out just what continent such specialties as El Mofofo Grill come from. Perhaps South America. Live music plays Friday and Saturday evenings. Beer and wine.

MI TIERRA CAFE AND BAKERY

Market Square, 218 Produce Row • Central • 225-1262 • Open at all times • No reservations taken • $–$$ • Cr. • W

This busy tourist spot keeps its eyes open 24 hours. Just outside the restaurant area is a large waiting room (which reminds one of the bus station in Chihuahua) that adjoins a bakery offering a wide range of Mexican bread and sweet rolls (*pan dulce*). The bakery is one of the attractions of the restaurant; many who eat at Mi Tierra take home a bag of crusty breakfast rolls or dessert goodies. The restaurant itself presents a fairly standard array of Mexican food, yet all aspects of the place give a feeling of Mexican-ness that makes Mi Tierra fun to visit. This is one place you can always enjoy serenading mariachis. But don't beckon them over unless you want to fork over some dinero. The service achieves exactly the kind of nonchalant but intense efficiency seen in restaurants all over Mexico. As for the food, many of the dishes are popular with tourists. *Chile rellenos* (stuffed peppers) here are the genuine Mexican kind—poblano peppers, not the easier-to-use Anaheim peppers. Combination plates run the gamut of sizes from large to huge—a big appetite is definitely an asset here. Mi Tierra sells some breakfast items all day. One of those specialties, huevos rancheros, is a real waker-upper. Bar.

PICO DE GALLO

111 S. Leona, at Buena Vista • Central • 225-6060 • Open daily $$ • AE, MC, V

The same family that brought you Mi Tierra and La Margarita has done it again, this time with a big, ebullient, family-style downtown restaurant where dishes are a bit more Mexican than Tex-Mex. Plenty of dishes have hot sauces that may make you think your tongue will take home scars, but there are plenty of more mild dishes, such as flautas or some of the enchiladas—just ask the waiters for suggestions. This place has shrimp enchiladas, and mariachis play at dinnertime. Bar.

ROSARIO'S

910 S. Alamo • Central 223-1806 • Open Monday through
Saturday, but hours vary • Reservations recommended for five or
more • $$ • Cr. • W

It takes a long look around the interior of Rosario's for one to be sure
this is Texas, not Mexico. This casual place looks south of the border.
The food follows suit, to the credit of this unpretentious spot. The chile
rellenos here are popular, as are the *camarones al mojo de ajo* (shrimp in
garlic sauce), which will remind one of how it is done along Mexico's
seacoast. Simple to the extreme, Rosario's is not for someone who
thinks that attentive and polished service is the main requirement for a
restaurant. The service will care for you, not pamper you. Nor is
Rosario's for someone who expects perfection in all dishes. Bar.

TACO CABANA

Locations all over town • Check telephone book for addresses
Open daily, some locations 24 hours • $ • No Cr.

This is San Antonio's answer to Taco Bell, though the food is much
better. In the past few years, Taco Cabana has grown from a single
location at San Pedro and Hildebrand to many locations. Some stay
open 24 hours and serve a moderately good selection of hearty Tex-
Mex food. Best of all, perhaps, is their version of fajitas, preferably with
guacamole and pico de gallo—a real fill-'er-upper when those 3 a.m.
hungries strike. Full Mexican plates, heavy with beans and rice, hold
down one end of the menu, while you can order tacos—both crisp and
soft—chalupas, enchiladas, and side orders to eat there or to whisk
away from the drive-up window. In the mornings look for breakfast
tacos, including ones with fresh-tasting scrambled eggs. What the
cooking lacks in finesse and subtlety it makes up for in convenience and
freshness. The drive-through lanes are always hopping. Beer and wine.

ORIENTAL

TONG'S THAI

1146 Austin Hwy., west of Exeter • Northeast • 829-7345
Open daily • Lunch and dinner on Monday through Friday, dinner
only on Saturday and Sunday • $$ • Cr. • W

Vietnam and Thailand both contribute to the menu here, and even
China gets into the act with a few dishes. You may find, though, that
the clearest, sharpest, and best flavors are in the Thai and Vietnamese
dishes. They have the light, well-defined tastes that mark those cuisines

and are seldom heavy or too filling. The kitchen treats both crab and shrimp well. The setting is as western (i.e., Texan) as it is oriental, and the service has a western practicality that gets the job done with no nonsense. The servers are especially accommodating to children.

DING HOW

4531 NW Loop 410, at Callaghan • Northwest • 340-7944
Open daily • Lunch and dinner • Reservations for eight or more
$$ • AE, MC, V

Every day at lunchtime, this restaurant is usually pretty busy. What is its secret? Location? Possibly, since it is just off Loop 410 at Callaghan. Decor? Probably, since every aspect of the interior is decorated with enough Chinese verve to cover eight ordinary restaurants. Walls and ceilings alike are coated with carved wood, oriental paintings, and the kind of Chinese artistry one will seldom see outside the Orient or the largest of western Chinatowns. Has old standbys, such as sesame chicken and cashew shrimp. Bar.

FUJIYA

9030 Wurzbach • Northwest • 615-7553 • Open daily
Lunch and dinner • $–$$ • Cr.

This longtime Japanese restaurant has moved from time to time, with its latest incarnation in the busy Wurzbach Road area. Tempura shrimp, delicately fried in a light batter, tastes quite good and is usually one of the lunch specials. Many varieties of sushi. For dessert, the Orange Delight is, well, delightful. Sort of an ice cream parfait made with orange liqueur.

GIN'S

5337 Glen Ridge, at Evers • Northwest • 684-7008
Open daily • $ • No Cr.

This restaurant has already expanded two or three times, as more and more people found out about it. I have heard that many in the Chinese community regard it, among all other restaurants in town, as having the Chinese food most similar to home cooking. Some of the specials at lunchtime are simple and stereotypical, but at dinner, the menu is a little more inventive. Look for smoked duck, shrimp with vegetables, and pan-fried pork dumplings. Expect nothing fancy or extravagant here—this is economical Chinese food at its best.

GOLDEN WOK

8822 Wurzbach Road, at Gardendale • Northwest
615-8282 • Open daily • $$ • Cr. • W

While the Golden Wok does have the specialties that seem obligatory for any Chinese restaurant, one of its main claims for attention is *dim sum*, that special weekend treat of small, varied dishes offered from carts pushed through the restaurant. Have a look at the dim sum menu when you go in, and then just point to the dishes on the carts as they roll by. When you've had your fill, a waiter will tote up the damage, and you can be off. Bar.

HSIU YU

8338 Broadway, at Greenbriar • North • 828-2273 • Open daily
On Saturday, dinner only • $–$$ • Cr.

Where old pizzerias die off, it seems oriental restaurants often follow. There must be a moral here, but I'm not quite sure what it is. Anyway, in this old pizza place near the traffic-loaded intersection of Broadway and Loop 410, Hsiu Yu came in and added a bright red Chinese door and is doing a lunch-crowd business. Reasonably priced lunches during the week cater to a lot of businessfolk in the neighborhood. Standbys such as Kung Pao chicken and spicy shredded chicken are good and even better considering the price.

KABUKI

15909 San Pedro • North • 545-5151 • Open Tuesday through Sunday • Lunch and dinner, but no lunch on weekends • $–$$
AE, MC, V • W+

The largest, most diverse, and most authentic-looking of San Antonio's Japanese restaurants, Kabuki offers western-style tables, cook-at-the-table grills, Japanese-style tatami mats, and a sushi bar. I have yet to be disappointed in anything on the long menu, but if any one area stands out, it is perhaps the sushi bar, where the range of sushi is rivaled only by its freshness. Tempura, teriyaki, mixed dinners, and special grilled dinners all add variety. The staff has the obliging courtesy so often seen in oriental restaurants. Beer and wine.

KOI KAWA

4051 Broadway, south of Hildebrand • Near North • 805-8111
Open Monday through Saturday • Lunch and dinner, except no lunch on Saturday • $$ • Cr.

Those who measure authenticity by the menu and kitchen, not the decor, swear by this little Japanese gem in the Boardwalk. Some dishes may be too unusual for the uninitiated, but standard Japanese fare, such as tempura and sukiyaki—even a unique seafood sukiyaki—is also available.

NIKI'S TOKYO INN

819 W. Hildebrand, near Blanco • Near North • 736-5471 • Open Tuesday through Sunday • Dinner only • $$ • AE, MC, V • W

Niki's offers a lot of what makes many people admire Japan. First, the service is courteous and considerate. Then there is the discretely romantic mien of the restaurant, with its choice of Japanese and western-style dining rooms, both decorated with the appealing restraint and sense of balance evident all over Japan. And, of course, there is Japanese food, including, best of all, a sushi bar. The restaurant's other dishes include sukiyaki, prepared at the table, and *tempura*, or shrimp fried with the lightest and airiest batter coating imaginable. For food, setting, and service, Niki's has it all. Beer and wine.

SAIGON GARDENS

**5505 Randolph Blvd. • Northeast • 654-8858 • Open daily
Lunch and dinner • No reservations taken • $ • MC, V**

You can't get more informal than this Vietnamese cafe off in the northeast corner of town. It specializes in folksy, simple food filled with intriguing flavors of the Orient, flavors that seem more mysterious than those in other Vietnamese restaurants. Look for the shrimp with hot sauce and barbecued pork with vermicelli (*banh hoi thit huong*, in case you were wondering), which comes with lettuce leaves that you use to enfold the spicy concoction, much as you might enfold Mexican food in a tortilla. The food itself, in all its ethnically riveting newness, is the only attraction here, but one that richly deserves a visit from the culinarily curious. The service is simply utilitarian, while the restaurant itself has about as much charm and glamour as a double-wide mobile home converted to a restaurant. Beer and wine.

TAIPEI

**2211 NW Military Hwy. • North • 366-3012 • Open daily
Lunch and dinner • $$–$$$ • Cr.**

If you're looking for a sedate dinner with a little more classy ambience and service in the evening, you might enjoy this Chinese restaurant, which is a little more fancy than many casual oriental places. Located in a Castle Hills shopping center. Some attractive shrimp dishes.

VIET NAM

**3244 Broadway, at Natalen • Northeast • 822-7461
Open daily • $$ • Cr. • W**

Spring rolls, the Vietnamese version of egg rolls, have a thinner cover and far more exciting flavor than any egg roll. Try them—they beat most egg rolls hands down. The spicy chicken, also very flavorful, has just the right amount of hot pepper. Crab Supreme, on the other hand, tastes mild, even subtle. Most visitors count it as the restaurant's masterpiece, with its noodles, crab, and mysterious oriental flavors and textures. Convenient to two colleges, Viet Nam is popular with college students, not only for its excellent food but also for its reasonable prices. The military contingent, as you might expect, also frequents this no-frills converted old house. Beer and wine.

SEAFOOD

PORTS O' CALL

4522 Fredericksburg Road, northeast corner of Crossroads Shopping Center parking lot • Northwest • 732-3663
Open daily • $$ • Cr. • W+

Nestled in a parking lot at the corner of I-10 and Loop 410, maybe the city's busiest interchange, Ports offers every kind of seafood from lunchtime shrimp salads to complete lobster dinners. Steaks and poultry dishes are there for those who must have them, but anyone looking for fine seafood, especially on a budget, would do better here. Bar.

SEA ISLAND

Two locations • 322 W. Rector at Ahern (North, 342-7771)
4323 Amerisuite Drive, at I-10 (North, 558-8989) • Open daily
No reservations taken • $$ • MC, V • W

Strap on the shoulder pads for a lunch here if you come on one of the crowded days. That means most days, incidentally, because Sea Island has won over the hearts of many northsiders. Little wonder, too, when you compare the food with that served in most of the surrounding fast-food emporia. Fresh oysters, a salad bar, and a couple of dozen other fish dishes are slung at high speed to the customers willing to order at the counter and wait for a table at lunchtime. The seafood always tastes fresh—indeed, it spends little time in the kitchen, thanks to the flow of customers.

WATER STREET OYSTER BAR

7500 Broadway, at Nacogdoches • Northeast • 829-4853
Open daily • $$–$$$ • Cr. • W

The Lincoln Heights Shopping Center isn't exactly the waterfront, but Water Street is proving to be the catch of the day on the local seafood scene. Trucks bring in fresh fish daily from the coast, and the daily special is marked on the blackboard in this large, brick building with a high ceiling and loft seating. The ceiling of exposed ductwork and metal beams may have the warehouse look, but the rest is casual slick. Wooden captains' chairs and wood-formica tables, with some greenery thrown in, overlook the see-through cooking area. A giant mural of a fisherman and a collection of fishing lures give the place its only nautical look. The blackened fish of your choice isn't overcooked, and the picayune shrimp are a spicy treat, broiled in a hot Cajun-style sauce. For dessert, the praline cheesecake has a good texture and isn't overly sweet. Bar.

STEAKS

BARN DOOR

8400 N. New Braunfels, inside Loop 410 • Northeast
824-0116 • Open daily • Saturday, dinner only • Reservations
recommended for large groups • $$–$$$ • AE, MC, V • W

"Keep the volume up" might be the motto here, where enough steak
is served every day to depopulate a small ranch. Nothing fancy—no
sauces, gimmicks, or special cooking—is offered. Instead, just steaks
with a kind of folksy, western friendliness. Service and setting evoke
West Texas towns and ranches. A favorite of locals, and yes, it looks
like a barn. Bar.

MORTON'S OF CHICAGO

Rivercenter Mall, enter from Crockett Street just behind the Menger
Hotel • Central • 228-0700 • Open daily • Dinner only • $$$$
Cr. • W+

This chain has opened up in the Rivercenter Mall, a magnet for visitors to the city. It specializes in steak, especially the expensive cuts.
You do get what you pay for, including excellent, attentive service and
a posh setting, but a steak may not really be worth that much fuss. Most
of the steaks are also bigger than all but the most ardent trencherman
could put away in one sitting, so many of the visitors walk out of one of
the city's priciest restaurants carrying doggie bags. Bar.

RUTH'S CHRIS STEAKHOUSE

7720 Jones Maltsberger, in the Concord Building just south of
Sunset Road • North • 821-5051 • Open daily • Dinner only
Reservations recommended weekends • $$$$ • Cr. • W+

Ruth's Chris, a determinedly upscale steak chain, boasts of having
some of the best beef in the country. Perhaps they do; certainly a sampling of the fare here does not give one reason to question that. But
whether unadorned beefsteak is worth that kind of fuss and prices is
debatable—broiled meat is broiled meat. But for those to whom a
grilled fillet or sirloin equals the ultimate in gastronomy, this may be
the ultimate in restaurants. Bar.

SAN FRANCISCO STEAK HOUSE

10223 Sahara, at San Pedro • North • 342-2321 • Open daily
Dinner only • Reservations recommended • $$$–$$$$ • Cr. • W

The steak tastes quite alright, served in a neo-Victorian, ornate San
Francisco atmosphere. For entertainment, a damsel pumps in a red vel-
vet swing suspended over the bar. The big crowd-pleaser comes when
she swings high enough to kick a bell hanging from the ceiling. Besides

the big beefy steaks, you get your very own block of cheese and loaf of sourdough bread. Live piano music. Bar.

U.R. COOKS

4907 NW Loop 410, in Loehmann's Village • Northwest 647-4846 • Open daily • Lunch and dinner, but lunch only on Saturday and Sunday • Reservations recommended for ten or more $$ • Cr.

Here, you can be totally sure that you will not have nasty comments for the cook when you get your steak, because here, the cook is the customer. Apparently not satisified with the trend of getting customers involved by letting them make their own salads, the impresario of U.R. Cooks had the inspiration of also letting them cook their own steaks, thus presumably cutting down on complaints and labor costs simultaneously, to say nothing of cutting out waiters and waitresses. But most important, does it work? Yes, apparently so. And it is kind of fun, standing side by side with other cooks of various degrees of enthusiasm and expertise, all preparing their own and their guests' steaks. The quality of the meat is fine. Thoroughly casual in style, U.R. Cooks fills on weekends with a mostly young and jovial crowd; you may often encounter birthday parties and big groups. If U.Rn't a cook, they'll cook it for you for a small fee. Bar.

Bars and Clubs

Finding a good bar or club is hardly a problem in San Antonio. Indeed, in some parts of town, such as the River Walk, the problem may be avoiding them. Some of the better bars and clubs, however, are hidden away where visitors are unlikely to stumble onto them. The River

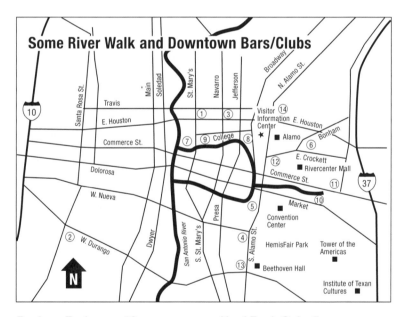

Some River Walk and Downtown Bars/Clubs

Bonham Exchange, 10
Cadillac Bar and Restaurant, 2
Champions, 11
Dick's Last Resort, 6
Durty Nelly's, 9
Esquire, 3

Hard Rock Cafe, 5
La Margarita, 1
Landing, 7
Menger Bar, 8
Planet Hollywood, 4

Walk, of course, is the main area for night spots, but another good hunting ground is the St. Mary's Street Strip, a couple of miles north of downtown. Many of the clubs featuring live entertainment have cover charges, but many of the more casual spots have none. The cover charges can vary drastically depending on the group playing. Not only do cover policies change; so do owners, kinds of entertainment, and closing days in some cases. Therefore, this book doesn't give specific information about cover charges and days open. Check ahead. The list of what is hot and what is not in San Antonio changes frequently. This book lists some of the clubs that have shown some staying power, but usually quite a number more spring up, catch the public's fancy, fade back after a few months, and then vanish. To find the current hot spots, check the newspaper's Friday weekend supplement or a periodical such as the *Current*.

BLUEBONNET PALACE

16842 I-35 North, a few miles northeast of San Antonio, in Selma Northeast • 651-6702

This is a Billy Bob kind of place for the real thing and those who aspire to be urban cowboys. You can two-step in the huge warehouselike dance hall to live country dance bands.

BLUE STAR BREWING CO.

1414 S. Alamo • Central • 212-5506

Tipple a brew in this combination restaurant-brewpub in the Blue Star Arts Complex area in Southtown, just south of downtown. Find a mixture of collegiates and artistic types.

THE BONHAM EXCHANGE

411 Bonham, at Travis • Central • 271-3811

The Bonham caters to the gay clientele, but straights are welcome. The spiffily restored building alone is worth a visit; it has greater historical interest than that of any other local bar, with the exception of the Menger Bar. In addition to a big, comfortable bar, there is also the dance floor with an electronically controlled sound and light system. The Bonham caters primarily to men; a corresponding bar for women is Nexus, at 8021 Pine Brook (341-2818).

CADILLAC BAR AND RESTAURANT

212 S. Flores • Central • 223-5533

Since it's not far from the Bexar County Courthouse, lawyers often drop by for drinks and to replay what went on in court in this attractively restored historic building.

CHAMPIONS

849 E. Commerce • Central • 226-7171

Sports fans get their kicks and dunks here in this combo sports bar and restaurant. Located downtown in Rivercenter Mall. Television screens proliferate for fans who prefer eating and watching sports on TV with big crowds instead of at home as a couch potato.

DICK'S LAST RESORT

406 Navarro, on River Walk • Central • 224-0026

The decibel noise meter always is on HIGH at this River Walk restaurant and night spot that caters to raucous revelers. Need I say, casual? Varied live music from R&B to rock.

DURTY NELLY'S IRISH PUB

Hilton Palacio del Rio, 200 S. Alamo, at Market • Central
222-1400

Calling itself an Irish pub, Durty Nelly's is the Hilton Palacio del Rio's contribution to nightlife on the river, a place to go for entertainment of the sing-along-and-be-merry variety. The piano player knows them all, and when you're in a loud kind of mood, pick this place to unwind. Even if you don't know the words, all is not lost—you'll find sheets of the most popular requests on most tables.

THE ESQUIRE

155 E. Commerce at St. Mary's • Central • 222-2521

The Esquire has been around far longer than most San Antonians. It is just what it appears to be, a straight, out-and-out no-frills downtown bar that attracts both blue and white collars in a time-worn setting. Mariachis on weekends.

HARD ROCK CAFE

111 W. Crockett, on River Walk • Central • 224-7625

Rock with burger and fries midst guitar displays and a hanging-from-the-ceiling, real Texas-size Caddy auto for decor.

LABORATORY BREWING CO.

7310 Jones Maltsberger • Northeast • 824-1997

The Lab is near the Quarry Market in yuppie land and has both a restaurant and bar (with an outside patio). A mixture of live music from R&B and soul to swing bands appeal to upwardly mobile and already arrived.

LA MARGARITA

(To imbibe some namesake margaritas at Market Square, see Mexican section in Restaurants chapter.)

THE LANDING

Hyatt Regency, 123 Losoya at Crockett • Central • 223-7266

Jim Cullum's Jazz Band and his Landing in the Hyatt Regency are the River Walk's best-known and most respected musical establishments. Traditional, irresistably rhythmic jazz fills the place almost every night. The large glass front of the Landing gives a full view of the crowded tables, the little balcony, and the band on the stage. The crowded tables and enthusiasm of the musicians may make conversation difficult, but one does not come to Jim Cullum's for conversation. A night on the town that includes the River Walk should include a stop here. The National Public Radio program *River Walk, Live From the Landing* is taped here, with live audiences.

MENGER BAR

Menger Hotel, 204 Alamo Plaza at Crockett • Central 223-4361

The Menger Bar is pure old San Antonio. According to local legend, Teddy Roosevelt recruited a number of his Rough Riders here in 1898 when he was encamped at Fort Sam Houston, although a more believable version has it that they came here to be wet down after training in the San Antonio heat. Another story with some local currency is that Ike brought Mamie here in their courting days. Perhaps one more believable legend is that, to bring some class to San Antonio, the bar was designed as a small replica of the bar in the House of Lords in London. Whatever the truth, the now-much-less-raucous Menger Bar, just a few moments' walk from the Alamo, offers a place to soak up a little of the spirit of old San Antonio.

PLANET HOLLYWOOD

245 E. Commerce on River Walk • Central • 212-7827

OK, so Planets are now everywhere in moviedom. But if you love movie stuff, go for the memorabilia, like Rocky's boxing shorts and *Planet of the Apes* monkey suits at this chain. Burgers and pizza. And of course, they'll try and sell you some souvenirs.

ST. MARY'S STRIP

An area containing dining and night spots, roughly in the 2400–3000 blocks of North St. Mary's, near the Highway 281 intersection • Near North

The St. Mary's Street Strip, as it has become known, is a strip of run-down old buildings that have been eclectically restored and turned into combination eating/entertainment establishments. Most are casual, noisy, and comfortably crowded on weekends with collegians and yuppies. The places change periodically, but the current ones include Tycoon Flats (an outdoor burger place with live music) and the White

Rabbit. Take your pick. If you don't like what's playing at one place, walk to the next. Parking is a real problem on busy nights.

STONE WERKS CAFE AND BAR
7300 Jones Maltsberger • Northeast • 828-3508

Stone Werks has become a popular place to meet and greet, whether it's businessfolk at lunch or happy hour time. Later, a younger crowd takes over. Simple fare, including burgers and pizza. Located in the Quarry area, which was a cement plant and has been redeveloped into an upscale shopping and eating complex; this spot was the old office. Casual. Patio.

WHITE RABBIT
2410 N. St. Mary's • Near North • 979-5950

This rock haven in the St. Mary's Strip area just north of downtown charges admission. Take St. Mary's exit off Hwy 281 and go west about one mile, and look for a gray and white building. Tickets available at local ticketmasters.

THREE NEARBY OUT-OF-TOWNERS

Several of the more amiable and atmospheric local entertainment venues sit just outside of town, within a short driving distance. While to some, these may represent an expedition rather than a casual trip, those who like their music live and often with a country accent have made these places into outstanding favorites. If you host a visitor from Maine (or anywhere else) to whom Texas authenticity matters more than bright lights, go to one of these clubs.

CIBOLO CREEK COUNTRY CLUB
8640 East Evans Road, behind the old Retama Polo Center
From the intersection of Nacogdoches and Loop 1604, go 1.75 miles north, then turn right on Evans, and follow to the CCC • **Far Northeast** • **651-6652**

Everything from porch-sitting to beer-sipping and music-listening goes on at this wonderful country establishment in a 100-year-old building. Light food. Mostly beer makes up the drinks. The inside is decorated with an eclectic melange of everything from ranch equipment to country club reminders. Cibolo Creek plays a variety of music besides country, but some evenings this place is just a friendly country beer hall out in the outskirts of the city, near the site of the first electric cotton gin in the state.

FLOORE COUNTRY STORE

14464 Bandera Road, Highway 16, in Helotes, a few miles northwest of San Antonio • 695-8827

You can't get much more country than this. The likes of Willie Nelson have played here. Dance away, either indoors or outdoors, to live country music on weekends at this country store turned dance hall.

HANGING TREE SALOON

18425 Second Street, in Bracken • *Go two miles north of 1604 on Nacogdoches, and turn right on Second Street in Bracken* • **651-5812**

A smalltown bar with mostly live music on weekends, the Hanging Tree would fit right into almost any western picture show you ever saw. You may notice an air of casual nonchalance about the western ambience—it's not something Hanging Tree seems to have striven to create. It's just there. Located only a mile or so from the Cibolo Creek Country Club—one expedition can easily take you to both.

ACCOMMODATIONS

First of all, remember that hotels change their names as often as banks and as quickly as our book ink dries. The names may change but not the other essential data. Keep that in mind. This book can't list all hotels/motels, but tries to give a range.

Most of San Antonio's better hotels are concentrated downtown and along the north side of Loop 410 from the airport, west to the intersection of I-10. The designation *W+* indicates that some of the rooms have special facilities for the physically challenged. Prices occasionally change, so instead of giving exact prices, the following codes will indicate general rate categories (for a double):

$: Under $45
$$: $46–$60
$$$: $61–$80
$$$$: $81–$100
$$$$$: Over $100

These are regular-rate price ranges. Be sure to ask about special rates or weekend rates that may save bucks at the big hotels. Note that there is also a hotel occupancy tax, together with sales tax. The room rates vary within hotels, sometimes for seemingly similar rooms, so call several hotels if price shopping.

Numerous hotels and motels in San Antonio belong to national chains. This guide doesn't list all of these because visitors will likely be familiar with them already.

While reservations are a good idea at any time, they become absolutely essential during Fiesta in April. Some of the hotels start to fill up almost a year before Fiesta, so make reservations as early as possible for that week. Since the downtown hotels are more convenient than outlying hotels for most of the Fiesta events, they fill up sooner than those located elsewhere around town.

WHERE TO GET A MORE COMPLETE LIST
OF SA ACCOMMODATIONS

Obviously this book can't list every hotel/motel, and I wouldn't want to anyway. But if you want a more complete list of what's available, along with prices, write or ask the San Antonio Convention and Visitors Bureau (see **For Your Information**) for its annual lodging guide.

RESORT HOTELS

HYATT REGENCY HILL COUNTRY RESORT

9800 Hyatt Resort Drive • Far Northwest • 647-1234 or (800) 233-1234 • W • $$$$$

This posh resort, in spite of its formidable 200-acre, 500-room size, has managed to capture some of the Hill Country's informal charm. In

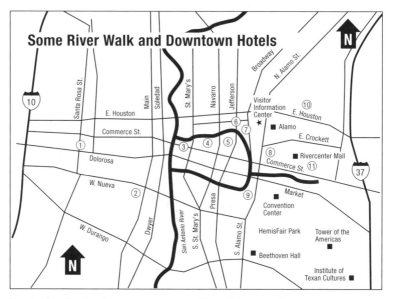

Camberley Gunter, 1
Courtyard by Marriott, 2
St. Anthony, 3
Fairmount, 4
Hilton Palacio del Rio, 5
Holiday Inn Crockett, 6
Holiday Inn River Walk, 7

Hyatt Regency, 8
La Mansion del Rio, 9
Marriott River Walk, 10
Marriott Rivercenter, 11
Menger, 12
Plaza San Antonio by Marriott, 13
Ramada Emily Morgan, 14

large part a golf resort with a lavish course, it also provides all conceivable amenities for meetings and nongolfing guests. The Hyatt offers programs and camping activities for children of various ages, tennis courts, a swimming area complete with a small water park, and a restaurant, Antlers, where classy cooking meets casual patrons. Convenient to Sea World. Its limestone construction and modest four-story height suggest the architecture the Hill Country.

WESTIN LA CANTERA RESORT

16641 La Cantera Pkwy • Far Northwest • 558-6500 • W+ $$$$$

Eighteen-hole golf course, landscaped pools, spa, etc., decorate this newer resort hotel next to Fiesta Texas.

DOWNTOWN

ADAM'S MARK

111 E. Pecan, at Soledad • Central • 354-2800 • W+ • $$$$$

Bank building turned sleek hotel, Adam's Mark is recent on the local hotel scene, with a different slant. It emphasizes entertainment and food more than most. Lobby area acts as a busy focal point for entertainment activity. On the river, but not the busier part of the River Walk.

GUNTER HOTEL

205 E. Houston, at St. Mary's • Central • 227-3241 • W+ • $$$$$

The Gunter has reestablished itself as a major downtown hotel, much as it was a generation ago, with renovations that turned things around. The rooms are larger than they were and are furnished invitingly in an essentially modern idiom, yet the hotel maintains its cachet of age. It combines the overall style of a hotel built when comfort was the main aim of builders with the conveniences of a modern refitting.

COURTYARD BY MARRIOTT

600 S. Santa Rosa • Central • 229-9449 • W+ • $$$–$$$$

For an alternative to the high-rise hotels and easier get-in-and-out parking (free too), here's another option from Marriott. Three stories and only several blocks from Market Square, where you can shop and eat in the Mexican experience. Restaurant and pool.

ST. ANTHONY

300 E. Travis, at Navarro • Central • 227-4392 • W+ • $$$$$

Fortunately, the St. Anthony has retained its name, unlike some hotels that are taken over by new management. For decades, the name has meant quality and elegance to old-line San Antonio. Here's where millionaires and celebrities alike stayed long before the new generation of hotels came on the scene to snatch away some business. A renovation restored the 1909 hotel to much of its previous persona. Oriental rugs, antiques, and chandeliers give it a quiet sumptuousness. The hotel has a fine view of landscaped Travis Park, which is just across the street and suitable for a stroll. Amenities include restaurant, bar, and a pool.

FAIRMOUNT HOTEL

401 S. Alamo, at Nueva • Central • 224-8800 • W+ • $$$$$

In a restored Victorian building, the Fairmount is the kind of small inn in which service, rather than size or physical opulence, attracts the high-budget clientele. The warm, upscale rooms are not particularly large (though most do have balconies), but you'll notice an unmistakable aura of Old World caring for the guest. The care shows in such features as 24-hour room service, complimentary shoe shines, and twice-daily maid service. Those who opt for even more luxury can select a suite, where prices can range up to around $500 per night. The hotel has one of the most fashionable restaurants in the downtown area. (See **Restaurants**.)

HILTON PALACIO DEL RIO

200 S. Alamo, at Market • Central • 222-1400 • W+ • $$$$$

This hotel sparked San Antonio's downtown hotel boom in time for HemisFair in 1968, and the speed with which it went up is still something of a legend around San Antonio. It has since been renovated and its commercial air replaced by more casual elegance. The rooms look inviting and comfortable; the views from them are among the best that San Antonio hotels afford. They look down over the center of the downtown area, the River Walk, and even La Villita. The location is also convenient—the Convention Center in HemisFair Park stands just across the street, and good restaurants and clubs are nearby.

HOLIDAY INN CROCKETT HOTEL

320 Bonham at Crockett • Central • 225-6500 • W+
$$$$–$$$$$

With the name of Crockett, you know this has to stand across from the Alamo. This smaller hotel is a hidden surprise many don't know about. It's convenient to everything on Alamo Plaza and the Rivercenter Mall. The 1909 structure has been completely restored, with modern rooms and a cheery atrium in the middle that serves as a courtyard cafe. It's large, yet small enough to give it a friendly feel. Be forewarned that some rooms are in a motel-type addition. Restaurant, bar, and pool.

HOLIDAY INN—RIVER WALK

217 North St. Mary's, at Houston • Central • 224-2500 • W+ $$$$$

This is a high-rise Holiday Inn on the River Walk (near Houston Street, away from the busier section of the River Walk). There's a swimming pool on the seventh floor, workout room, and restaurant on the river side. This makes a good choice for those who want to stay on the river but can stand to be a few minutes' walk from the center of the action.

HYATT REGENCY

123 Losoya, at Crockett • Central • 222-1234 • W+ • $$$$$

The Hyatt is one of the busiest of the downtown hotels. This modern hotel is much more than a place to stay, eat, or meet. It is also a gathering place on the river of downtown San Antonio. People neither staying at nor visiting the hotel pass through and mingle with guests and those attending parties as well as with those visiting the businesses in the hotel. Some of the businesses account for much of the traffic—Jim Cullum's Landing, for example, steadily draws in passersby from the River Walk (see **Bars and Clubs**). If all this makes the Hyatt sound a little less than relaxing, that certainly can be true. Those looking for a quiet getaway should look elsewhere. The rooms are efficient and comfortable, and many of them have a view into the central atrium that faces the river. Conventions, meetings, and special events are held frequently at the Hyatt.

LA MANSION DEL RIO

112 College, at Navarro • Central • 225-2581 • W+ • $$$$$

La Mansion del Rio is located on the River Walk, and its style of accommodation abides in harmony with San Antonio's more relaxed way of living. La Mansion del Rio emphasizes the Hispanic heritage of the city. It represents a little more casual and less busy alternative to some of the other hotels in the area. Rooms are comfortable. Most people think well of La Mansion's dining room, Las Canarias (named in honor of the city's first civilian settlers). On Sunday mornings the dining room sets up a fine brunch.

MARRIOTT RIVERCENTER

101 Bowie, at Commerce • Central • 223-1000 • W+ • $$$$$

It's hard to miss this high rise hotel, all thirty-eight stories of it standing out on the skyline. The twin towers of this dramatic structure definitely make a statement that this hotel takes on a big chunk of convention business, with its 1,000 guest rooms and numerous conference rooms. Slick and smart, it fits in with the upscale Rivercenter Mall next door. Just across the street is its older sister hotel, the Marriott River Walk. Atrium lobby, piano bar, executive health club, and whirlpool all add to the attractions.

MARRIOTT RIVER WALK

711 E. River Walk, between S. Alamo and Bowie • Central 224-4555 • W+ • $$$$$

The Marriott River Walk is a mostly businesslike, convention-oriented hotel. Located directly across from the Convention Center, this Marriott is as conveniently situated for conventions as any of the hotels and is also a few minutes' stroll from the center of the River Walk. A full range of amenities, from sauna to restaurant.

MENGER HOTEL

204 Alamo Plaza, at Crockett • Central • 223-4361 • W+ $$$$–$$$$$

The Menger's history goes back to 1859, when it became the first major hotel in San Antonio. Its imposing front offers a unique view of Alamo Plaza. The older rooms are far from luxurious, but those overlooking the courtyard and tropical garden have a certain charm. There are newer rooms in the newer section. Because of its central location, the Menger is one of San Antonio's more popular hotels. The grandeur of the old Menger is apparent inside the south lobby, called the rotunda. There, decorative arts of the nineteenth century have been preserved in full glory, giving ample evidence of why the hotel was known as one of the most sumptuous between New Orleans and the West Coast. The peaceful atmosphere of the lobby makes it a fine place simply to sit and talk or read. Another feature of the hotel is its famous old bar (see **Bars and Clubs**).

PLAZA SAN ANTONIO HOTEL BY MARRIOTT

555 S. Alamo, at Arceniega • Central • 229-1000 • W+ • $$$$$

Although not the biggest, the most convenient, the oldest, or the most traditional hotel in San Antonio, somehow the Plaza has quietly drawn to itself the cachet of desirability. Its reputation rests on a remarkably good restaurant, the Anaqua Room (see **Restaurants**), excellent service, and finally, an atmosphere of tranquility that belies a location just a couple of blocks south of the heart of downtown. All of this charm is achieved without a hint of stuffiness. True, one must expect to pay for such pampering and for facilities such as tennis courts and a pool. Modern rooms, warmly comfortable rather than impersonal, are generous in size although not palatial.

RAMADA EMILY MORGAN

705 E. Houston, at Avenue E • Central • 225-8486 • W • $$$$

The Emily Morgan, only shouting distance from the Alamo, is both convenient to the Rivercenter shopping complex and a few minutes' amble from the River Walk. A hotel in an older, restored building that's more relaxed and congenial than the more commercial River Walk hotels a few blocks away, the Emily Morgan is popular for smaller meetings and conferences. The lobby and rooms are modern and smartly furnished, in contrast to the architecturally ornate building. A swimming pool and health club are the main amenities. Slightly more reasonably priced than many of the other downtown hotels, the Emily Morgan is nevertheless comfortable.

NORTH SIDE

AIRPORT HILTON

611 NW Loop 410, at San Pedro • North • 340-6060 • W $$$$$

The Hilton gussied up its lobby and caters to businessfolk. The rooms, comfortable but conventional, are smaller than those at the Hilton's larger neighbors, but they have better views if you can get one on an upper floor. Conventions and meetings, as is usual at urban hotels, account for much of the business; the airport is only a five-minute drive from the hotel.

BEST WESTERN OAK HILLS MOTOR INN

7401 Wurzbach, at Babcock • Northwest • 614-9900 • W+ • $$

This motel caters to those visiting the South Texas Medical Center as patients, as patients' friends or family members, as doctors, or as sales representatives for medical suppliers. Certainly nothing is any more convenient to the sprawling center, although some places may be a little more spectacular. Bar, restaurant, and several small shopping centers lie within easy driving distance.

CLUB HOTEL BY DOUBLETREE

1111 NE Loop 410, at Broadway • Northeast • 828-9031 W+ • $$$

Here on the fringe of the airport lies a ten-story hotel of a sensible commercial type. While more economical, this place is neither Spartan nor excessively simple and has a few more amenities than some motels. Not only is it close to the airport, it has an airport transport service (as do most hotels in this section). Restaurant and bar.

DOUBLETREE

37 NE Loop 410, at McCullough • North • 366-2424
W+ • $$$$$

Convenience to the airport and north side combines with more appeal than people usually associate with hotels near airports here in this major Loop 410 hotel. You'll notice Hispanic influence in the architecture, which features several floors of rooms opening onto a large courtyard dominated by a pool and sunbathing area. Rooms are generous in size, nearly suites. Also look for the inviting hotel bar, much less frenetic than most of its ilk. This hotel is popular for meetings and small conventions yet also draws plenty of customers who want guaranteed comfort.

EMBASSY SUITES

7750 Briaridge, near Callaghan and I-10 (Northwest, 340-5421)
10110 US 281 North, near Isom Road (Northeast, 525-9999)
W+ • $$$$$

All Embassy Suites follow the same general plan: an enclosed central court or atrium onto which the rooms open. The San Antonio examples use that interior open space to the best advantage. The lofty central court at the Briaridge location—colorful, graceful, and exuberantly decorative—sets the scene for a daily breakfast buffet and an evening cocktail hour, both free to guests. The rooms are all suites. The sitting room of a typical suite includes a minute kitchenette, complete with small refrigerator, thus making the rooms fine for entertaining. While the Embassy Suites does not fall in the low-price class, its breakfasts and evening bar, together with its amenities (such as an indoor pool), make it stand out as good value.

HOLIDAY INN SELECT

77 NE Loop 410, near McCullough • North • 349-9900
W+ • $$$$

This Holiday Inn stands a cut above most Holiday Inns in its design and atmosphere. The lobby and restaurant, a set of spaces leading naturally into each other, are architecturally interesting and visually pleasing. The rooms live up to Holiday Inn standards—comfortably furnished but fairly characterless.

MOTEL 6

9400 Wurzbach • Northwest • 593-0013 • $–$$

This Motel 6 is a cut above most and in a desirable location near I-10 also. Plus the more economical rate, which you can't find elsewhere in the same area. Pool.

OMNI

9821 Colonnade (exit I-10 at Wurzbach) • North • 691-8888
W+ • $$$$$

Most of San Antonio's major northside hotels cling to the access roads of Loop 410, but not the Omni, the north side's most noticeable hotel. Jutting above its surrounding commercial establishments, the Omni is a popular center for conventions, training programs, and meetings, as well as for visitors to San Antonio. While many visitors might prefer to stay downtown by the river, others may welcome the proximity to the Medical Center and commercial areas of I-10. In any case, the elegant and modern hotel has a well-equipped athletic club, a superior coffee shop, and comfortable rooms with some of the best views of the city. On the top floor is a meeting room with windows looking down over all of San Antonio's north side, a view leading to the skyline of downtown San Antonio.

PEAR TREE INN BY DRURY

143 NE Loop 410 • North • 366-9300 • W+ • $$

The Drury Inn chain has rooms that are modest in size, simply furnished, and spotlessly clean. A pool is the only visible concession to the demands of those who need more than the basics, unless one counts the continental breakfast included in the price of a room. Small meeting rooms are available as is a bus to the nearby airport. The Drury aims at the traveler on a budget who wants something more than the bare minimum of a bed in a box.

SEVEN OAKS RESORT AND CONFERENCE CENTER

1400 Austin Hwy., near Harry Wurzbach • Northeast
824-5371 • W • $$

This older hotel straddles the fence between hotel and motel. Fairly basic. Many of the rooms loom out over a nine-hole golf course, but others look out over an uninspiring section of one of San Antonio's less appealing commercial streets. Seven Oaks is particularly convenient to parts of Fort Sam Houston.

OTHER AREAS

LA QUINTA INNS

Various locations about city • (800) 687-6667 • $$$–$$$$$

It's hard to miss La Quinta—you'll see one in practically every area of town. The one near Lackland Air Force Base is a likely place to stay in that area. There is one near the Convention Center downtown, and the one a few hundred yards from the airport is just right for a layover between flights. The general rule at any of the La Quinta motels is basic rooms and comfortable beds, though they do have pools. For those wanting a room less expensive than the "big hotels," a La Quinta is an option. San Antonio used to be La Quinta's corporate headquarters.

BED-AND-BREAKFAST/HOSTEL

As a big tourist town, naturally San Antonio has its share of numerous bed-and-breakfasts. In fact, so many exist that this book can't begin to list or rate them. Some of the more interesting ones in grand old homes tend to be in, of course, downtown or the King William Historic District, just south of downtown. So, if you want to be centrally located near the downtown sites, inquire about what's available down there. Also inquire about the current owners and the upkeep. Sometimes, owners have great expectations but then may not have the funds to continue good upkeep.

You can also find B&Bs in other, not necessarily old and historical areas of the city. And San Antonio does have a hostel. Listed below is a B&B service for the city that can tell you what's available.

And be forewarned that no longer do B&Bs necessarily keep prices economical. Particularly in the big city, rates may rival the big hotels.

BED AND BREAKFAST HOSTS OF SAN ANTONIO

B&B referral service • 824-8036

Call for access to many of the local B&Bs in and around San Antonio. While not all of the local establishments are on this service's lists, many are. Bed and Breakfast Hosts of San Antonio can make reservations and tell you about the various B&B guest rooms in homes about the city.

SAN ANTONIO INTERNATIONAL HOSTEL

621 Pierce • Northeast • 223-9426 • $–$$$ • W

This fine, old early 1900s neoclassical mansion (the Bullis House) has been turned into a B&B and hostel in a workingclass neighborhood next to Fort Sam Houston. Homey, high ceilings, very clean, and big rooms. The inexpensive hostel dormitory is in an adjacent building.

MARKETS AND MERCHANTS

SHOPPING

Shopping in San Antonio is much like the city—textured and diverse. While San Antonio has its share of posh stores in assorted mammoth shopping malls and tourist-minded hotel environs, an entire spectrum of merchants exists, from homey Mom-and-Pop shops that speak only Spanish to elegant specialty stores that speak only money. This section touches lightly on some of the larger malls and then points out some of the shops popular with natives and old-timers. And some even they may have missed. It also mentions where to find offbeat items and offbeat places and where to save some dinero.

This is not intended to be an all-encompassing list of shopping places in San Antonio. Obviously, there's not enough room in a chapter, or even a whole book, for that. A lot of familiar stores are not included precisely because they *are* familiar or carry routine merchandise. In addition to commenting on malls and department stores for the newcomers, this book tries to point out lesser-known specialty fare, unusual items, or bargains.

LARGER SHOPPING MALLS

CENTRAL PARK MALL
Loop 410 at San Pedro • North • W

San Pedro and Loop 410 is mall city, with North Star Mall on the east and Central Park Mall on the west. Like most malls, Central Park has a starkly functional design, with anchor stores Sears and Dillard's. One of the few malls owned by a local developer, it has the usual assortment of smaller stores and an informal eating area offering fast foods.

CROSSROADS
Loop 410 at Fredericksburg Road • Northwest • W

This rejuvenated older mall (in another life, its name was Wonderland Mall) is now Crossroads. It includes Palm Pavilion food court and a waterfall. Tenants include Montgomery Ward and an upscale discount store, Stein Mart. Also in Crossroads is San Antonio's multiscreen theater most likely to show foreign films, art films, and films whose success has been greater with critics than with the public.

INGRAM PARK MALL
Loop 410 at Ingram • Northwest • W

Besides an abundance of teenagers, shoe stores, and jewelry shops, Ingram Park has large department stores, such as Dillard's, Foley's, J.C. Penney, and Sears.

NORTH STAR MALL
Loop 410 at San Pedro • North • W

As new mini-mall after mini-mall has opened in San Antonio, one established mall has fought back with vigor. North Star Mall has expanded to include a wide range of fancier stores. Apparently, when many of the country's upscale retailers had a good look around, they decided that San Antonio's buying power was coming of age and moved into North Star Mall's enlarged spaces. The result has been a resoundingly successful retail operation that sometimes leads to parking garage and traffic gridlock. In any case, the variety of stores, anchored by Macy's, Saks Fifth Avenue, Dillard's, and Foley's, is the greatest in town. When looking for items that used to be available only in Dallas, Houston, or maybe San Francisco or Boston, start your search here.

QUARRY MARKET
Basse at US Hwy 281 • Northeast • W

Just look for the Old Alamo Cement Co. smokestack looming skyward at the side of Hwy 281. Not your usual mall experience, the Quarry Market houses various free-standing buildings with the parking lot in the middle. Whole Foods Market, Whole Earth Provision, Office Max, and Old Navy are just some of the mostly upscale retail entities. Sprinkle in assorted restaurants such as Canyon Cafe, Joe's Crab Shack, and EZ's, and you've got an intesting mix on this 50-acre site that was in its past life, you guessed it, a quarry.

RIVERCENTER

Commerce at Bowie • Central • W

Whereas most urban downtowns are struggling, San Antonio has a glitzy regional shopping center in its inner city. But more than that, it's also a dining and entertainment complex, with the huge IMAX Theatre, featuring a movie about the Alamo. Rivercenter has something going for it that other malls don't—the San Antonio River. The river has been extended, and an arm of it flows into the horseshoe-shaped, three-level Rivercenter, thereby giving it a glassed-in view. This unusual ten-acre complex includes more than 120 specialty shops and restaurants, plus a Marriott Hotel, Foley's, and Dillard's (which bought out the old Joske's store adjoining the site). More stores here than at other malls seem to aim at souvenir shoppers, impulse buyers, and visitors to the city.

ROLLING OAKS MALL

Loop 1604 at Nacogdoches • Northeast • W

You'll find this newer mall out in the hinterlands on the fringe of town. It has Dillard's, Foley's, and Sears in addition to the range of smaller stores that populate any mall.

WINDSOR PARK MALL

I-35 at Walzem • Northeast • W

Windsor Park Mall is appealing inside, with its warm colors, plants, and fountain displays. Many of its shops target the younger set. Anchor stores are Dillard's, Montgomery Ward, and J.C. Penney.

DEPARTMENT STORES

Aside from Sears, J.C. Penney, and assorted chain discount stores usually implanted in a city, here are some of the more frequented ones, both nationally known and homegrown.

DILLARD'S

North Star Mall, Loop 410 at San Pedro, and other locations
North • 341-6666 • W

This upscale department store has locations downtown and at North Star, Ingram Park, North Star, Rivercenter, and Windsor Park malls. It features the usual department store fare, plus portrait galleries and a decorator service. Carries better name brands.

FOLEY'S

North Star Mall, Loop 410 at San Pedro, and other locations
North • 340-4308 • W

A department store that has migrated from Houston, Foley's has few of its own brands and instead selects from the higher end of well-known brands, with merchandise running the gamut from clothing to cameras and home computers. Also at Ingram Park, Rivercenter, and Rolling Oaks malls.

MACY'S

North Star Mall, Loop 410 at San Pedro • North • 979-0333 • W

Another northern carpetbagger has come to town in the form of Macy's, which supplanted Marshall Field's in North Star Mall. This well-known chain currently only offers clothing at this store.

SAKS FIFTH AVENUE

North Star Mall, Loop 410 at San Pedro • North • 341-4111 • W

I'm glad they didn't tear down my favorite boots sculpture when they let Saks squeeze in at North Star. San Antonians might do without New York chichi but never their boots roots. Look for designer accessories and clothes, including sportswear, in this exclusive store.

SCRIVENER'S

8502 Broadway, at Loop 410 • Northeast • 824-2353

While not exactly a full-line department store, Scrivener's carries an extraordinary variety of items, from hardware to fabrics and patterns to unique Christmas decorations. First-time visitors to Scrivener's sometimes wonder how they could have overlooked it for so long. One reason is that this extraordinary department store does little advertising. Perhaps it does not have to—it has an established clientele and a range of merchandise that makes finding just what you need easier here than anywhere else. Scrivener's started out as a lumber store; now you can buy gifts, silver, clothes, and even eat lunch at its small restaurant. Scrivener's has a superb china and crystal department and, just a few steps away, a hardware and garden tools department. Throughout the store is evidence of good taste and care in selecting the merchandise.

ULTIMATE OUTLET

639-B Lanark at Loop 410 • Northeast • 655-9696

The loading dock entrance gives you the first clue this isn't exactly Macy's. It's not on the railroad lines for nothing, it's freight claims sales. Not exactly a department store, but Ultimate Outlet does serve up some possible savings in big items like refrigerators, mattresses, and furniture. You never know what's going to turn up. But be sure to compare prices. (I liked it better when they used to carry all sorts of things, from canned goods to office supplies, it was more fun to dig around.)

ANTIQUES, DECOR, AND GIFTS

ACCENTS
199 W. Sunset • Northeast • 826-4500 • W

True to its name, Accents offers a mixture of interior decor items. Gifts, furniture, antiques, china, and accessories.

ANTIQUES DOWNTOWN MALL
515 E. Houston, at Alamo Street • Central • 224-8845

As the name says, this antique mall is downtown, right around the corner from the Alamo. Presumably, it doesn't have any priceless Alamo antiques to sell, but it does have a variety of collectibles, silver, and furniture, all sold under one roof by a group of dealers.

BASIL N. SCALJON ORIENTAL RUGS INC.
2420 N. Main, at Woodlawn • Near North • 734-3711

Basil Scaljon's store is the closest thing to a gallery of oriental rugs in San Antonio. Scaljon's is renowned for its knowledge of old oriental rugs. The vast selection has all sizes available. Prices vary, and though oriental rugs are generally pricey, some are distinctly reasonable. Before visiting the mass merchandisers of new oriental rugs, visit here, not only to see gems of the past but perhaps also to be surprised by the affordability of some of them.

CENTER FOR ANTIQUES
8505 Broadway, at Loop 410 • Northeast • 804-6300

A bunch of dealers in an old discount chain store building. Antiques, collectibles, books, silver, etc.

GARDEN RIDGE
17975 I-35 North • Northeast • 599-5700 • W

Talk about BIG—you can easily lose a family member while shopping in these gigantic warehouselike buildings, covering seven acres a few miles northeast of town. Rows and rows of discount merchandise include such categories as glassware, candles, pottery, brass, baskets, and dried flowers. Imports make up much of the merchandise.

HANLEY WOOD
5611 Broadway, at Austin Highway • Northeast • 822-3311 • W

Hanley Wood's niche is firmly in the upper end of the gift shop range. A lot of what goes out the door turns up as wedding presents, whether it be china, silver, or crystal. The selection of merchandise suggests that the shop's buyers have unusually good taste.

JANAL WHOLESALE COMPANY

1942 North St. Mary's • Near North • 225-3367

Try looking for seasonal decorations here, in the way of silk flowers, ribbons, baskets, and arrangements.

TUESDAY MORNING

6808 Huebner Rd., and several other locations • Northwest 680-6641

Tuesday's buys closeouts and other good deals and then passes them onto you. Carries a big variety, from decorative gift items and brass to towels and rugs. Several more locations around town than the one listed above. Open only certain periods of the year, so call ahead.

BOOKSTORES

ANTIQUARIAN BOOK MART

3127 Broadway, at Eleanor • Northeast • 828-4885
Annex, 3132 Avenue B, at Ira • Northeast • 828-7433

In a sense, these two bookstores form one business managed by father and son, yet they are two distinct shops. The address on Broadway is a used bookstore, with paperbacks, fiction, and many shelves of academic and semiacademic works in addition to the general trade books. The Annex, located in back of the main building, offers a treasure trove of rare and semirare books. The diverse subject matter ranges from modern fiction and travel to cooking and drama. Military history (as befits a rare bookstore owned by a retired colonel) is one of the strong areas; others include Texana and modern history. The Annex, the much more interesting shop of the two for collectors, is open only a few hours a day, so call before visiting.

BARNES AND NOBLE BOOKSELLERS

321 NW Loop 410, at San Pedro • North • 342-0008
12635 W. I-10 • Northwest • 561-0205
6065 NW Loop 410 • Northwest • 522-1340

Forget the bus station. If you're homeless, you might find a home here and never have to leave. B&N, a very large national chain, has found its niche in the retail business by making customers feel comfortable and giving them a huge selection of thousands of new books. Chairs are scattered about the stores so you can read and browse to your book's content. Everyday discounts and a large magazine and newspaper section. Even a cafe with coffee and snacks.

BOOKETERIA

5530 Evers Road, near Glen Ridge • Northwest • 680-8555

It would be a waste of time to come here looking for rare first editions, but in the book trade one can never be sure just where any given item will turn up. Many novels, mostly forgotten and with good reason, line the shelves here, as do numerous nonfiction books. Booketeria has no major specialty, just shelves and shelves of moderately well-sorted and organized miscellany, with lots of paperbacks.

BOOKSMITHS OF SAN ANTONIO

209 Alamo Plaza, at Crockett • Central • 271-9177

So you want a book about Davy and the rest of the defenders of the Alamo? Just cross the street or Alamo Plaza and browse Booksmiths, which, while carrying all general topics, leans heavily toward Texana and regional books. It also has children's books and a place for readings and book signings. Independent, retails new books.

BOOKSTOP

6496 N. New Braunfels, at Brees • Northeast • 828-9046

Volume and discount are the two key words to these huge retail bookstores. One passes up selectivity and personal service in return for wide variety and good discounts on all books. To get the best discounts, you must join, pay a fee, and then show a card with every purchase. Since the average reader will quickly earn his membership fee back, it may prove worthwhile. All areas except textbooks seem well represented, and the selection even covers some technical areas, such as personal computers. A computerized inquiry system lets the clerks find out quickly whether they have (or can get) a book you want.

BOOK WORM BOOKSTORE

4707 Blanco, at Hillwood • Northwest • 342-4258

The Book Worm falls in the great divide between used and rare bookstores. Most of the stock is used books, well organized and sorted. An extensive collection, divided into several rooms, is displayed advantageously for browsing. You'll find different categories in different rooms, and although some of the categories are a little idiosyncratic, there are some treasures and unexpected moderate rarities waiting to be had. The Book Worm's reputation as a rare bookstore is helped by its willingness to search for out-of-print titles for a customer.

BORDERS BOOKS AND MUSIC

11745 W. I-10 • Northwest • 561-0022

Another retail chain moves in to entice booklovers to hang out. With a cafe that serves soups and sandwiches, you can eat and greet—and read. Music department and sometimes live music and poetry readings.

BRENTANO'S BOOKSTORE

Rivercenter Mall, Commerce at Bowie • Central • 223-3938

Tourists can whip into Brentano's if they crave some reading material between doing what tourists do—walking and eating a lot. Though it has stores across the nation, Brentano's likes to think of itself as more than just a chain bookstore. This full-service general bookstore has varied regional, fiction, and art sections.

CHEEVER BOOKS

140 Carnahan, at Broadway • Northeast • 824-2665

Cheever Books is one of the city's most pleasant used bookstores to visit. Instead of narrow aisles between crowded bookshelves, Cheever Books is in an old house and has rooms with shelves along the walls and some open space in the middle. Cookbooks and children's books are important areas and so are art, history, and mysteries. The store tries to cover most of the bases, and in doing so creates a remarkably appealing place to browse or do some serious searching.

DONALDSON'S BOOKSTORE

2421 North St. Mary's, at Ashby • Near North • 732-0496

Donaldson's collection of books pertaining to San Antonio and Texas qualifies this shop as a rare bookstore, although much of the rest of the collection falls into the used-book category. Particularly strong sections include sports and cooking, which have a sufficiently fast turnover to make visits every few months worthwhile for the true devotee. Another strong section is fiction, including used, rare, and children's books. Paperbacks also account for much of the business, although few, if any, have attained rare book status. Among local book collectors, Donaldson's has the reputation of being somewhat quixotic about prices—one might see rather rare books at very low prices and undistinguished, uncollectable books at naively optimistic prices. Stacks and stacks of books delight the die-hard browser but make it hard to retrieve certain titles.

HALF PRICE BOOKS

3207 Broadway, at Ira • Northeast • 822-4597
7959 Fredericksburg Rd., at Medical • Northwest • 692-8868
2106 Military Dr. NW, near West Avenue • North • 349-1429
4919 NW Loop 410, at Summit Drive • Northwest • 647-1103

Magazines, paperbacks, and publisher's closeouts fill many of the shelves here, but some of the books, especially those at the Broadway store, are more interesting. General used books, with less fiction than at some used bookstores, might best describe the merchandise, which is priced rather well for the buyer.

L&M BOOKSTORE

1716 N. Main • Near North • 222-1323

L&M is across from San Antonio College and so features all sorts of used and new college textbooks, including nursing and professional ones.

THE TWIG BOOK SHOP

5005 Broadway, at Mary D. • Northeast • 826-6411

The folks who run this independent retail bookstore know their books and give helpful, personal service. The staff keeps up to date with new books and stocks the best of older ones, particularly regional books. They'll also gladly special order. If you're looking to meet some author, local or national, the Twig is the most likely place to sight them, at one of its many author book-signing parties. Next door, the Twig's cheery sister store, The Red Balloon, specializes in children's and youth's books and related merchandise.

CATERING AND PARTY HOUSES

CATERING BY DON STRANGE

1551 Bandera, at Hillcrest • Northwest • 434-2331

Strange does a lot of the large, social parties in town. He can move in with food booths or tents and stir up a large assortment of dishes that rival or surpass those that restaurants, with their immobile kitchens, can turn out.

CATERING BY ROSEMARY/THE R.K. GROUP

1220 E. Commerce, at Cherry • Central • 223-2680

Rosemary Kowalski knows how to throw a big party and smaller parties as well. Her firm does the catering at the San Antonio Convention Center and many a political shindig, including those for some of the state's recent governors. She even once served 10,000 at one meal, but she doesn't sacrifice quality for quantity.

CLOTHING

ADELANTE BOUTIQUE

6414 N. New Braunfels, at Sunset Ridge • Northeast 826-6770 • W

Adelante's merchandise ranges from handwoven women's clothing from Mexico, India, and Guatemala to jewelry and carved wood.

HAROLD'S OF SAN ANTONIO

5424 Broadway, at Austin Highway • Northeast • 828-2378

Harold's features stylish southwestern casual wear for those who can afford to splurge from time to time. Look for really colorful clothes for women, such as Native American pullovers, concho belts, Mexican silver jewelry, and Guatemalan goods.

KALLISON'S WESTERN WEAR

123 S. Flores, at Nueva • Central • 222-1364

This isn't some urban cowboy store, pardner. Real cowboys and farmers go to old-time Kallison's for work duds. Another branch of Kallison's, at 616 Southwest Military Drive, has the largest stock of jeans I have seen—those who are hard to fit may find uncommon sizes there.

KATHLEEN SOMMERS

2417 N. Main at Woodlawn • Near North • 732-8437

Kathleen Sommers not only manufactures and sells women's clothes, she also designs them. The clothes in her store that she has not designed usually come from sources other than the sources most such stores use. Consequently, her clothes have a distinctively stylish appearance—they look simultaneously simple, sophisticated, and natural. In addition to the clothes, look for hair and skin products, women's gifts, including a few books, and jewelry, especially that made by local artists.

LARRY MAZER TAILORING

120 W. Mistletoe, near Main • Near North • 735-6144 • W

Men who cannot (or will not) wear clothes that come in standard sizes off the rack or who occasionally want something that fits better and looks better go to Larry Mazer, San Antonio's tailor extraordinary. With the exception of the neckties, anything that comes from Mazer is custom made of excellent material and with the benefit of skill and years of experience. The shop also performs custom alterations, from minor changes to complete retailorings, of men's and women's clothes. Whenever a job is too much for the corner tailor (a vanishing breed, to be sure), take comfort in knowing that one place in town can take care of it without a hint of difficulty.

LITTLE'S BOOT COMPANY

110 Division, at S. Flores • South • 923-2221

Go in and get your feet fit for some custom-made boots from this longtime bootmaker family. They may cost more than mass-produced boots, but for a perfect fit, nothing can surpass custom boots.

MEXICAN CLOTHING

Numerous shops about town carry Mexican dresses, from casual to wedding styles. They likewise feature the casual guayabera shirts for men. The most obvious place to look is at Market Square, where many vendors sell these goods. So price around while you're looking.

PARIS HATTERS

119 N. Broadway, at Travis • Central • 223-3453 • W

The range of merchandise here, everything from a Sherlock Holmes deerstalker to formal western hats, only tells part of the story. Perhaps more important is the knack the older clerks have for matching up head and hat in just the right way. Many times a clerk here has given a customer a canny glance of appraisal and then selected the style of hat that seems just right for that person. The storefront may make Paris Hatters look a little old—but don't be put off. It's only old with experience.

SHEPLER'S

6201 NW Loop 410, at Ingram • Northwest • 681-8230 • W

Western goods are big business at Shepler's. In a store almost as big as most shopping centers, Shepler's sells everything from boots to western hats and most of the things in between. It's not all for dudes and drugstore cowboys, either—much of the merchandise, such as the saddles and tack, is for working ranches. The emphasis leans toward western clothes, but Shepler's has considered every aspect of ranch life, from kitchen to corral.

TALBOT'S

718 North Star Mall, Loop 410 at San Pedro, lower level
North • 348-8385

Signs are increasing that San Antonio is losing its identity as a low-income annex among high-rolling Texas cities. The evidence includes the number of upscale stores that have come to town. Talbot's, long favored by the country's high priestesses of prep as a place to be outfitted, offers well-tailored and stylish clothes for those who want to find something on the less formal side. Some of the clothes are definitely sportswear; others fall into a kind of ill-defined but attractive limbo that one might describe as sportswear derivatives.

RESALE STORES

BAUBLES AND BEADS

2267 NW Military Hwy., at West Avenue • North • 341-8491

Used clothes never had it so good in this upscale secondhand store. It specializes in designer stuff, including evening wear, sportswear, and furs. The woman who wants to go first class but pay only third class should know this place. Another store is located on Basse Road in Lincoln Heights Shopping Center.

BOYSVILLE THRIFT SHOP

307 Olmos, at Howard • Near North • 826-2195 • W

This small shop occasionally has some unusual collectibles and off-beat items; many donors live in nearby Olmos Park. Stocks used clothing, jewelry, knickknacks, and furniture.

CLOTHES ENCOUNTERS FOR THE SECOND TIME

1856 Nacogdoches, at North New Braunfels • Northeast
822-2902

This pleasant, upscale store in Richmond Oaks Shopping Center has attractive resale clothing and accessories for women.

GOODWILL BARGAIN STORE

3401 Fredericksburg, and several other locations • Northwest
736-1373

This warehouse-type building is one of the largest of the Goodwills about town. Assorted clothing, dishes, appliances, furniture, and toys.

GREEN DOOR

1030 Nacogdoches, at Broadway • Northeast • 826-7111 • W

This is one of my favorite secondhand clothing shops. Good selection of brand-name men's and women's clothing and other quality merchandise. The volunteers from the Episcopal Church who run this shop are fairly picky in what they accept for consignment. Merchandise includes jewelry and a few knickknacks along with the clothes. The store's hours vary, so call ahead before going.

FORT SAM HOUSTON THRIFT SHOP

Fort Sam Houston, Bldg. 230, Liscum • Northeast • 225-4682

Don't go running out to Fort Sam Houston without calling first to check the store's hours. It's open only a couple of days a week. Second-hand items bought by military personnel all over the world can be found here, plus clothing, furniture, and toys.

JUST FOR KIDS RESALE

1576 Babcock Road, at Callaghan • Northwest • 340-8949

KIDS' JUNCTION RESALE

2267 NW Military Hwy. • North • 340-5532 • W

These two resale shops are lumped together not because of any association they have with each other, but because they have such similar merchandise and mien. Both offer baby accessories, toys, and children's clothes for ages from infancy to about middle school. The merchandise at both stores is in good condition and well-displayed. You can find good prices and a wide variety of clothes in each size.

PAYLESS USED OFFICE FURNITURE
9311 Broadway • Northeast • 826-4495

Because so many businesses don't make it, why not take advantage of their losses and buy used office furniture? Maybe if they'd bought theirs used they would have cut their overhead and not gone down the tubes. Desks, bookcases, chairs, files, and so on.

SALVATION ARMY THRIFT STORE
1324 S. Flores, at S. Alamo Street • Central • 223-6877
2711 West Ave. • Northwest • 342-4731 • W

These are two of the larger stores, but there are stores at other locations in town. The main store (on South Flores) has a large display space for clothing, furniture, appliances, and books. Clothing at both stores is low-priced, but antique furniture may be overpriced and no longer a bargain. The West Avenue store is very clean, with rows and rows of clothes, plus furniture, appliances, and jewelry.

SECOND LOOKS
1804 Nacogdoches, at New Braunfels • Northeast • 826-6121 • W

The idea of a secondhand clothing store for men unfortunately carries with it a hint of the less-than-respectable, of clothes that might not be acceptable on all occasions. Second Looks fights that impression by accepting clothes that are "gently worn." Of course, not all sizes or styles are available at any one time, but when the store has the right size, you can get excellent clothes at spectacular savings. Some of the best labels in men's clothes turn up here, together with the less distinguished ones. Merchandise moves pretty quickly, so those who want to find something in particular should check every week or so.

THRIFT TOWN
12247 Nacogdoches • Northeast • 656-8696

A neat and fairly large thrift shop in a strip shopping center. Large selection of clothing with plenty of dressing rooms. Appliances, books, knickknacks, jewelry.

TOO GOOD TO BE THREW
7115 Blanco, at Loop 410 • North • 340-2422

This large consignment store specializes in "pre-owned" designer clothing. Besides the usual women's items, it also carries men's and kids' wear. Although most of the items are marked with the size, some sizing can be unreliable—it's a good idea to try on what you like, since the marked size is only approximate.

SERVICES

AERIAL PHOTOS-WEISSGARBER
627 Many Oaks, at Wolf Creek • North • 494-7727

Tony Weissgarber will go up, up in his flying machine and take a photograph of whatever your heart desires—whether it's a development, palatial mansion, farm, ranch, oil rig, or corporate headquarters. For his minimum charge, he'll fly anywhere in the San Antonio, Austin, Corpus Christi, or Rio Grande Valley area and take an aerial photo. Weissgarber also has stock aerial shots of the city.

AVSAT
557 Sandau, at Jones-Maltsberger • Northeast • 828-0551

Here's a good anniversary idea or a way to show newcomers the town. Take a sunset flight and watch the city lights come on. It's a romantic way to see San Antonio. A chartered tour takes about one hour and circles over the downtown area and other landmarks. Cost varies with number of persons and type of airplane.

VILLAGE SMITHY
21384 Milsa. *Take I-10 north about twenty miles to Leon Springs*
Northwest • 698-2412

Kurt Pankratz may not shoe horses anymore, but he works out of a realistic blacksmith shop in an old barn in Leon Springs. If you need a branding iron, he'll design one for you. If you want to brand steaks, he'll make a miniature branding iron with your initials on it to show off at cookout time. Pankratz does all kinds of metal working (weather vanes, fireplace equipment), woodworking, and antique furniture repair. He also works with interior designers on custom items. And if you happen to have an old buggy in the garage, the Village Smithy can repair that, too.

SPECIALTIES AND MISCELLANEOUS

A BRIGHTER CHILD
7115 Blanco, at Loop 410 • North • 366-2286

Toys and educational supplies are mixed together here, with one category shading into the other. Puzzles, blocks, trains, and kites—the toys are crowded and numerous, but so are the cutouts, science kits, display boards, and books more typical of schools than playrooms.

ACADEMY SPORT COMPANY

2727 NE Loop 410, at Perrin Beitel • Northeast
590-0500 • W

The concept of shopping in vast warehouse stores has spread to sporting goods stores. Academy has an enormous sales floor on which you can find equipment and clothes for just about every sport. Fishing, running, biking, baseball, football, pumping iron, and camping are just the more obvious sports covered. A big footware section, with both boots and shoes, is also included. Prices are lower here than at most sporting goods stores, but you'll also find fewer helpful clerks here.

AMOLS SPECIALTY COMPANY

710 S. Flores, at Arsenal • Central • 227-1457 • W

So you're throwing a birthday party for fifty of your kid's nearest and dearest friends. Or the school carnival is coming up, and you've got to supply the tickets and trinkets for the fishbowl booth. Go to Amols in search of bargain-priced party favors and theme decorations. Buy by the bag or gross.

ARCHITECTURAL ANTIQUES

403 Dawson St., at Houston • Central • 226-6863

This is where house and building wreckers send the decorative details they strip off the interiors of older houses. Paneling, carved wood, fireplaces, mantel pieces, and the like await their next destination stacked and piled in profusion. It is probably worth a stop for those who are remodeling, because most of these kinds of things are either no longer made or are much more expensive new than they are here. While lots of the items seem unlikely to be used again anywhere, some strikingly handsome pieces may surprise you from time to time.

ARTISANS' ALLEY

555 Bitters, at Tomahawk Trail • North • 494-3226

The Alley is a potpourri of about twenty small shops in a rustic decor, all intertwined by a winding indoor hallway. Browse for a gift item and have lunch at the small tearoom. Artists, potters, and weavers are in residence, and merchandise includes plants, metal sculptures, baskets, antiques, collectibles, stained glass, jewelry, candles, and brassware. Someone here will even tell your fortune if you're not afraid of cosmic connections.

B & J BICYCLE SHOP

8800 Broadway, at Ceegee • Northeast • 826-0177

San Antonio's climate and terrain make the city ideal for bicycling in all but the hottest of summer months. A dozen or more good bicycle shops dot the city, but this one has become especially popular with the city's more serious cyclists. In addition to a range of bicycles, from knockaround-town utility cycles to semicustom touring cycles with the latest and lightest alloy components, B & J carries a line of accessories and replacement parts that spans a range of quality, lightness, and price. B & J can also turn out a set of racing wheels to order. The customer, perhaps with the advice of the wheel builder, specifies the hub, the rim, the spokes, and the lacing desired and—presto! A day or so later, a set of custom wheels will be ready, at a price suited to their quality. The quality that B & J builds into its wheels indicates how seriously it takes the bicycle business.

FERGUSON'S MAP

610 W. Sunset • North • 829-7629

Getting lost on San Antonio's meandering streets? Ferguson Map Company knows its way around and publishes keyed map books of the city. If you are going to be in town for long, you should probably buy the map book sooner rather than later. Keep it in your car, and you'll never be caught off guard. You can also get maps of all sizes, shapes, and colors. Geological, nautical, residential, or topographical. Ferguson's handles fishing and canoeing maps, even plats of the county, such as a map of San Antonio de Bexar in 1852.

FLAG CENTER HOBBY AND GAME SHOP

1326 Austin Hwy. • Northeast • 824-6242 • W

The Flag Center of Texas is fun to browse in. It has state flags, national flags, historical flags, and battle flags. Historical societies get many of their flags here, as do hobbyists and collectors. Also historic games.

HOUSE OF INTERNATIONAL FRAGRANCES

4711 Blanco, at General Krueger Boulevard • North • 341-2283

Just follow your nose to this perfumery and sniff out some savings. The laboratory brews up reproductions of brand-name perfumes, calling them "likeness fragrances." House of International Fragrances markets a list of around fifty fragrances that correspond to familiar name brands, at a much lower cost. Purchase here or by mail order.

JAMES AVERY CRAFTSMAN

7120 Blanco, at Loop 410 • North • 342-3412 • W

James Avery turns out beautifully crafted silver and gold jewelry. Avery's jewelry is Texas-oriented, such as armadillo rings and Brangus tie pins. But he also designs many pieces with religious motifs, particularly lovely crosses. The company's headquarters are in nearby Kerrville. Several other store locations.

LA VILLITA

South Alamo at Nueva • Central • 207-8610

Specialty shops and artisans call this historic area home. At same time you're looking at crafts and artwork, you can relive some history of San Antonio. (See **Points of Interest** and **Historical Places**.)

LAMM ENTERPRISES

6462 New Sulphur Springs Road, two miles east of Loop 410, Exit 37 (Southcross exit) • South • 648-2452

LOS PATIOS

2015 NE Loop 410, at Salado Creek (Starcrest exit) • Northeast 655-6171 • W with assistance

Houston may have its Galleria, but San Antonio has Los Patios. This unique shopping area occupies acres of unspoiled land on Salado Creek. Shop at leisure in various shops and galleries whose Southwest architecture of stucco and wood fits in comfortably with the landscape. Los Patios started out as a plant nursery and gallery but grew into what now includes two restaurants (the Gazebo and Brazier) and assorted classy shops specializing in furniture, crafts, women's clothing, and gifts. Be sure to have lunch at one of the restaurants (availability for dinner has varied over the past few years, but the restaurants are usually available for private parties). And if it's a pretty day, sit on one of their patios or verandas overlooking the rustic scenery. At one time, an old tavern stood out here. Deer still roam, and it's a popular place for weddings, especially at the old-fashioned gazebo. Los Patios is a frequent side trip for convention tour groups.

MARKET SQUARE

W. Commerce at Santa Rosa • Central • 207-8600

For a lively time in shopping, head for Market Square downtown. You'll encounter numerous stores and vendors, particularly in the area of El Mercado, a Mexican market. Haggle over prices of many Mexican goods, both cheap and pricey. (See **Points of Interest**.)

NATURE COMPANY

North Star Mall • North • 341-8171

Now here's a store that knows how to present natural history with a sense of whimsy. Besides natural history books, fossils, and mineral collections, you'll also find inflatable versions of the giant beasts.

QUALITY WOOD PRODUCTS

18487 Bandera Road, 5.7 miles northwest of Loop 1604 Northwest • 695-8400

These two businesses, located in diagonally opposite corners of the county, form a pair for would-be barbecue chefs—aficionados of the long, slow, old-fashioned pit-smoking of meat and poultry. Real smoke barbecue takes hours—about an hour a pound for turkeys and all day for a brisket. The art of barbecue, say the experts, is stewardship of the fire. The four essentials are good technique, good meat, good wood, and a good pit. This book won't help you with technique, but these two businesses will set you up with a pit and wood to turn out real barbecue.

A good pit requires a firebox where one can stoke, refuel, and tend the fire as needed and a smoking chamber where the smoke, on its way to the chimney, passes over the meat to cook and flavor it. The welders and blacksmiths at Lamm Enterprises make a number of different pits, in sizes suitable for backyards and patios, that allow full control of the fire, the smoke path, and the meat. Sturdy, well made, practical, and handsome, their pits are much more versatile (and more expensive) than the usual split and hinged barrels that many use for barbecuing.

Once one has a pit, one must find appropriate wood, and for that I've found no source better than Quality Wood Products on Bandera Road, northwest of Helotes. Mesquite and oak, the favorites of most local bar-becuers, are available there but so are pecan, applewood, wild cherry, and the wood most favored in the Southeast, hickory. Along with the wood, you can also get, at no extra charge, some pretty sage advice; listen up to polish your barbecue technique a bit.

SALAS AND COMPANY
1350 E. Southcross • South • 733-1269

The phrase *architectural millwork*, displayed prominently on Salas and Company's cards, hardly begins to describe the work the company does. Salas and Company custom-builds furniture by either copying an existing piece or creating a new piece to a customer's specifications. These craftsmen can copy antique furniture so well that people often find it hard to tell the original from the reproduction. Whether the work is done in pine, plywood, or hardwood, depending on the needs of the customer, it will likely be well made and solid. Finally, the company makes carved and ornate solid wood doors, the kind that mass production has made almost extinct.

SOUTHERN MUSIC COMPANY
1100 Broadway, at Jones • Near North • 226-8167 • W

Southern Music's slogan ("Everything in Sheet Music") is not wrong by much. Musicians around the Southwest know that if anyone has it, Southern does. Musicians from any but the largest of cities will be over-whelmed by the riches one can find along the corridors and stacks. It definitely helps to know what you want before you go, because the stock is not laid out to make browsing easy. If it's worth playing, South-ern probably has it. In addition to the music, Southern has a large selec-tion of books.

SPORTSMAN'S BAILIWICK

6011 Broadway, at Montclair • Northeast • 824-9649

Are you ready for a wedding dress made of military camouflage fabric? Well, neither am I, though Sportsman's Bailiwick has had one for sale. But that's not all. Sportsman's Bailiwick might be described as a gentleman's sporting good store, with all the trappings that name implies. In addition to camping, hunting, and fishing gear, the store has gifts, outdoor books (both practical and the armchair variety), and prints. The clerks are divided between outdoor types and ones who seem better equipped to help you pick a duck print for your living room than a backpack for a two-day hike in the Gila National Forest. In any case, the sheer diversity of the stock practically guarantees that you will find what you need for an outdoor venture, whether it be as mundane as shotgun shells or as silly as a mustache-and-beard grooming set.

SPURS SOUVENIR SHOP

600 E. Market • Central • 704-6798

Fans of the San Antonio Spurs basketball team can dribble into this store and pig out. Besides jerseys of their favorite players (some of the more famous NBA players too), Spurmania can manifest itself in all sorts of items, such as caps, jackets, and keychains. You can walk out all Spur-dudded up.

TEXAS DEPARTMENT OF TRANSPORTATION

4615 Loop 410, at Callaghan Road • Northwest • 615-1110

No, that's not a misprint above. The highway department has one of San Antonio's least-known bargains for sale. Maps of local counties prepared by and for the department cost less here than anywhere else in town. The most practical size, at a scale of about half an inch to the mile, was recently selling for less than fifty cents. The maps show virtually every road (paved or unpaved), bridge, river, and large natural feature in a county. Though not topographic maps (and therefore minimally useful for off-road travel, such as hiking or hunting), they are essential for such activities as poking around the Hill Country, finding access to rivers for canoeists, getting started on hunting trips, or just general exploring. The really intrepid can spend about twenty-five dollars for a bound volume of the entire set of the state's county maps— kind of the ultimate state map to carry in your trunk (it would never fit in a car's glove compartment). A more concentrated source of information about Texas' geography probably doesn't exist.

TEXAS LAPIDARIES

1910 East Pyron Road, at South Presa • South • 533-7778 • No W

The Harrouns, proprietors here, really know their stones. They also know how to select, polish, and set them to show them off to best advantage. Their large and attractive showroom, about as far off the beaten track as any in town, shows the art of lapidary at its most appealing. Whether as jewelry or as decor, these gleaming stones provide excellent examples of the lapidarist's art. The hours are a bit unpredictable, so give them a call before venturing so far.

A COOK'S TOUR

Eating out is fine, but what if you prefer to cook your own vittles? This section is devoted to the interests of those amateur chefs, regardless of whether they specialize in La Haute Cuisine or in Tacos Tipicos. I have included a few food stores and specialty shops for unusual or ethnic ingredients and several good wine and beer stores. Finally, there is a section on where to look for cooking equipment that characterizes a well-equipped kitchen.

PRODUCE

FARMERS' MARKET

In a field at Jackson-Keller and McCullough and other locations in town on certain days of the week • For information about locations and hours, call 820-0288

The Texas Department of Agriculture, at the above number, can tell you about various farmers' markets that set up about town during harvesting season (roughly between May and October). The farmers drive in with trucks laden with produce and stay only until it's all sold out. Since everything is fresh from the farm—usually picked just the day before—quality is topnotch. Popular items include squash, tomatoes, peaches, blackberries, cucumbers, and onions.

FARM TO MARKET

1133 Austin Hwy., at Mount Calvary • Northeast • 822-4450 • W

Over the past years, Farm to Market has grown from a small produce shop to one of the city's best-stocked gourmet shops. It still has extensive, though often more expensive, produce, but now it also has cheeses, meats, wines, specialty vinegars, oils, fresh herbs, and spices. Allow plenty of time to browse, for shelves contain numerous unexpected surprises, including unusual soup mixes, various syrups, and endless varieties of crackers and bread (freshly baked and excellent).

HEB MARKETPLACE

5601 Bandera, at Loop 410 • Northwest • 647-2700 • W+

In San Antonio, this is the mother of all supermarkets. HEB, the city's dominant grocery chain, has put together a new kind of store—vast, varied, and, to judge by its popularity, entirely successful. Its inclusion in this section is mainly because of its remarkably complete produce department. It has a most extensive selection of Mexican chile peppers, both fresh and dried. It carries numerous oriental vegetables, its selection of mushrooms is excellent, and even out-of-season fruits and berries are usually available. Other departments are similarly well stocked. The meat department has been known to carry items as diverse as rattlesnake, buffalo, rabbit, and cabrito. The fish market is extraordinary; there is a sushi bar; fresh tortillas are made right in the middle of the store; the cheese selection is huge; HEB has departments for herbs, flowers, and deli items; and even the selection of ordinary groceries is amazing—the variety of, for example, mustards is staggering. Visit you must, but allow plenty of time. This is no convenience store.

NATURE'S HERB FARM

**7193 Old Talley Road, off Route 471 (hard to find—call ahead)
Northwest • 688-9421 • No W**

Call before you go—sometimes the retail hours are temporarily curtailed, but for fresh herbs in profusion and variety, you can't beat this place. Restaurants and markets buy from Nature's, and so do many local chefs. Herbs are never cheap, but prices here are lower than those in grocery and specialty stores.

SAN ANTONIO PRODUCE TERMINAL MARKET

1500 S. Zarzamora, at Laredo • West • 223-1235

Here's where to go if you're buying produce in quantity, say for a neighborhood co-op. Wholesalers sell to grocers and institutions here, and you can get into the act, too. Most of them will sell only by the sack, flat, or similarly outsized measure, so you may need to band together with friends. Get there before noon; work starts as early as 5 a.m. Watch out for the truck traffic pulling in and out.

VERSTUYFT FARMS

**14819 I-35 South, in Von Ormy just beyond 1604 • South
622-3423**

I have found this the most rewarding of local farms that sells produce straight to customers. Verstuyft has more variety than most farms—corn, beans, peas, melons, fruit—and everyone who works here is helpful and friendly.

SPECIALTIES

CRUMPETS
3920 Harry Wurzbach • Northeast • 821-5454

Crumpets restaurant has a European-style bakery that has freshly baked items every day. Real butter and whipped cream will tell. The croissants taste excellent. Other caloried sins include fruit tarts, Black Forest cake, and Danish pastries. Special orders accepted.

FRESH FROM TEXAS
3602 High Point, at Nacogdoches • Northeast • 654-3963

All kinds of sprouts sprout here. Most of the customers are the big users—salad bar restaurants, health food stores, and sandwich shops. If your order isn't too small, maybe you can get it filled here. Call before visiting. Also sells tofu, egg roll skins, etc.

INDIA STORE
5751 Evers, at Wurzbach • Northwest • 681-3100

More arcane herbs and spices than you knew existed are hidden away at this shop. Even for those who do not plan to buy anything, a visit will prove worthwhile just to smell the intriguing air and puzzle over labels. In short, the India Store is worth knowing. After all, when nothing other than Foul Mudammas will fill the bill, where else in town can you go?

NADLER'S BAKERY AND DELICATESSEN
7053 San Pedro, at Maplewood • North • 340-1021

Nadler's, which combines a restaurant and a deli, has a large selection of deli meats and cheeses. The shelves are filled with specialty canned and bottled goods, while the bakery offers desserts both ready made and made-to-order. Nadler's also makes specialty party trays.

NEW BRAUNFELS SMOKEHOUSE
6450 N. New Braunfels, at Sunset Ridge • Northeast • 826-6008

Long known in New Braunfels as a source of sausage and other meat specialties, the New Braunfels Smokehouse has opened a store in San Antonio with a nice range of food specialties, from light lunches to fancy jams and jellies. At Christmas, the store is full of chocolates and other Christmas candies. It always has plenty of pâtés and cheeses, and, most important of all, the smoked meats and sausages that used to be available only in New Braunfels are now available in San Antonio. The sandwiches are uncomplicated but good—smoked turkey, for example, may consist of nothing more than bread and turkey.

PALETTA IMPORTED FOOD
202 Recoletta, near San Pedro • North • 828-0678

If an Italian recipe calls for an unusual item, you can probably get it here. Thick, fragrant olive oil, pasta in scores of shapes, pine nuts, oil-cured olives, and Mediterranean goods of every description crowd the shelves. Cheeses and some meats. In the back, tables await those who want to order a sandwich and enjoy it on the spot.

SCHILO'S DELICATESSEN
424 E. Commerce St. • Central • 223-6692

Schilo's is set up more for serving sandwiches on the premises (see **Restaurants**) than as a take-out deli, but the staff is happy to cut meats or cheeses to go.

SUN HARVEST FARMS
2502 Nacogdoches, near Loop 410 • Northwest • 824-7800
8101 Callaghan • North • 979-8121
7243 Blanco Road, at Lockhill Selma • North • 342-3822

Sun Harvest is a supermarket specializing in natural foods. Fresh fruits and vegetables, whether organically grown or not, look better here than they do at most places, and sometimes cost a bit less. The store offers a full range of whole grains, fresh cheeses, herb teas, nuts, and dried fruits, plus special syrups, oils, wines, and even fresh fish and meats. Though it doesn't carry near the range of items of a regular grocery, it does sell more bulk items than anywhere else. Just dip in the bin and get dried apricots or generic cookies.

TNK ORIENTAL GROCERY
1901 N. New Braunfels • Northeast • 226-1739

This is one of my all-time favorite hidden retail stores in San Antonio. If nothing else, go just to look around at this old-fashioned grocery store, cluttered from floor to ceiling with all kinds of oriental goods. Located right off Fort Sam Houston, TNK is out of the usual shopping zones. Thousands of items range from frozen oriental food to a bewildering array of rices, Chinese plates and bowls, vases, parasols, rice vinegar, and porcelain; even cooking equipment lurks in the crowded, musty spaces.

WHOLE FOODS
255 E. Basse • Northeast • 826-4676 • W

Whole Foods, a slick supermarket of natural and organic foods, has everything from produce to tofu. Grains, herbs, pastas, couscous, canned goods—it's all there, but in far, far greater variety than one usually associates with health food stores. A deli makes sandwiches and serves hot dishes and a prodigious array of salads whenever the store is open. Whole Foods has tables if you want to eat there, or you can carry out.

WINE AND BEER

DON'S AND BEN'S (WINE LAND)

9305 Wurzbach, at I-10, and various locations • Northwest 690-8011 • W

Among local liquor stores, Don's and Ben's has San Antonio covered. Most of the branches have good selections of wine. Don's and Ben's holds frequent sales, and even when the wine is not on sale, the prices go no higher than the norm. Be sure to look around to find out what is being closed out—some of the best bargains in the store are in the closeout bins.

FINE SPIRITS

416 Austin Hwy., between Broadway and New Braunfels Northeast • 828-8333 • W

Wines and spirits are both featured here, where the selection and quality of the stock are more impressive than its sheer breadth. Wines are available in a wide range of prices, lacking only the very inexpensive, and the proprietors seem to have gone out of their way to find particularly good wines in every price category. They also seem to know their stock well and can make appropriate suggestions when customers ask.

HILL'S AND DALE'S

15403 White Fawn, at Loop 1604 • Northwest • 695-2307 • W

Hill's and Dale's may look just like a hundred other ice houses in San Antonio, but it has hundreds of brands of beer available—quite possibly the largest selection in the city. Every major beer-producing country is represented. Also ale.

KITCHEN EQUIPMENT

When it comes to kitchen utensils, there is nothing like good solid no-nonsense hotel and restaurant supply equipment. In San Antonio, looking for that kind of thing means taking a trip down to South Flores Street, where several stores are located. I especially like Ace-Mart.

ACE-MART RESTAURANT SUPPLY COMPANY
411 S. Flores, at Durango • Central • 224-0082

Ace-Mart, although only one out of several hotel and restaurant supply stores in the area, seems to have the most appealing displays and, often, the most appealing prices. Hotel and restaurant equipment lasts longer and often does a better job for home cooking chores than the kind of merchandise found at most retail stores. Ace-Mart carries everything from ranges to teaspoons, with plenty of items of the right size for home kitchens. Bowls, knives, saucepans, stockpots, and accessories, all made to take the hard daily use of a professional kitchen, fill the shelves here.

MUSEUMS

San Antonio's museums range from a gem of an art museum, the McNay, to one heavy in local color, the Texas Pioneers, Trail Drivers, and Rangers Museum. Some have received national attention, such as the architecturally distinctive San Antonio Museum of Art. Others, like Hangar Nine, doze in the shadows, away from the limelight.

In addition to the museums listed below, there are small, specialized exhibits at places of interest covered elsewhere in this guide, such as the Alamo Museum, Carver Community Cultural Center, the Fifth Army Museum, the missions, Navarro Historical Park, the Spanish Governors' Palace, and the Steves Homestead.

HANGAR NINE (MUSEUM OF FLIGHT MEDICINE)

Brooks Air Force Base, Bldg. 671, Lindbergh Drive • South 536-2203 • Monday through Friday 8–4 • Free • W • Temporarily closed, call ahead

The museum focuses on space travel, along with new problems in medicine or in adapting to the demands of the new environment. One of the few surviving Jenny aircraft, a World War I biplane used for training, is usually here. Attractions include mementos of the early days at Brooks and relics from the pioneer moments of flight. The building itself is historically significant—it is the oldest surviving aircraft hangar at any U.S. Air Force base. Although built as a temporary structure in 1918, it has turned out to be permanent. The museum is maintained as a memorial to astronaut Edward H. White, a native of San Antonio. When you enter Brooks Air Force Base, the guard on duty will give you directions to the museum. (Note that this base and Hangar Nine Museum might close in later years because of military budget-cutting.)

HERTZBERG CIRCUS MUSEUM

210 W. Market, at S. Presa • Central • 207-7810 Daily (call for hours) • Adults $2.50, children $1

This museum brings back a bit of the glamour and excitement of the days when the circus provided the ultimate in entertainment. Somehow, the static exhibits can't quite spark the same enthusiasm that the big top did, but a lot of nostalgia lurks under the museum's roof. Tom Thumb's carriage, circus posters, colorful costumes, and artifacts of circus life make up the exhibits. A favorite is a scale model of a complete circus, just as it might have been set up on the outskirts of a town anywhere in the country. Also a noncirculating library of circus literature facilitates browsing and reference.

HISTORY AND TRADITIONS MUSEUM

Lackland Air Force Base, Orville Wright Drive • South
671-3055 • Monday through Friday 8–4:30 • Free • W

Designed for the orientation of Air Force recruits, the History and Traditions Museum will also appeal to the general aviation aficionado. Engines, scale models, and dioramas go back to the ballooning days of aviation in the Civil War. Among the exhibits that repay close study is the skeleton of a Curtiss JN-4D, the plane better known as the Jenny, the mainstay of American aviation during World War I. The wooden skeleton of the Jenny shows how the spruce frame was drilled and hollowed for lightness, as well as how marvelously intricate and beautifully constructed the old biplane's internal structure had to be. Other exhibits include historically significant photographs, models of the Wrights' flyers, and newer jet engines and guided missiles.

But don't miss the real stuff! The inside of the building is not all there is to this museum. OUTSIDE really makes up the big part of it, where almost forty real-live planes from the World War II and Vietnam eras line up on nearby parade grounds and areas. Don't miss these; the kids will love them. You can walk up and see them closely.

INSTITUTE OF TEXAN CULTURES

HemisFair Park, Bowie and Durango • Central • 458-2300
Tuesday through Sunday 9–5 • Adults $4, children $2 • W

For children or for adults, this offers one of the greatest treats in the city. This place lovingly tells the story of Texas and the different groups that have made up its history. The exhibits cover almost every ethnic group that had anything to do with the founding, settling, or growth of Texas. Pioneer life, the tribulations of the immigrants, the struggles of African-Americans, and the importation of native customs from all parts of the world form the subject matter of the displays. Included are letters and writings by the settlers, which give a good feeling of just how isolated Texas was in the middle of the last century. Among the more intriguing sights, you'll see reminders of German shooting societies, displays of patent medicines, spinning wheels and looms, and early modes of transportation. Standard exhibits include ones about the Spanish, Native Americans, Germans, Tejanos, and African-Americans. Officially part of the University of Texas, the institute maintains research facilities, including a good library. Slide shows and movies, directly or indirectly related to an exhibit, frequently enliven the dome in the center of the exhibit hall. A visit to the gift shop also proves worthwhile. It sells good books about Texas and other items of high quality. Every August the institute hosts the Texas Folklife Festival (see **Annual Events**), one of the biggest events in San Antonio.

McNAY ART MUSEUM

6000 N. New Braunfels, at Austin Highway • Northeast 824-5368 • Tuesday through Saturday 10–5, Sunday 12–5 Free • W

The McNay provides a wonderful jaunt for art lovers. Ensconsed in an attractive old mansion on beautiful grounds, the museum is heavy on American and European art, particularly by expressionists. The museum's reputation goes well beyond San Antonio. It has paintings and sculptures by Gauguin, Cezanne, Van Gogh, Picasso, Degas, Matisse, Rodin, Hopper, Manet, Corot, Andrew Wyeth, Calder, etc. The museum also has a large graphic arts collection, plus the Tobin Collection of Theatre Arts, which includes costume designs and rare books about theater arts. The McNay also hosts occasional special exhibits. Although the core collection belonged to Marion NcNay, the exhibits have expanded since the museum opened in 1954. The museum building itself, on its splendid surrounding grounds, is one of the most attractive structures open to the public in San Antonio. Originally McNay's residence, it has been enlarged several times to hold the growing collection. Yet the alterations have not changed the character of the building; it remains a perfectly proportioned small mansion that incorporates elements of southwestern architecture and Mediterranean style. The central courtyard, or sculpture garden, looks especially attractive.

SAN ANTONIO CHILDREN'S MUSEUM

305 E. Houston • Central • 212-4453 • Tuesday through Saturday 9–6, Sunday 12–5 • All persons $4, children under 2 free • W

Here's a downtown spot to take the kids, especially those aged two to ten. Lots of colorful and interactive exhibits designed for the wiggly generation. Kids can sit in a plane cockpit, sit in a saddle, take out an account at a kid-friendly bank, or ring up a sale at a grocery store. All designed to be entertaining and educational.

SAN ANTONIO MUSEUM OF ART

200 W. Jones, between Broadway and St. Mary's • Central
978-8100 • Monday through Saturday 10–5, Sunday noon–5
Adults $4, children $1.75 • W+

A nineteenth-century brewery, once the state's largest and now part of the past that San Antonio is so adept at preserving, has been transformed into a spectacularly well-designed and thought-out museum. The galleries are well lit, with high ceilings and open, airy spaces. The feeling of antiquity transformed to a modern functionalism permeates the entire structure—including the elevators. Even those who do not like art will enjoy a visit to this museum, for here the museum is the message. The museum is located close to downtown, on the banks of the San Antonio River. Its collections include Spanish colonial, pre-Columbian, eighteenth- to twentieth-century American, Latin American, Chinese and Asian, Greek and Roman, Egyptian, and European art. And the museum often hosts special national traveling exhibits that may not stop elsewhere in the region, with thousands of art lovers trekking to San Antonio to attend.

In the years since the museum's opening, its holdings have been enormously enriched by the acquisition of major collections of oriental art, western antiquities, and folk art. The oriental collection is primarily one of Chinese porcelains, and the western antiquities, a gift of Gilbert M. Denman, Jr., include an important collection of Greek antiquities. But the big attraction is the recent three-story additon of its Nelson Rockefeller Center for Latin American Art. Heralded as the most complete Latin American collection in the U.S., it colorfully showcases folk (much from the namesake Rockefeller), pre-Columbian, Spanish Colonial, and comtemporary art.

TEXAS PIONEERS, TRAIL DRIVERS, AND RANGERS MUSEUM

3805 Broadway, at Tuleta • Near North • 822-9011
Open daily; 11–4 in fall and winter, 10–5 in spring
and summer • Adults $2, children 50¢

Texas trail drivers and Texas Rangers have joined to show artifacts relevant to the history of both. Trail drives were a fixture of the West from the beginning of cattle-ranching days until it became more profitable to send cattle to market by rail than drive them up the trail. The Texas Rangers, an arm of the law, sometimes broadly interpreted, helped create some of the key aspects of Texas legend.

U.S. ARMY MEDICAL DEPARTMENT MUSEUM

Fort Sam Houston, Harry Wurzbach and Stanley Road
Northeast • 221-6358 • Tuesday through Sunday 10–4 • Free

This museum, whose new quarters were built with donated (not appropriated) funds, traces the history of army medicine since 1775. As in any military museum, uniforms, insignia, and medals make up part of the collection. But you'll also see photographs, scale models, ambulances, and memorabilia from prisoners of war and an interesting exhibit of medical material taken from medics and medical supplies captured by U.S. Armed Forces in combat.

WITTE MUSEUM

3801 Broadway, at Pershing • Northeast • 357-1900 • Monday through Saturday 10–5, Sunday noon–5 (open until 6 in summer) Adults $5.95, children $3.95 • W

The Witte, a museum of natural and local history and science, interprets this designation broadly. The exhibits change from time to time, offering additional variety. Visiting exhibits, some of major scientific or historical significance, add to the appeal of the basic collection. Artifacts of Southwest Indians and three houses, significant because of their historic past, all make up parts of the Witte's eclectic collection. The Witte has a number of hands-on displays that particularly appeal to kids. Other exhibits show the animals and plant life of the South Texas region, dinosaurs, and the Indian rock art of the lower Pecos in West Texas. Over the years, Witte has had exhibits on the Alamo, kites, and antiques, with an emphasis on both education and entertainment. This is a comfortable, family-oriented museum. The gift shop sells books and items related to the exhibits, as well as some crafted items.

A colorful Science Treehouse is a recent attraction added to the museum's facilities. Four levels, this science center has all sorts of hands-on fun activities for kids of all ages. The museum admission fee includes the treehouse.

ART GALLERIES

Unfortunately, art galleries have a history of finding it tough to last economically. Space permits this guide to only list a representative few and some who have persevered through the years.

ART INCORPORATED
9401 San Pedro, just north of Loop 410 • North • 340-1091

While many visit here because of the excellent choice and service in framing, Art Inc. also has a series of changing exhibits. The art is eclectic, with themes running all the way from traditional to abstract.

ARTPACE
445 N. Main • Central • 212-4900

The ArtPace Foundation for Contemporary Art has international artists come and live in residence and then displays their work. This nonprofit organization also shows local and regional artists.

BLUE STAR ARTS COMPLEX
1400 block of S. Alamo • Central

This old warehouse area in Southtown, an urban conclave south of downtown, houses a contemporary and nontraditional arts complex, where old warehouses have been converted into art studios, galleries, living quarters, etc. The area has received some national attention. Several galleries homestead in the complex, which, besides displaying some well-known artists, has given lesser-known regional ones a chance to get shown and sold. Several of the more established galleries in the complex are listed below.

BLUE STAR ART SPACE
116 Blue Star • 227-6960

This nonprofit gallery, the largest in the complex, has helped local and less traditional artists show their work. Contemporary.

MARTIN-RATHBURN GALLERY

132 Blue Star • 229-9609

This spacious, open gallery, in the building locally known as Baja Blue Star, shows mostly Texan artists. The works are contemporary and vary from the studious to the droll. Since the artists whose works are on display at any given time may have nothing in common with each other, a visit can reveal widely divergent styles and subject matter.

SAN ANGEL FOLK ART

110 Blue Star • 226-6688

San Angel exhibits mostly Mexican folk art but includes the art of other Latin American countries as well. With its wide range of style, prices, and subject matter, almost everyone can find something here that interests them. Wood carvings, painted tins, ceramics, and brightly painted papier-mache objects are on exhibit in startling profusion. Small decorative candleholders may be next to dramatic dragons; ornate Mexican mirrors may share space with carved fish. Many of the artists shown are represented in museums.

BRIGHT SHAWL

819 Augusta • Central • 225-6366

The Junior League sponsors regular art shows and always has some area art work displayed in its headquarters. Top-notch artists, particularly in watercolor, show here. You can come in and browse or attend the special shows.

COPPINI GALLERY

115 Melrose, at McCullough • North • 824-8502

Coppini is a special place for those who appreciate sculpture, although painting is featured here as well. Pompeo Coppini was one of San Antonio's and Texas' great sculptors. The Littlefield Fountain at the University of Texas at Austin is one of his best-known works; another is the sculpture on the Alamo Cenotaph at Alamo Plaza. He also created the Texas Ranger statue on the grounds of the state capitol and the frieze on Sam Houston's grave. A naturalized citizen, he strove to make Texas a cultural mecca reminiscent of his native Italy. His foster daughter and student, Waldine Tauch, became a noted artist who sculpted the statue of Moses Austin in Military Plaza. There is an art school (Coppini Academy of Fine Arts), studio, and small gallery here. Much of Coppini's work is on exhibit, as is work of the school's students.

GALERIA ORTIZ

102 S. Concho, at Market • Central • 225-0731

Galeria Ortiz shows art that many feel represents the fine work that Texas southwestern artists are now doing. The gallery carries the work of many artists, but most prominent among them is Amado Peña, a Texan-born artist. The gallery has shows of his work, which combines elements of Indian art with Mexican and American artistic traditions. The paintings, jewelry, sculpture, and posters present fresh images and viewpoints. The range of prices is unusually wide.

GALLERY OF THE SOUTHWEST

13485 Blanco Road, just south of Bitters Road • North • 493-3344

This gallery specializes in Indian art and jewelry, especially from the Navajo, Hopi, and Zuni tribes. Sand paintings, rugs, fetishes, and a few baskets are among the many offerings. Some silver jewelry. All of the pieces are shown to good effect and are well lit.

LOVE TEXAS GALLERY

International Airport, Terminal I • North • 824-2424

What? Art taking to the crowded skies? Yes, it's become popular to display art at airports, and San Antonio is no different. And really, this regional gallery shows many fine professional local artists, from oils to watercolors and other media, in its shop and on concourse walls. In fact, you'll probably find the broadest display of good area artists as can be found anywhere in town. You may find handcrafted items from Mexico or South America.

NANETTE RICHARDSON FINE ART

426 E. Commerce, at Losoya • Central • 224-1550

A classy gallery with mainly traditional but also some contemporary and western art. Oils, watercolors, sculpture and pottery. Local, regional, and some national artists. The gallery is on the street level with a balcony overlooking the River Walk. Another gallery location in Lincoln Heights shopping area.

RATTLESNAKE AND STAR

209 North Presa • Central • 225-5977

Native Indian, primarily southwestern pueblo, art makes up the collection here, plus some fine jewelry (mostly silver). The owners buy from Indian artists, new and upcoming as well as long-established ones, in their home villages and thus often end up with objects of outstanding quality. While prices are higher than one would pay for mass-produced or tourist-oriented art, they are reasonable for work of this quality.

RIVER ART GROUP GALLERY

510 Paseo de la Villita • Central • 226-8752

This small gallery is in a restored house in historic La Villita. Area artists in the River Art Group display quality, professional wares, including oils, watercolors, pottery, jewelry, and drawings. Subject matter leans heavily toward local sites and scapes. If you're looking for a bit of San Antonio color to take home, try here.

SAN ANTONIO ART LEAGUE

130 King William, near S. Alamo • Central • 223-1140

The office of the Art League also has a small gallery, where shows often feature local artists. Works from the league's larger collection are occasionally on exhibit in the gallery, but shows vary from special one-artist shows, such as that for the artist of the year, to exhibits for the Watercolor Society.

SOL DEL RIO GALLERY

1020 Townsend • Northeast • 828-5555

This longtime small gallery has well-selected contemporary painting, sculpture, weavings, and some jewelry. While none of the offerings is avant-garde or experimental, neither is it excessively traditional. Sol del Rio's Alamo Heights location is a little off the beaten gallery track, but the quality and selection may make a visit worthwhile.

SOUTHWEST CRAFT CENTER

300 Augusta, at Navarro • Central • 224-1848

The buildings of the old Ursuline Academy (see **Historical Places**) now house not only the Southwest Craft Center (see **Continuing Education Classes** in **Education** chapter) but also a gallery that exhibits the art of students, faculty, and outside artists. The distinction between arts and crafts has always been blurry; here the exhibits may seem to be either or both—ceramics, textiles, weaving, calligraphy, and glass have all been on exhibit from time to time.

TEXAS TRAILS GALLERY

245 Losoya, at Commerce • Central • 224-7865

Here's another gallery on street level with a perch and balcony overlooking the River Walk. This longtime gallery in a triangular-shaped building is where you'll find the regional genre, some typical western art, landscapes, wildlife, and bronzes. Also American Indian paintings.

PERFORMING ARTS

Ever since frontier days, San Antonio has entertained itself with gusto. Saloon entertainment and vaudeville acts proliferated in this wide-open city. But it also sported elegance. In 1886, the plush Grand Opera House was built on Alamo Plaza and was thought the grandest one between New Orleans and San Francisco. The likes of Edwin Booth and Sarah Bernhardt played here, and the *Express* even quoted Bernhardt as calling San Antonio the "art center of Texas." Today the city still offers a strong cross section of performing arts. Though arts funding is less than in Dallas or Houston, the town attracts artists and thus some innovative performances. San Antonio, for instance, was the site of the Texas premiere of the Virgil Thomson-Gertrude Stein opera, *The Mother of Us All*. And as an ethnically mixed city, with a strong Mexican culture, San Antonio has two nationally known centers that promote their particular performing artists: Guadalupe Cultural Arts Center (Hispanic) and Carver Community Cultural Center (African-American), listed below. Also, San Antonio has sometimes been called the Nashville of Tejano music. This regional music has been growing in popularity, and San Antonio is home to many Tejano stars and several recording studios. Even if you live on a budget, the town offers plenty of free entertainment. (For informal live music, see **Bars and Clubs**.) Sometimes no phone number or address is listed for small arts groups because they may lack permanent offices—call the city's Arts and Cultural Affairs Department (222-2787) for more information.

Remember also that San Antonio's colleges and universities sponsor numerous concerts and performances. A call to a college's public relations office can often put you on a list for announcements of concerts, plays, and lectures. Many shopping malls have a cultural bent, putting on concerts and theatrical events to pull in the crowds.

HOW TO FIND OUT ABOUT
SCHEDULED EVENTS

One way of keeping abreast of what events are happening when is to check the weekend entertainment section of the daily newspaper and the calendar of events in *Texas Monthly* magazine and the San Antonio *Current* weekly newspaper. In addition, a San Antonio Arts Line (207-2166) has recorded information about dates and costs of current events.

The Texas Commission on the Arts publishes a free bimonthly newsletter of cultural events covering the entire state. To request a copy, write P.O. Box 13406, Austin 78711. Or call toll-free 1-800-252-9415.

GENERAL ARTS CENTERS AND ASSOCIATIONS

ARTS! SAN ANTONIO
222 E. Houston, at St. Mary's • Central • 226-2891

Two former organizations, the San Antonio Performing Arts Association and San Antonio Festival, in the name of the decreasing cultural funds dollar, merged to form Arts! San Antonio. With its year-round season, it brings in national and international performing arts groups, from classical to pop. Various venues about town are utilized, from the Majestic Theater to Laurie Auditorium. A variety of music, dance, and theater to appeal to various age groups. You'll find the likes of a Moscow chamber ensemble, Isaac Stern, or the Dance Theater of Harlem.

CARVER COMMUNITY CULTURAL CENTER
226 N. Hackberry, at Center • East • 207-2234

This is one of San Antonio's most stimulating surprises. Because it does so much, it's difficult to pigeonhole. The center not only serves the African-American community; it offers a wealth of cultural events for the whole city. Continuous art exhibits and classes are held here, and nationally known artists are brought in to perform and give workshops. The center has sponsored jazz greats, multicultural dance and drama, Smithsonian exhibits, gospel singers, puppet shows, international dance groups, and other delights. Various season ticket packages are available.

GUADALUPE CULTURAL ARTS CENTER

1300 Guadalupe, at Brazos • Northwest • 271-3151 • W theater

The Guadalupe Center isn't one of the largest Hispanic arts institutions in the nation for nothing. It has a lot going on over there, all the time. It primarily showcases Chicano and Hispanic visual and performing artists, but anyone can take its many classes in everything ranging from pottery to drama. Ongoing events, such as art exhibits, films, and concerts, make up much of the program; some events are free. The center also sponsors arts festivals, such as the popular Tejano Conjunto Festival and CineFestival (international Latino film festival). The center has an annual book fair that pulls in national big-name authors.

INSTITUTO CULTURAL MEXICANO

600 HemisFair Park • Central • 227-0123 • W

The institute, funded by the Mexican government, offers a mixed bag. Besides many free art exhibits and workshops, it sponsors performing arts groups and a free film series. Naturally, the emphasis is Mexican, and you can often see exhibits here that you would otherwise have to travel to Mexico to see.

MAJESTIC THEATER

226 E. Houston, at St. Mary's • Central • 226-3333 • W downstairs

The fine old Majestic Theater has been handsomely renovated and brings touring productions of current Broadway hits and other big-name entertainment to San Antonio. The old theater is a unique production in itself, with its nostalgic, ornate Moorish decor and simulated clouds and stars on the ceiling. Currently the home of the San Antonio Symphony, this period piece almost got away, but San Antonians, as they have done with so many historically significant buildings, rescued it and now point with pride to one of the country's few surviving theaters of this genre.

PARKS AND RECREATION DEPARTMENT

Various locations • 207-3000 • Free • W

Throughout the year, look for fun entertainment from the cultural elves at the Parks and Rec Department. These events will likely be anywhere in the city—outdoors, of course—and often free. Take, for instance, Brown Bag Days, which provide free entertainment in downtown parks weekly during the spring and fall. It's a perfect place to take your bag lunch for a respite from claustrophobic work environs or for harried mothers who have to get the kids out of the house. P&R also presents a weekly Mexican musical review on the River Walk at the Arneson River Theater during the summer.

DANCE

Since so many dance companies come and go or change their phone numbers, I'm not going to list any individual dance groups. But assorted professional ones perform in the city, particularly of the Mexican folkloric and Spanish dance variety. (You can see such Hispanic entertainment nightly during the summer at the outdoor Arneson River Theater on the River Walk.) Several dance-oriented organizations in town can point you to the various dance groups, whether they be of the classic ballet or the folkloric variety: San Antonio Dance Umbrella (212-7775) and City Dance (822-2453), both city-associated.

MUSIC

ALAMO METRO CHORUS—SWEET ADELINES INC.
Various locations • 493-7383

A barbershop singing group affiliated with Sweet Adelines Inc., this large chorus presents an annual show, sings for conventions, and delivers singing telegrams. No, the whole chorus doesn't show up on the doorstep for the telegram, just a quartet.

ARNESON RIVER THEATER
On River Walk, at Presa, in La Villita • Central • 207-8610
Admission

Look for nightly entertainment during the summer every day of the week at this outdoor theater on the River Walk. Some local groups are always performing Mexican and Hispanic music and dances. (See **Annual Events.**)

BEETHOVEN MAENNERCHOR AND DAMENCHOR
Beethoven Home, 422 Pereida, at S. Alamo Street • Central
222-1521 • Admission • W

The Maennerchor goes all the way back to 1867. Even poet Sidney Lanier once visited one of the group's rehearsals in 1873 and played along, with his flute. These German choirs perform at their headquarters, the Beethoven Home, an old remodeled 1850s German residence. In its early life, the singing society built the old Beethoven Hall on Alamo Street, a center of music and opera in San Antonio in that era. Look for outdoor concerts followed by a dance every third Friday, from May through September.

CHILDREN'S CHORUS OF SAN ANTONIO

Various locations • 826-3447

This group provides training for children, and it performs locally at various venues. The children practice at the Alamo Heights United Methodist Church.

JIM CULLUM'S JAZZ BAND

The Landing at the Hyatt Regency Hotel, 123 Losoya • Central
223-7266 • Admission

Although the Landing is listed in the **Bars and Clubs** chapter, Jim Cullum's Jazz Band is so well known, both locally and nationally, that it deserves a mention here. The band has its own popular National Public Radio show called *River Walk, Live From the Landing*. The show is broadcast nationally from July through December, and if you're lucky (big crowds and a small club), you might sit in on a taping of the show. But anytime, from Monday through Saturday nights, you can catch the band performing in its club in the Hyatt Regency Hotel on the River Walk level.

KING WILLIAM WINDS

Various locations • 436-3421

The Winds, a quintet, performs a variety of classical music at various area locations, including St. Mary's University.

SAN ANTONIO CHAMBER MUSIC SOCIETY

Incarnate Word University, 4301 Broadway, at Hildebrand
Near North • 829-6000 • Admission

The society brings renowned chamber music groups from all over to play at Incarnate Word College. Usually four or five performances occur per year. Of all local musical groups, this has one of the best track records for consistently high artistic standards.

SAN ANTONIO CHORAL SOCIETY

Various locations • 641-7582 (ask for the director, Gary Mabry)
Admission

This choral group concentrates on works from classical choral literature, both sacred and secular. Its repertoire ranges from early music to Randall Thompson and even more contemporary composers. It gives approximately four concerts a year at various locations in the city.

SAN ANTONIO SYMPHONY

Majestic Theater, 226 E. Houston, at St. Mary's • Central
554-1010 • Admission

You can mix and match with the San Antonio Symphony's seasonal offerings. Generally running from September to May, you can choose from the classical series and the pop series or the mini versions of both, where you can opt for a smaller package of concerts rather than a full series. Despite the occupational hazards of many orchestras—funding and management turnover—the San Antonio Symphony survives and gives credible account for itself. Recently the symphony has had a succession of talented younger conductors who have gone on to the larger, more visible orchestras. Concerts are usually held at the Majestic Theater and often feature visiting artists. The symphony also gives student concerts and some educational programs for the schools. This symphony dates back to 1939, when San Antonio brought in Max Reiter, a conductor and refugee from Hitler-torn Europe, to direct it. But this wasn't the town's first effort to organize a symphony. At the old Beethoven Hall, built in 1895 by the German contingent in town, opera companies and orchestras performed between 1906 and 1916. It was proclaimed the best concert hall in the Southwest.

TEXAS BACH CHOIR

Various locations • Admission

This polished local choir specializes in mostly sacred choral music, particularly the works of Bach and other masters. It has received good reviews for its performances and is frequently accompanied by its own orchestra consisting of many San Antonio Symphony members. Approximately four or five concerts a season.

TRINITY SYMPHONY ORCHESTRA

Trinity University, 715 Stadium Drive, near Hildebrand • Near North • 736-8211

This all-student orchestra is made up of Trinity students but not restricted to music majors. It performs several concerts a year.

TUESDAY MUSICAL CLUB

Various locations • 732-5411 • Admission

One of the oldest clubs in town sponsors this classical series that usually brings in national and international artists several times a year. Not surprisingly, the performances usually take place on Tuesday afternoons at various locations.

WINTERS CHAMBER ORCHESTRA

Ruth Taylor Concert Hall, Trinity University • 736-8211

This local wind symphony gives several classical concerts a year at Trinity University.

YOUTH ORCHESTRAS OF SAN ANTONIO

Various locations • 737-0097

This is an outlet for young local musicians, with several different age-group orchestras performing public concerts. Sponsored by the

Parks and Recreation Department, the organization also offers workshops and classes.

OPERA

SAN ANTONIO OPERA COMPANY
Various locations • 524-9665 • Admission

Because arts funding is a chronic problem, local opera companies have come and gone. But avid opera fans still abound, and this latest company has helped sponsor some national touring operas here, plus given sampler/dinners, and staged its own occasional local productions.

THEATER

ALAMO STREET RESTAURANT AND THEATRE
1150 S. Alamo, at Wicks • Central • 271-7791 • Admission

Maybe there are no collection plates or hymnals, but you'll still feel like saying amen. Because, in fact, in this old 1912 church, the stage is in the former sanctuary, and you dine in the choir room. Professional company does both comedies and drama. Some by Texas authors.

HARLEQUIN DINNER THEATER
Fort Sam Houston, Bldg. 2652, Harney Road • Northeast
222-9694 • Admission • W

The Harlequin is part of Fort Sam Houston's theater and recreation program. Before-show. Reservations necessary.

INCARNATE WORD UNIVERSITY
Maddux Theater and Cheever Downstage, 4301 Broadway, at Hildebrand • Northeast • 829-3800 • Admission

Student productions range from Shakespeare to modern plays. This theater has the reputation of putting on consistently good productions.

JOSEPHINE THEATRE
339 W. Josephine, at St. Mary's • Near North • 734-4646
Admission

Housed in the renovated old Josephine Theater, this theater presents local professional productions of musicals and comedies. Usually four productions a year.

JUMP-START THEATER

108 Blue Star • Central • 227-5867 • Admission

Whether it's funky, sociopolitical, or controversial, Jump-Start doesn't shirk from it. Sometimes presents new pieces by company members. In the Blue Star Arts Complex.

MAGIK CHILDREN'S THEATRE

420 S. Alamo • Central • 227-2751 • Admission

Aimed at kids, this one calls itself a family theater. Productions range from *Willy Wonka* to *The Red Shoes.*

MAIN AVENUE STUDIO

1608 N. Main Avenue • Near North • 227-2872 • Admission

They call it an alternative theatrical experience, and I won't argue. Located on the fringe of San Antonio College, Main Avenue Studio offers up everything from improvisational comedy to spoofs and satirical productions.

SAN PEDRO PLAYHOUSE

800 W. Ashby, at San Pedro • Near North • 733-7258
Admission • W

This community theater may be the nation's oldest continually operating one. It started in 1925, moving to the present site in San Pedro Park in 1930. Drama, comedy, and lots of musicals. Productions occur year-round, and most play for four to six weeks. San Pedro Playhouse has been renovated, and this is a comfortable theater, large enough to seat plenty but small enough to give a good seat anywhere and a feel of nearness to the stage. Performances Friday and Saturday nights and Sunday afternoons. The more popular productions often sell out, so do not count on buying tickets at the door.

STEVEN STOLI'S PLAYHOUSE

11838 Wurzbach • North • 408-0116 • Admission

Year-round productions in this small, intimate theater in an upscale shopping center, The Elms. Comedy to drama.

TRINITY UNIVERSITY

Ruth Taylor Theater One and Attic Two, 715 Stadium Drive, at Hildebrand • Near North • 999-8515 • Admission

Paul Baker started something here when he took over the fledgling drama department in the 1960s. Now Trinity has an excellent theatrics plant, with stimulating productions throughout the year in Theater One and Attic Two.

LIBRARIES

San Antonio has libraries that are public, educationally or governmentally affiliated, and private. In most local libraries, the holdings are neither extensive nor unique, but you will most likely find what you need. Some local specialized libraries, such as the Daughters of the Republic of Texas Library at the Alamo, are extraordinary and may even be the best of their kinds anywhere.

On the whole, the quality of the research libraries is better than that of the public libraries. San Antonio, by almost any metropolitan standard, tends to underfund its public libraries, and unfortunately, the result shows in the size, quality, and accessibility of the collections. However, the more recently built new central library (with its enchilada-red facade) is an outstanding addition to the system. The research libraries, on the other hand, tend to meet the standards necessary for professional scholarly research. The universities, of course, all have their libraries, most of which are open to the public for use, if not for borrowing. Several government institutions have first-rate research libraries, although these are less well known and are operated mainly for the benefit of the staff at the host institution.

Those with specialized needs who cannot find the right material can get in touch with the Bexar Library Association, the organization for professional librarians in the San Antonio area. The staff is helpful, and the association also publishes an annual directory of local libraries and librarians. Either the Bexar Library Association or the San Antonio Public Library can provide more information about local libraries. Most local research libraries can find, by computerized inquiry, whether any local library has a given document or journal.

Counting the various university, institutional, and military libraries in San Antonio and surrounding communities, there are close to thirty research libraries. Those libraries have affiliated with each other to form CORAL, the Council of Research and Academic Libraries. Scholars or students who are authorized to use any one of the affiliated libraries automatically have at their disposal the resources of all of them. Thus, although there is no single outstanding library in San

Antonio for research purposes, CORAL makes available the resources of a far more extensive library than any single institution can offer.

BEXAR COUNTY SPANISH ARCHIVES

Bexar County Courthouse, Main Plaza • Central • 220-2125

You might call this going back to the basics—basic research, that is—because these fascinating old Spanish records go back to the 1700s and 1800s. As you might expect, these precious archives aren't out for browsing with soda in hand; you need to see the archivist. You'd best call ahead to the courthouse and the county clerk's office before venturing forth.

BROOKE ARMY MEDICAL CENTER MEDICAL LIBRARY

Fort Sam Houston, New Braunfels and Grayson
Northeast • 916-2182

The library serves the needs of the large medical facility at Fort Sam Houston on Roger Brooke Drive.

DAUGHTERS OF THE REPUBLIC OF TEXAS LIBRARY

Alamo Plaza • Central • 225-1071 • W with assistance

The library at the Alamo serves as a repository for books, documents, letters, photographs, maps, and other material relevant not only to the Alamo but also to the history of Texas. The library is a research library containing much rare and unique material. As a result, scholars must register upon entering, and the stacks are not open for browsing.

INSTITUTE OF TEXAN CULTURES LIBRARY

HemisFair Park, Durango at Bowie • Central • 458-2228 • W

The Institute of Texan Cultures Library maintains an extensive collection of published and unpublished writings relevant to the state's cultural history. The library's collection of books and documents about Texas is an important aspect of the institute (see **Museums**).

LEON VALLEY PUBLIC LIBRARY

6425 Evers, at Poss • Northwest • 684-0720

The library for the community of Leon Valley has a small but excellent general collection.

McNAY ART MUSEUM LIBRARY

6000 N. New Braunfels, at Austin Highway • Northeast
824-5368

The collection of the McNay Library is a general art collection but is particularly strong in those areas most relevant to the museum's holdings. The library's holdings thus increase the value of the McNay Art Museum (see **Museums**) as a scholarly resource. The library is available for use by the public, not just members of the museum. The extensive Tobin Theater Arts Library is also here.

MIND SCIENCE FOUNDATION LIBRARY

7979 Broadway, Suite 100, at Sunset Road • Northeast
821-6094

The Mind Science Foundation investigates mainstream mental sciences, both medical and behavioral, as well as more arcane and problematic fields, such as extrasensory phenomena and telekinesis. For that research, the foundation has assembled a considerable library, including a number of journals that go back to very early investigations of these phenomena.

OBLATE SCHOOL OF THEOLOGY LIBRARY

285 Oblate, near Blanco • North • 341-1366

Theology, as you might expect, forms the backbone of the collection at the Oblate School Library. Probably the city's largest theological collection. Use of scholarly material at the library is available to all.

OLD SPANISH MISSIONS HISTORICAL RESEARCH LIBRARY

Our Lady of the Lake University, 411 SW Twenty-fourth St., at Commerce • Northwest • 434-6711 • Call for appointment

This special collection contains material relevant to the founding, maintenance, and decline of the missions in San Antonio. Scholarly research based on material in the collection is contributing a new understanding of this important feature of the area's history. Many of the documents are unpublished letters and diaries. Most are in Spanish, although some are available in translation.

OUR LADY OF THE LAKE UNIVERSITY LIBRARY

411 SW Twenty-fourth St., at Commerce • Northwest • 434-6711
W ground floor

Our Lady of the Lake University has a general university library of moderate size. The collection is distinguished by a good collection of Texana and a special collection relating to the missions (see above).

ST. MARY'S UNIVERSITY LIBRARY

One Camino Santa Maria, at Cincinnati • Northwest
436-3441 • W

St. Mary's University is particularly well known for its law and business schools, and the library reflects the quality of those programs. The law collection is housed separately from the main collection and may have different hours, so call ahead. Local lawyers frequently use the library for research needed for their cases.

SAN ANTONIO COLLEGE LIBRARY
1300 San Pedro, at Dewey • Near North • 733-2487 • W+

For a two-year college, San Antonio College has a fine library. Though naturally basic, it serves the area's largest enrollment and has several rare book collections. It also houses collections of Southwest genealogical data, Texana, and western Americana.

SAN ANTONIO CONSERVATION SOCIETY LIBRARY
107 King William, at St. Mary's • Central • 224-6163

The Conservation Society maintains a small library of books and documents relevant to the preservation and protection of buildings and places significant to San Antonio's history. The library also has a large collection of photographs from San Antonio's past.

SAN ANTONIO PUBLIC LIBRARY SYSTEM
600 Soledad and various branch locations • Central
207-2500 • W+

In recent years, a modern, tomato-red (or enchilada-red, as they like to call it in Tamaleville) central library building burst onto the scene with a lot of national hoopla about the color and architecture. Whatever you think about the design, it provides a popular new central library with modern facilities and computer services. With a computer and modem, you can dial up the library's catalog to see what's available at which branch. (Just under twenty library branches are scattered about town.) Aside from some of the usual topics, the library has good sections on genealogy and Texana. And it has circus literature in its separate Hertzberg Circus Museum, also located downtown.

STAKE GENEALOGICAL LIBRARY
2103 St. Cloud, near Babcock • Northwest • 736-2940 • W

The Mormon Church operates this library for the use of those doing genealogical research.

TEMPLE BETH-EL LIBRARY
211 Belknap • Near North • 733-9135

The temple has a strong collection of Judaica: thousands of titles, most of which are appropriate for study or research. The large majority of the collection is in English, though volumes in Yiddish (see also UTSA Library, this section) and Hebrew are available also. Nonmembers of the temple are encouraged to use the collection.

TRINITY UNIVERSITY LIBRARY
715 Stadium Drive, near Hildebrand • Near North
999-8126 • W

The library serves the Trinity community as a general university-level research library. The government documents section contains one of the particularly strong collections. Other collections include Texana, English and American literature, and space exploration.

UNIVERSITY OF TEXAS AT SAN ANTONIO LIBRARY
6900 Loop 1604 • Northwest • 458-4585 • W+

This is another general university library. Beyond its general collection, it has collections on archaeology, Mexican government, Texana, and western Americana. It also has one of the country's finest collections of Yiddish literature.

UNIVERSITY OF TEXAS HEALTH SCIENCE CENTER AT SAN ANTONIO LIBRARY
7703 Floyd Curl, at Medical • Northwest • 567-2450 • W

The medical research library is particularly strong in its collection of journals in the fields of medicine and health care. The library conducts computer searches for references related to topics in medicine, a service that is remarkably inexpensive.

EDUCATION

Looking to take some college courses or just increase your noggin's IQ on the likes of physics or car mechanics? The city offers many choices, from a large junior college system (Alamo Community College District) to several impressive state and private universities (where you can also learn to become a doc or legal eagle). Just peruse the Ivory Towers section for these.

And many more institutions or organizations serve up continuing education classes, as noted in the Continuing Education section.

IVORY TOWERS

San Antonio's abundance of Catholic colleges is due to the sisters and brothers having been instrumental in settling San Antonio and starting schools early in the city's history. But the Presbyterians, Episcopalians, and secular educators got into the act in later years, so San Antonio has abundant ivory towers. This section also includes institutions that carry out research or combine functions of teaching and research, such as the University of Texas Health Science Center, which has several medical and allied health schools under its umbrella. In fact, San Antonio is a contender for leadership in the biotech research field.

Note that the Alamo Community College District is the governing body for four public junior colleges in the city (San Antonio, St. Philip's, Palo Alto, and Northwest Vista). They are spread about in different geographical areas to allow local students easy access.

NORTHWEST VISTA COLLEGE
3535 N. Ellison • Northwest • 348-2000

This is the newest junior college campus of the Alamo Community College District. Out near Loop 1604 and Sea World, it should be open by the time of this printing.

OBLATE SCHOOL OF THEOLOGY

285 Oblate, at Blanco • North • 341-1366

Oblate is a small Catholic college that formerly trained men for the priesthood. However, it has undergone a recent name change and opened its doors to men and women of all faiths for graduate theology studies. Founded in 1903 as the San Antonio Philosophical and Theological Seminary and later called Oblate College, it now offers several master's degrees.

OUR LADY OF THE LAKE UNIVERSITY

411 SW Twenty-fourth St., at Commerce • Northwest
434-6711 • W variable

This Catholic college is steeped in history. Although it didn't actually offer college-level study until 1911, these old buildings with their fine-crafted wood and marble go back to 1896. One of the most beautiful is the Sacred Heart Chapel. With the chapel's wooden pews, marble altar, carved wood, gold leaf, and stained glass windows imported from the Frei studios of Munich, few things this side of Europe are as exquisite. The nuns sold their needlework to pay for this chapel. Completed in 1923, the steeple is the landmark of Our Lady of the Lake. Viewed from across nearby Elmendorf Lake, it makes a good picture postcard scene. The Congregation of the Sisters of Divine Providence founded Our Lady of the Lake. Members first settled in nearby Castroville in 1868 and then moved to San Antonio in 1896. This college has a history of being attuned to community needs. During the Depression, it set up a food line at the convent kitchen for the hungry poor. Today, situated in a low-income, minority neighborhood, it emphasizes programs for minorities, particularly Hispanics. It also has some of the most progressive approaches of any of the city's colleges, including a weekend college for working people. Its school of social work is well thought of, and graduate programs in education, business administration, and counseling are available. Total enrollment is about 3,500. Visit the college's annual festival, Spring Jam, in the fall. It features food, music, and kiddie rides and is open to the public.

PALO ALTO COLLEGE

1400 Villaret, at Palo Alto Road • South • 921-5000 • W variable

In the Alamo Community College District, this two-year college is designed to give the south side greater access to collegiate education. While it offers traditional arts and sciences, Palo Alto hones in on some pragmatic technical programs, such as aviation, computers, and agribusiness. It has around 7,600 students.

ST. MARY'S UNIVERSITY

One Camino Santa Maria, at Cincinnati • Northwest
436-3011 • W variable

The beginning of St. Mary's, another Catholic college in San Antonio, can be traced to several French brothers of the Society of Mary who rode into town on the stagecoach from Indianola in 1852. These intrepid brothers started a boys' school in rooms over a livery stable near Military Plaza. Later, in 1853, they moved to a spot on the San Antonio River (on College Street), where they started building what would be known as St. Mary's College, or "the French school." The brothers grew a garden and grapes but supposedly drank only the water of the San Antonio River. In 1894 they opened a new school called St. Louis College in the northwest section of town. The school's football coach in 1916 was none other than Second Lieutenant Dwight Eisenhower. Eventually, the whole college moved to this location, the present campus. Some of the original buildings downtown on College have been preserved and incorporated in what is now La Mansion del Rio hotel. St. Mary's, with a student body of about 4,000, offers bachelor's and many graduate degrees. Many local attorneys graduated from its law school. It has business and engineering schools and a computer science program. Dormitory housing is available. St. Mary's sponsors the annual Oyster Bake during Fiesta in April. This is a giant family picnic, with thousands attending.

ST. PHILIP'S COLLEGE
1801 Martin Luther King Drive • East • 531-3200 • W

St. Philip's in east San Antonio has some 8,900 students and dates back to 1898, when it began as an Episcopal school for African-American women. The two-year college, now part of the Alamo Community College District, has an occupational-technical emphasis. It offers, for instance, hospitality management and career training in health care and the automotive/construction trades.

SAN ANTONIO COLLEGE
1300 San Pedro, at Dewey • Near North • 733-2000 • W variable

This two-year college anchors the Alamo Community College District, with about 21,000 students. It's also one of the largest junior colleges in the state. San Antonio College started out in 1925 as a night school for local students who needed to work part-time and acquire a low-cost college education. Though it has grown by leaps and bounds since then, it's still pretty much a basic, modern, urban campus for the same commuter student. That doesn't mean, however, that it skimps on faculty or facilities. For instance, it has a large computer program, and its radio, TV, and film department has trained personnel for many local stations. The college had its beginnings at old Main Avenue High School and spent twenty-five years in the German-English School buildings on South Alamo Street near the Plaza San Antonio Hotel. Its present campus is on forty-four acres on San Pedro, just north of downtown. One unique place to explore on campus is the planetarium on

Myrtle, just east of San Pedro. Travel through space or see 4,000 stars projected in this multimedia presentation with special sound effects. For information or to arrange special group shows, call 733-2910. Another place of interest is the Koehler House, a Victorian home now used for college activities. Otto Koehler, a German who helped organize what ultimately became Pearl Brewery, built the house at the turn of the century high on a hill (now 310 W. Ashby) so he could have an unobstructed view of his brewery. Supposedly, Koehler could sit on his front porch and tell whether his men were working by the color of the smoke belching out of the brewery stacks. The property was later deeded to the Alamo Community College District. Be sure to look for interesting national speakers that San Antonio College brings in. The events are free and open to the public.

SOUTHWEST FOUNDATION FOR BIOMEDICAL RESEARCH
7620 NW Loop 410 at Military Drive • Northwest • 674-1410

SOUTHWEST RESEARCH INSTITUTE
6220 Culebra, at Oakhill • Northwest • 684-5111

These aren't colleges, so don't go motoring up to enroll for your sheepskin or visit. But they're such renowned think tanks that I'm including them along with the regular ivory towers. Many townsfolk don't even realize these two distinct research organizations exist, located on gently rolling old ranch property in northwest San Antonio. Obviously no longer a ranch, this land just inside Loop 410 is being put to more modern use as a site for biomedical, industrial, and governmental research. There is still unused land in the parcel, and you'll see pleasant countryside midst modern administrative and research buildings. Both organizations were started by oilman Tom Slick, Jr., who set aside 1,500 acres of the Essar Ranch for their use. However, they have different governing boards and are considered two separate, independent organizations, although their staffs often work together on projects that call for joint talents and facilities. The organizations also sometimes work in tandem with the University of Texas at San Antonio and the University of Texas Health Science Center.

The **Southwest Foundation for Biomedical Research,** a nonprofit institution first started in 1941, does basic biomedical research. Researchers focus on the detection, cause, cure, prevention, and elimination of disease. They have studied, for instance, alcoholism, hypertension, long-acting contraceptives, and the link between estrogens and cancer. And currently they are in the forefront of AIDS research. The foundation has a large research colony of baboons. Needed for testing human diseases and environmental problems, the baboons have even been trained to puff on cigarettes and measure their own blood pressures. The foundation, incidentally, is linked to an exclusive private dinner club in town, the Argyle (see **Points of Interest**), which provides some financial support for the foundation's research.

Southwest Research Institute, on the other hand, is an applied research organization. It works on contract with private industry and the government. The engineering and scientific activities going on out here have included such diverse topics as finding out why an offshore drilling rig collapsed, testing electric cars, studying energy alternatives and synthetic fuels, and designing equipment for the inspection of nuclear power plant systems. Slick founded this organization in 1947, with it first operating out of an old ranch house called the Cable House, named after a railroad president who bought the ranch in 1886. The institute continued to use the house, a showplace in San Antonio in the 1890s, even after it expanded but unfortunately opted to tear it down some years ago.

These research organizations are not open to the general public.

TRINITY UNIVERSITY

715 Stadium Drive, near Hildebrand • Near North • 999-7011
W variable

Trinity is located on high, bluff countryside near Alamo Stadium, just north of downtown. Although originally founded in 1869 by Texas Presbyterians, it has since had several lives in different cities, finally ending up in 1952 at the present campus designed by San Antonio master architect O'Neil Ford. The university used to call itself the Skyline Campus, because you can view downtown from the attractive campus, which has retained its Hill Country landscaping. Some buildings worth seeing include the chapel and library. Trinity, which offers bachelor's and graduate degrees, has a strong education department, and the Communications Center includes color television studios and a student-operated FM radio station. A Texas chapter of Phi Beta Kappa is located here. While Trinity doesn't emphasize a lot of big sports, it does well in a few. Its tennis and skeet teams have racked up many national championships over the years. This private school has attracted many National Merit Scholars, plus more affluent students. Enrollment is around 2,300. Trinity's Distinguished Lecture Series has attracted prominent speakers and is free and open to the public, but go early because popular speakers attract crowds.

UNIVERSIDAD NACIONAL AUTONOMA DE MEXICO

HemisFair Park • Central • 222-8626 • W

A branch of the University of Mexico here in San Antonio offers extension courses in Spanish and the history and culture of Mexico. (For more details, see Educational Opportunities under **Mexico in San Antonio**.)

UNIVERSITY OF TEXAS AT SAN ANTONIO

6900 N. Loop 1604 • Northwest • 458-4011 • W

UTSA, being state supported, is BIG, getting bigger. Already the 600-acre campus has around 18,000 students. The school opened its doors in 1973 on land that some people thought too far north and inaccessible to students in south and central San Antonio. But the city has grown northward, and UTSA's interesting campus rises out of the rugged Hill Country terrain. The buildings are modern in both architecture and facilities, contrasting starkly, but somehow fitting in, with the rolling terrain. Part of the huge University of Texas system, the University of Texas at San Antonio offers bachelor's and master's degrees, plus some doctorates, and provides the city with a much-needed engineering-degree program. Its Center for Archaeological Research has several field dig sites and has received publicity for unearthing a skull at the Alamo dating back to the historic battle. The library has good rare book collections pertaining to the Texas Republic, western Americana, and J. Frank Dobie. A branch of the campus has recently opened in downtown San Antonio to make it much more convenient to those students who don't live on the north side.

UNIVERSITY OF TEXAS HEALTH SCIENCE CENTER AT SAN ANTONIO

7703 Floyd Curl, at Medical • Northwest • 567-7000

This immense medical complex, on 100 acres in the South Texas Medical Center, provides the setting for all sorts of exciting health research in fields ranging from cancer and cardiovascular disease to geriatrics and why smokers can't stop smoking. This modern center is also busy cranking out fledgling doctors, dentists, and nurses. It's actually five schools: the Medical School, the Dental School, the Graduate School of Biomedical Sciences, the School of Nursing, and the School of Allied Health Sciences. Bachelor's, master's, and doctoral degrees are granted, besides two-year programs in dental hygiene and dental laboratory technology. Enrollment is around 2,700. The extensive facilities include television studios where a teleconference network broadcasts to hospitals and health centers in Texas and other states. The Health Science Center welcomes visitors. Take a self-guided tour (a map is provided at UTHSC) through the medical library, multidisciplinary labs, and nursing school. Even the cafeteria is open to the public. Or call to arrange a group tour, which can be tailored to meet special interests, whether it's to see the Dental School, nutritionists, or lab experiments. Faculty physicians for the Health Science Center come from the supervising medical staff at the University Hospital and the Audie Murphy Memorial Veterans Hospital, the primary teaching hospitals. UTHSC's Speakers Bureau will arrange for experts to speak to community groups free about all sorts of subjects, such as acupuncture and biofeedback.

UNIVERSITY OF THE INCARNATE WORD
4301 Broadway at Hildebrand • Northeast • 829-6000 • W

This venerable Catholic college has a fascinating history. Fortunately, its founders, the Sisters of Charity, were astute enough to snatch up the 280-acre estate of George Brackenridge when he sold it back in 1897. All this prime land (now at busy Broadway and Hildebrand streets) was just part of his large holdings, which also included the land eventually donated for Brackenridge Park and Fort Sam Houston. Brackenridge's marvelous old home (built around 1886) still stands intact on the college grounds. Brackenridge insisted his land remain as nature had made it. Even after selling his estate, he frequently checked up on the sisters to be sure they hadn't pruned one tiny limb from any of the trees. The headwaters of the San Antonio River are located on this property, where Indians camped long ago. Incarnate Word boasts its own archeological dig, with artifacts dating back some 10,000 years. The college was actually established in 1881 by the Sisters of Charity of Incarnate Word at another site. These same industrious sisters also founded Santa Rosa Hospital. Consequently, the liberal arts college, with an enrollment of about 3,200, has a strong nursing school and allied health program. It has a respected drama department and offers graduate degrees in nutrition, education, business administration, communication and other fields. This peaceful old campus with its wooded grounds makes an ideal place for a walk or picnic lunch.

CONTINUING EDUCATION CLASSES

There's a brave new world out there for revitalizing the tired mind and reluctant body. Whether you're interested in constructing your very own solar heating system to belly dancing, you can find a class about it somewhere in town. Some are extension courses for regular college credit, and others are continuing education courses. The rest are simply for fun. Most of these courses require fees. However, the Parks and Recreation Department and several department stores offer many free classes. Also check the adult education programs offered by the various school districts in town.

GUADALUPE CULTURAL ARTS CENTER
1300 Guadalupe • Northwest • 271-3151

The center offers a fine variety of courses heavy on Chicano and Hispanic culture and arts, ranging from art and writing to music.

OUR LADY OF THE LAKE UNIVERSITY
411 SW Twenty-fourth St., at Commerce • Northwest
434-6711 • W variable

A cross section of classes is offered, from computing and country and western dancing to fitness.

PARKS AND RECREATION DEPARTMENT
Various locations • 207-3000 • W

The city offers numerous classes for all ages at various community centers and parks around town—ranging from dancing to guitar, bridge, and sports. The Parks and Recreation Department also has a good senior citizens program, particularly at the Commander's House at 647 South Main. It even serves lunch. Most of these city classes are gloriously free. Call the above number or look in the blue pages of the phone book under "City Government, Parks and Recreation Department, Recreational Facilities" to locate the center nearest you.

SAN ANTONIO COLLEGE
1300 San Pedro • Near North • 733-2635 • W

Some good practical courses are offered here—law enforcement, business, computer, and others. The college is also strong in women's courses (see Women's Center, below).

SOUTHWEST CRAFT CENTER
300 Augusta, at Navarro • Central • 224-1848 • W

The center, located in the historically significant buildings of the old Ursuline Academy, has had such courses as painting, drawing, sculpting, weaving, ceramics, jewelry, enameling, and photography, to name a few.

TEXAS A&M UNIVERSITY, ENGINEERING EXTENSION SERVICE
Several locations • 208-9300

Basic employment courses offered in the past have included automotive mechanics, electronics repair, welding, and major appliance repair.

TRINITY UNIVERSITY
715 Stadium Drive, near Hildebrand • Near North • 999-7601
W variable

Trinity's Brown Bag series on literature is popular. Otherwise, the continuing education department only offers review and cram courses for popular standardized college examinations and helps with the coordination and arrangements for group conferences at Trinity.

WITTE MUSEUM
3801 Broadway • Northeast • 357-1900

The museum offers interesting excursions and programs. Go on a fossil hunt, take a bus trek to Lost Maples, or learn Chinese cooking. Whatever, the museum makes it fun and informative for children and adults.

WOMEN'S CENTER
1300 San Pedro • Near North • 733-2299 • W

San Antonio College's program aims at helping women. It has offered classes, workshops, and counseling in career planning, employment preparation, upward mobility, and life transitions, such as transitions experienced by homemakers going back to work.

YOUNG MEN'S CHRISTIAN ASSOCIATION
Various locations • 246-9622 • W Westside and Alamo branches only

Classes vary at the YMCA's six branches, so call the nearest one for details. Fitness, youth sports, and karate are some of the topics taught.

YOUNG WOMEN'S CHRISTIAN ASSOCIATION
503 Castroville • South • 433-9922

Swimming, aerobic dancing, and other topics are taught at the YWCA.

Health, Safety, and Community Services

MEDICAL AND HEALTH SERVICES

That old standby, the Alamo, once doubled as the city's first makeshift hospital. In 1806, then an abandoned mission, it had thirty beds with cattail mattresses and served soldiers, Indians, and the Spanish governor.

Medical facilities have changed a bit since then. San Antonio is now a major regional center for health care, both civilian and military. The large South Texas Medical Center complex in northwest San Antonio includes hospitals, clinics, labs, schools, and research facilities. And with the UT Health Science Center, Southwest Foundation for Biomedical Research, Institute of Biotechnology, and Texas Research Park, the city has become a leader in medical research, biotechnology, and education. Numerous civilian hospitals fill the city. The first one, started in 1869 by the Sisters of Charity of the Incarnate Word, ultimately became the present-day Santa Rosa Hospital. Military hospitals and research centers also contribute to the quality of health care in the area. Brooke Army Medical Center, one of the army's largest hospitals, and its burn center, to which victims are flown from all over the world, are located at Fort Sam Houston, along with the army's Health Services Command. The huge Wilford Hall USAF Medical Center is located at Lackland Air Force Base. The Aerospace Medical Division is based at Brooks Air Force Base, along with the U.S. Air Force School of Aerospace Medicine (see **Military Bases**).

MEDICAL COMPLEXES

SOUTH TEXAS MEDICAL CENTER
Bounded by Fredericksburg Road, Babcock, and
Louis Pasteur Drive • Northwest • W variable

The 683-acre South Texas Medical Center encompasses the giant
University of Texas Health Science Center, hospitals, clinics, labs,
research centers, and assorted professional buildings where many of the
city's physicians have their offices. Everything from A (Audie Murphy
Memorial Veterans Hospital) to V (Villa Rosa Hospital) is located out
here. For more information, call the San Antonio Medical Foundation
at 614-3724.

UNIVERSITY OF TEXAS HEALTH SCIENCE CENTER AT
SAN ANTONIO
7703 Floyd Curl • Northwest • 567-7000

This huge complex has five schools in various medicine-related sciences and is a leader in basic biomedical research. (See Ivory Towers
section in **Education** chapter for details.)

HEALTH TELEPHONE SERVICES

EMERGENCY MEDICAL SERVICE
Dial 911

In emergencies, EMS technicians are dispatched to the scene to
begin treatment. A city-county service, EMS works closely with hospitals to provide ambulance transportation and emergency service.

ASK-A-NURSE
Santa Rosa Health Care • 704-4844

A handy 24-hour service, where you can discuss your symptoms, and
a professional nurse advises when you need to consult a doctor. The
nurses can also give you general information about illnesses from reference books.

EXPRESS-NEWS LINE
554-0500

The *Express-News* newspaper has a recorded line with various news
and info topics, including health and fitness. Check or call the newspaper for a list of numbers to key in on the phone.

HEALTH LINE

Methodist Healthcare • 377-4884

Methodist Healthcare and other hospitals in the city occasionally offer informative community health programs or courses, some free, some for a fee.

TEL-MED HEALTH INFORMATION SERVICE

225-HEAL (225-4325)

Baptist Memorial Healthcare provides this handy service. Phone this number at any time, day or night, and get recorded tape messages about various illnesses or health topics, from glaucoma to anemia.

HOSPITALS

This is by no means a complete list of all hospitals in the city. This guide only attempts to touch on the bigger ones that have wide ranges of services. Numerous others specialize in services for such areas as psychiatric, cancer, geriatric, and drug abuse problems. Also the large, state-run San Antonio State Hospital provides mental illness services in south San Antonio.

AUDIE MURPHY MEMORIAL VETERANS HOSPITAL

7400 Merton Minter • Northwest • 617-5300

This huge VA hospital is located in the South Texas Medical Center. In addition to its general hospital, it has a rehabilitation unit and an active research program.

BAPTIST MEMORIAL HEALTHCARE SYSTEM

Several hospitals across town make up this Baptist system:

Baptist Medical Center
111 Dallas • Central • 297-7000

The Baptists' largest facility is downtown near where San Pedro intersects with Main.

North Central Baptist
520 Madison Oak Drive • North • 297-4000

Near Loop 1604 and Highway 281.

Northeast Baptist
8811 Village Drive • Northeast • 297-2000

Just off Northeast Loop 410, near the fashionable Marymount residential area.

St. Luke's Baptist Hospital
7930 Floyd Curl • Northwest • 297-5000

Like many others, this hospital is in the South Texas Medical Center. It has a burn care center.

Southeast Baptist
4214 E. Southcross • East • 297-3000

Near Southside Lions Park. Includes a sports medicine clinic.

METHODIST HEALTHCARE SYSTEM

Methodist Hospital
7700 Floyd Curl Drive • Northwest • 575-4000

This large hospital is situated in the South Texas Medical Center complex and has many specialties, including a pediatric intensive care unit and hyperbaric medicine.

Metropolitan Methodist Hospital
1310 McCullough • Near North • 208-2200

Located just north of downtown, this general services hospital also has a sleep disorders center.

Northeast Methodist Hospital
12414 Judson Road • Northeast • 650-4949

Near I-35.

San Antonio Community Hospital
8026 Floyd Curl Drive • Northwest • 692-8110

This large hospital in the South Texas Medical Center has a leading transplant program and various specialty units, such as its diabetes center and urology center. The renal transplant center has transplanted many kidneys over the years.

NIX HEALTH CARE SYSTEM
414 Navarro • Central • 271-1800

This old-line hospital downtown was one of the first (in 1930) to put a hospital, doctors' offices, drugstore, and parking all in one twenty-four-story building. For years, it has served the South Texas carriage trade. Besides the usual, it has occupational medicine and sports medicine clinics.

SANTA ROSA HEALTH CARE

This Catholic-run system encompasses several hospitals, including Villa Rosa, a psychiatric hospital.

Santa Rosa Children's Hospital
519 W. Houston • Central • 704-2011

This downtown hospital offers extensive care for kids, including centers for cancer research and treatment, hemophilia, birth defects, muscular dystrophy, and cystic fibrosis.

Santa Rosa Hospital
519 W. Houston • Central • 704-2011

This granddaddy of all local hospitals predates all the rest. Downtown, alongside Santa Rosa Children's Hospital. Beyond the general medical and surgical services, it also has a natural childbirth/birthing room.

Santa Rosa Northwest Hospital and Rehabilitation Hospital
2827 Babcock • Northwest • 705-6300

Aside from the usual services, this hospital offers rehabilitation medicine. At the South Texas Medical Center.

SOUTHWEST GENERAL HOSPITAL
7400 Barlite Blvd. • South • 921-2000

Not too many hospitals are located in south San Antonio. This one is not far from South Park Mall, where I-35 intersects with Southwest Military Drive. It offers general services and outreach community programs. Most of the staff is bilingual.

UNIVERSITY HEALTH SYSTEM

Consists of several tax-supported health care organizations:

University Health Center—Downtown
527 N. Leona • Central • 358-3400

Located downtown, this outpatient center is one of the largest of its kind in the state. Numerous specialty clinics fall under this one umbrella center.

University Hospital
4502 Medical Drive • Northwest • 358-4000

As a county teaching hospital (staff comes from the nearby UT Health Science Center), it provides a broad range of services. The emergency center is a level I trauma center and can receive trauma victims by helicopter. It has been the site of several organ transplant firsts for the region.

MILITARY HOSPITALS

BROOKE ARMY MEDICAL CENTER
Fort Sam Houston • Northeast • 916-6141

This longtime army hospital now has a newly built complex and a full range of services and also does medical research and education. The renowned burn center, to which victims are flown from throughout the world, is here.

WILFORD HALL USAF MEDICAL CENTER
Lackland Air Force Base • South • 292-7100

This enormous hospital center is the air force's largest medical facility anywhere. Numerous specialty fields treat not only patients from the huge local community of active and retired air force personnel and their families but also patients who may be sent here from other air force installations.

GETTING HELP . . . COMMUNITY NUMBERS

Numerous agencies exist in San Antonio to call on for help, whether for an emergency, mental health problem, or consumer complaint. It's impossible to list them all, but I have tried to include some representative ones.

EMERGENCY
Dial 911

The number to call when you need the fire department, the police department, or medical aid. This number is for emergencies only.

PERSONAL PROBLEMS
227-HELP (227-4357)

A 24-hour hot line to help you cope with personal problems. This United Way service offers counseling in suicide prevention, rape crisis, depression, drug abuse, and child abuse. These counselors can also help you solve other problems, whether financial, emotional, or medical, by giving information about local agencies.

POISON CENTER
(800) 764-7661

A 24-hour service that gives information about how to deal with suspected poisonings and drug interactions.

TIME AND TEMPERATURE
226-3232

Frost Bank has provided this service for years.

WEATHER SERVICE FORECAST
225-0404

Unfortunately, you've got to listen to a commercial before you get the forecast. If this line is busy, try the KENS-TV weather information line (470-5367).

AGRICULTURE

COUNTY AGENT
930-3086

The agent's office can provide information about horticulture, livestock, crops, and home economics. Gardeners find it useful, but so do home cooks and canners who need a bit of arcane information.

ALCOHOLISM

ALCOHOLICS ANONYMOUS
828-6235

ALCOHOLIC TREATMENT PROGRAM AND CRISIS LINE
225-5481

A service of the Bexar County Center for Health Care Services.

SAN ANTONIO COUNCIL ON ALCOHOL AND DRUG ABUSE
225-4741

ANIMALS

ANIMAL CARE HUMANE SOCIETY
226-7461

The Humane Society operates a shelter for healthy animals and helps with the adoption of dogs and cats.

ANIMAL CONTROL FACILITY
737-1442

This facility enforces the city's leash law by picking up strays.

DEAD ANIMAL REMOVAL

522-8831

EMERGENCY PET CLINIC

8503 Broadway • 822-2873

For small-animal emergencies occurring when regular veterinary clinics are closed (the facility is staffed nights and weekends).

WILDLIFE RESCUE AND REHABILITATION

698-1709

Picks up and rehabilitates injured nondomestic animals to return them to the wild.

CHILDREN

CHILD ABUSE HOTLINE

(800) 252-5400

A 24-hour toll-free number sponsored and staffed by the Texas Department of Human Services.

CHILDREN'S SHELTER OF SAN ANTONIO

223-6281

Adoption services, foster care, and emergency shelter.

CONSUMER COMPLAINTS

ATTORNEY GENERAL CONSUMER PROTECTION DIVISION

224-1007

To either report a complaint against a business or inquire about complaints against one.

BETTER BUSINESS BUREAU OF SAN ANTONIO

828-9441

The BBB keeps complaint records of San Antonio businesses and helps consumers file complaints. Some suggest checking with the BBB before signing a contract with an unknown business.

CREDIT

SAN ANTONIO RETAIL MERCHANTS' ASSOCIATION

224-6121

Supplies individuals with information about their own credit history.

CRIME

CRIME STOPPERS
207-STOP (207-7867)

To report a crime or related information about one without giving your name, call this number at the police department.

DENTAL CARE

METROPOLITAN HEALTH DISTRICT
207-8895

Operates dental clinics about town for children from low-income families. Very nominal fee.

UNIVERSITY OF TEXAS HEALTH SCIENCE CENTER DENTAL SCHOOL
567-3222

Operates an outpatient clinic, with work done by supervised dental students. Patients are accepted who have dental problems suited to current instructional needs. There may be a waiting list for services, and a fee is charged for materials used.

DRUGS

DRUG TREATMENT PROGRAM AND CRISIS LINE
225-5481

A service of the Bexar County Center for Health Care Services.

EMPLOYMENT

TEXAS EMPLOYMENT COMMISSION
222-8484

Several branches around town offer free job placement, counseling, and testing. The commission maintains extensive lists of available jobs.

FAMILY

FAMILY SERVICE ASSOCIATION
226-3391

The association provides counseling for individuals, couples, and families. Homemaker services, family life education, and family sex abuse counseling are among the services offered.

GARBAGE

CITY PUBLIC WORKS DEPARTMENT
522-8831

Garbage and brush collection. Dead animal removal.

HOME ECONOMICS

COUNTY AGRICULTURAL EXTENSION SERVICE
930-3091

Questions about home economics, in all of its branches, are fielded here, where they can tell you anything from how long to barbecue a turkey in a south Texas smoke oven to whether canning tomatillos in a boiling water bath is safe.

HOUSING

SALVATION ARMY
226-2291

Provides emergency lodging.

SAMM SHELTER
224-5838

Emergency lodging for the homeless.

INFORMATION AND REFERRAL

CITY INFORMATION
207-7080

City Hall can direct you to the proper city agency to take care of almost any situation. Various departments are listed in the blue pages of the phone book.

COUNTY INFORMATION
220-2011

The county courthouse refers you to a suitable county government department.

FEDERAL INFORMATION

(800) 688-9889

Information about federal government agencies.

STATE INFORMATION—GOVERNOR'S ASSISTANCE

(800) 252-9600

Provides information about state agencies.

UNITED WAY

352-7000

The United Way provides information and referrals concerning social service agencies in San Antonio and Bexar County.

LEGAL

LEGAL AID ASSOCIATION OF BEXAR COUNTY

227-0111

The Legal Aid Association provides low-income county residents with legal services that they could not afford on the open market. There is a means test to determine eligibility.

LEGAL ASSISTANCE—PEER COUNSELING FOR SENIOR CITIZENS

228-0334

A free service for people over age sixty.

MENTAL HEALTH

CENTER FOR HEALTH CARE SERVICES

226-9241

The center provides counseling for emotional, alcohol, drug, and retardation problems at various county treatment centers.

SAN ANTONIO STATE HOSPITAL

532-8811

STATE SCHOOL

532-9610

The above two state-supported hospitals serve the mentally ill and retarded.

RAPE

HELP-LINE
227-HELP (227-4357)
This rape crisis counseling and referral service is sponsored by United Way.

RAPE CRISIS CENTER HOT LINE
349-7273
This 24-hour hot line gives immediate help and support when a victim needs it.

SEXUAL ASSAULT CRISIS AND RESOURCE CENTER
521-7273
This center not only provides the above hot line but also provides counseling and public education.

SENIOR CITIZENS

LEGAL ASSISTANCE—PEER COUNSELING FOR SENIOR CITIZENS
228-0334
A free service for people over age sixty.

METROPOLITAN HEALTH DISTRICT
207-8802
Clinics throughout the city provide various kinds of health care.

NUTRITION PROJECT
207-8780
This project provides lunches at nutrition centers around town for persons sixty years of age or older. It requests a voluntary contribution, but free meals are available.

VOTER REGISTRATION

VOTER REGISTRATION
978-0362
Applicants for voter registration can obtain the necessary forms at local public libraries; further information is available from this office.

WOMEN'S SERVICES

BATTERED WOMEN'S SHELTER OF BEXAR COUNTY
733-8810

Temporary shelter, counseling, and referrals for victims of family violence are available through this number, which is a 24-hour help line.

SAN ANTONIO COLLEGE WOMEN'S CENTER
733-2299

This office specializes in providing counseling, information, and referral services for women wanting to return to college or making life changes.

COMMUNITY CLUBS AND HOBBIES

Like any city, San Antonio has innumerable clubs and organizations, ranging from large to small, from exclusive to all embracing. Here is just a sampling of the less well known, the more arcane, the more interesting, and the more hobby-oriented ones, many of which came (with updatings as needed) from an extensive clubs and organizations directory by the San Antonio Chamber of Commerce. Although the directory is expensive, local libraries carry copies.

In cases where an organization does not have an office, this book lists the address or telephone number of a contact person who can provide more information about club activities and meetings. Remember that almost all these organizations are volunteer groups, so the contact person may change frequently and home numbers may be listed. Many of the organizations listed here have regular meeting times and places, but since they are subject to change without notice, this guide does not usually include this information. Check with the contact persons to verify details of meetings.

ALAMO AQUARIUM SOCIETY
Hazel Hall • 822-9848

The fish fanciers meet monthly for discussion, learning, and bowl shows. Members take an interest in both saltwater and freshwater aquaria and gather for lectures, movies, slide shows, and other educational activities.

ALAMO AREA SQUARE AND ROUND DANCE ASSOCIATION
Paul and Kathy Rigsby • 637-7490

This association consists of numerous square and round dancing organizations all over the San Antonio area. Call to find a dance organization that meets in a place convenient to you.

ALAMO AREA WOOD CARVERS ASSOCIATION
Lloyd Johnson • 494-3957

Promotes wood carving as an art form.

ALAMO BRIDGE CLUB
8709 Botts Lane, at Ceegee • 822-2223

This is more of a studio than a club—a place to go to play for a small fee. Call for schedule of games.

ALAMO CITY CLIMBING CLUB
Call Sun and Ski Sports, 494-0429, for current information sheet about club activities and contact person about climbing opportunities in the Alamo City area.

ALAMO CITY RIVERMEN
Gib Hafernick • 822-8901

The Rivermen specialize in running local rivers by canoe and kayak. They take frequent trips, mostly on the gentler local rivers, although the whitewater canoeists have their day also. Trips include day outings as well as weekend jaunts, and instructional courses are also part of the program. Occasional longer trips, such as the lower Rio Grande, an 83-mile wild river trip, fill out the program.

ALAMO COIN CLUB
Wayne Gordon • 494-6824

This numismatic group meets several times a month.

ALAMO PC ORGANIZATION INC.
375-7300

Surfing the net can be more fun in numbers. This huge IBM computer compatible club has all sorts of specialized meetings about different topics and software during the month, both for novices and the truly wired. At various locations in town. Check the Sunday business section of the *Express-News* newspaper, where topics and meetings are announced in the computer bulletin board.

BEXAR AUDUBON SOCIETY
822-4503

The Bexar Audubon Society, a chapter of the National Audubon Society, has an active schedule of meetings and birding trips. Also active in local conservation issues, it currently meets monthly.

BEXAR GROTTO
Linda Palit • 699-1388

This group of spelunkers visits local caves and occasionally makes longer trips to pursue their underground activities. They also play an active role in cave conservation, an activity important in Bexar County, which sits over or near enormous deposits of limestone.

CONFEDERATION OF CHARROS IN SAN ANTONIO
Colonel Maximo Virgil • 824-1217

The confederation works to keep intact the traditions and customs of charros and the skilled horsemanship that descended from Spanish settlers. Members have their own horses and participate in *charreadas*, displays of skill and proficiency in horsemanship.

FIRE ON THE MOUNTAIN CLOGGERS
Linda Carolan • 344-2557

The Fire on the Mountain Cloggers, whose dancing descended from an Appalachian dance form, perform not only locally but have also taken international tours. The members dance for the love of doing so, but they are also available for performance at festivals and conventions. New members are recruited from those who take classes from the group or already know the dance form.

GREATER SAN ANTONIO QUILT GUILD
695-8737

The Quilt Guild is devoted to keeping alive one of the great folk arts of the Southwest. The organization promotes this handicraft through judged shows, lectures and demonstrations, and quilt sales from time to time. The organization's members are quilters, but they provide information about quilting and shows to nonmembers.

MAHENDRA RING #18, INTERNATIONAL BROTHERHOOD OF MAGICIANS
For information, call Dennis Martin • 212-6056

Perhaps the most mysterious of all organizational goings-on takes place at the meetings of the Mahendra Ring. Some meetings are open to visitors; others are not, so call before showing up and being disappointed. About seventy enthusiastic prestidigitators of all ages make up the membership.

NORTHSIDE NEWCOMERS' BRIDGE CLUB
Call Northern Hills Country Club for contact person • 655-4148

Here is a club for card players who are new (within two years) to the city's north side. The club meets monthly at the Northern Hills Country Club.

PARENTS WITHOUT PARTNERS
2700 NE Loop 410 • 871-4052

Parents Without Partners is concerned with the problems of raising children in a single-parent home. The issues may be social, practical, legal, financial, or emotional; the group's approach to those problems is primarily educational. The local chapter is affiliated with the national organization.

POLISH FOLK DANCERS OF SAN ANTONIO
Genny Kraus • 533-7865

The Polish Folk Dancers perform in authentic costumes at the Folklife Festival and numerous other events around Texas. Membership is open to anyone interested in dancing and in enhancing and spreading knowledge of Polish heritage. The club also teaches the dances to new members.

SAN ANTONIO ANTIQUES CLUB
June Carter, 433-5609

Antique lovers unite and learn more about, what else, antiques.

SAN ANTONIO ART LEAGUE
130 King William • Central • 223-1140

Although not formally organized until 1912, the meetings of this, San Antonio's oldest arts organization, stretch back a century. Devoted to the promotion of the visual arts in San Antonio, the Art League's members, who include both patrons and artists, sponsor an artist of the year award, have a number of shows, and maintain a gallery in the King William area (see **Art Galleries**). There are also lectures and other activities for members.

SAN ANTONIO ASTRONOMICAL ASSOCIATION
Rick Frankenberger • 681-2276

This association of amateur stargazers has an observing site near Center Point, well away from the star-dimming city lights. Educational events and observing trips make up much of its activity. Meetings are monthly.

SAN ANTONIO CALLIGRAPHERS GUILD
Darla Peek • 736-3942

The guild meets monthly to promote and encourage interest and skill in calligraphy. Two or three workshops a year feature well-known calligraphers from other parts of the country.

SAN ANTONIO CHESS CLUB
Contact San Pedro Library • 733-1454

The chess club has weekly meetings at San Pedro Library.

SAN ANTONIO HANDWEAVERS' GUILD
Barbara Geisewite • 493-5050

The handweavers explore every phase of the art of weaving, from spinning and dying to the making of lace. Monthly meetings give the members a chance to compare and exchange techniques. Sometimes members' creations are sold at the Southwest Craft Center.

SAN ANTONIO LIVING HISTORY ASSOCIATION
Thomas Jackson • 822-4292

An educational living history organization that portrays San Antonio and Texas history, particularly battle reenactments of the Texas Revolution Era.

SAN ANTONIO MODEL RAILROAD ASSOCIATION
Chuck Booth • 567-4370

Model railroad enthusiasts meet monthly to compare notes about model making, layouts, and other activities related to their interest in miniature trains. The club also has an open house or demonstration from time to time; the quality and detail of the members' work is extraordinary.

SAN ANTONIO RADIO CLUB
Contact American Red Cross to find out meeting day

Amateur radio operators (hams, not CB users), make up the membership of this, the oldest radio club in the city. The group assists the American Red Cross by providing communication when necessary. Meetings are held at Red Cross headquarters.

SAN ANTONIO ROAD RUNNERS
John Delgado • 648-4729

The Road Runners provides a rallying point for runners of all ages and various capabilities—from neighborhood joggers to trained marathoners. The club holds meetings, fun runs, and competitive events. One of the group's major events is a ten-kilometer race held every year in conjunction with Fiesta.

SAN ANTONIO STAMP COLLECTORS
Call Alamo Heights Stamp Shop for info • 826-4328

Meetings are held weekly at St. Luke's Lutheran Church. Stamp collectors gather to find out what is new or, perhaps more to the point in their specialty, what is old. The meetings may be the site of swaps, lectures, or exhibits.

SAN ANTONIO WHEELMEN
826-5015 (Call this hotline for rides info.)

This bicycle touring club sponsors several activities. Of greatest interest to avid cyclists are the tours of anywhere from five to sixty miles, at paces that reflect the ability of those in the group. San Antonio also has a bicycle racing club; for more information inquire at one of the city's cycle shops.

SAN ANTONIO WRITERS' GUILD
Louise Stewart • 554-5725

The guild is an association that looks after and promotes the interests of some of San Antonio's writers. The group's activities include meetings, which may involve critiques of members' work or lectures relevant to writing. Meetings are held monthly at St. Andrew Presbyterian Church, 8231 Callaghan.

SIERRA CLUB, ALAMO GROUP
222-8195

The local group of the Lone Star chapter of the Sierra Club meets monthly. The meetings consist of committee reports, the discussion of club projects, and usually a lecture or slide show. The members are interested in both conservation and outings.

SKI CLUBS

The amount of snow that falls annually in San Antonio would hardly support one ski on a run down the hill in San Pedro Park, but neither the lack of snow nor the lack of mountains deters the city's ski clubs from promoting an interest in skiing. The clubs—all members of the Texas Ski Council, an umbrella organization that promotes skiing and helps keep skiing costs reasonable—sponsor trips to ski areas all over the country and in Europe. Some even have summer meetings, perhaps for a barbecue or for waterskiing. There are several different clubs, with slightly different orientations:

Alamo Skiers, a small, predominantly African-American ski club affiliated with the National Brotherhood of Skiers: Dorothy Carroll, 661-9188

Los Amigos, a large, congenial club proud not only of its club trophies, but also of its après-ski life: hot line, 494-7669

San Antonio Ski Club, a smaller club whose membership is weighted toward professional people: 699-1062

SOUTHWEST GEM AND MINERAL SOCIETY
William H. Lee • 690-1355

Promotes exchange of info regarding earth sciences among people interested in lapidary art and the collection of minerals, fossils, and artifacts.

TEXAS CAMEL CORPS
Witte Museum • 357-1900

Although officially a group formed in support of the programs and exhibits of the Witte Museum, the Camel Corps is more than that, with its travel program (including even a bicycle trip through China), support of archeological and scientific field trips, and monthly meetings. The meetings are generally given over to a talk on an archeological or natural history topic, quite often presented by a professor or an investigator of the site being discussed. The members span different ages, interests, and degrees of familiarity with archeology; what they share is their interest in the subject.

VOLKSSPORTS—SAN ANTONIO CHAPTER N.D.T.A.
American Volkssport Association • 659-2112

A *volksmarch* (literally, "people's walk") is a noncompetitive walk of from six to twenty miles. The sport originated in Germany but has taken root in the United States. San Antonio has several separate groups of volksmarchers, out of the many that have formed around the country. Call the national headquarters for information about a local club.

WOODLAWN CAMERA CLUB
Jan Mueller • 622-3945

The Woodlawn Camera Club meets several times a month. Regular activities at the meetings include lectures or demonstrations of techniques for competition and perhaps a travelogue or other entertainment. The club also sponsors occasional field trips.

MILITARY BASES

Soldiering and the military have played more than a bit part in San Antonio's history. Practically every big-name military luminary has either trained or been stationed here at one time or another—from Robert E. Lee and Teddy Roosevelt to John "Black Jack" Pershing, Billy Mitchell, and Dwight D. Eisenhower. In San Antonio, Lee, then army inspector general in Texas, decided to throw his hat in with the South at the onset of the Civil War. Roosevelt trained his Rough Riders here before making his bully way to Cuba, often, local lore has it, bellying up to the bar at the Menger Hotel. After all, the town started out as a Spanish military garrison and mission in 1718. The Alamo later became a U.S. Army quartermaster's depot, serving as a supply center for frontier forts to the west and south. So it's no surprise that today five bases call San Antonio home and represent the biggest employer in town (though one, Kelly AFB, is due to be phased out).

FORT SAM HOUSTON
New Braunfels and Grayson (main gate) • Northeast
221-1211 • W variable

Fort Sam Houston is the oldest and most picturesque of the bases. Drive at leisure along its tree-lined boulevards with officers' Victorian homes, and you will feel the history of the place: Mamie and Ike courting on one of the verandas; military decisions being made in a slower age. Thank goodness the army had the good sense to retain these marvelous old buildings of character. Dating back to 1876, this is one of the most charming forts around.

Stop in to see the Quadrangle, located near the main gate; it houses the headquarters for the Fifth Army. This old limestone structure and courtyard is where Geronimo and thirty other Apaches were confined for forty days in 1886 after being captured. It's also the depot that outfitted Teddy Roosevelt's Rough Riders in 1898. A National Historic Landmark, the Quad and its courtyard, with tame deer and peacocks, makes a pleasant spot for a picnic lunch. At the Quadrangle, pick up a map showing the main points of interest on the base. Drive by the Pershing House and Eisenhower's old quarters, which aren't open to the public. However, visitors are welcome at the Fort Sam Houston Military Museum on Stanley Road (221-0019) and the U.S. Army Medical Museum on Stanley Road (see **Museums** chapter of this guide).

At Arthur MacArthur Field, use your imagination to conjure up the birth of the forerunner of the air force. Here, the Aero Squadron, consisting of one plane and one pilot, was formed. Using a Wright Type A biplane shipped here in crates and assembled by the pilot himself in 1910, Lieutenant Benjamin D. Foulois made one of the first military flights, a seven-minute thriller and his first solo flight. "Coming down is the most critical part of flying," Orville Wright had helpfully warned him. That was scant advice for a pilot who had mainly learned to fly by corresponding with Wright. Foulois went on to become chief of the fledgling Army Air Corps, all six planes of it.

Besides the Fifth Army, Fort Sam (as people in San Antonio universally call it) is also home to the Army Medical Command, Brooke Army Medical Center (one of the army's largest), and an internationally known burn treatment center. Look for the fireworks display during Fiesta.

BROOKS AIR FORCE BASE
SE Military Drive, just off I-37 • South • 536-1110 • W variable

Visit antiquated Hanger Nine at Brooks and get some idea of San Antonio's role in aviation. Hanger Nine, the oldest aircraft hangar in the air force and now a National Historic Landmark, is a museum of flight medicine and base history but is temporarily closed. The museum features a delightful old photograph of Charles Lindbergh, who was a flying cadet there in 1922. Also on exhibit is one of the original Jennys, the first planes to fly here. The base was established in 1917 because the army needed a place to train pilot instructors during World War I. At one time, Brooks was a balloon and airship school, and the technique of mass paratroop drops was first tried out here in 1929. Today those runways are no longer used for flights. Brooks is the home of the Aerospace Medical Division and the U.S. Air Force School of Aerospace Medicine. Research here helped the first manned space flights by simulating space cabin conditions. Brooks has also studied everything from stress and environmental problems to unique treatments for gas gangrene, decompression sickness, and carbon monoxide poisoning. Elsewhere on the base, at the Armstrong Laboratory, is the air force's main concentration of talent in the behavioral sciences. Here, research projects on personnel selection, classification, and utilization are initiated and carried out. You can tour some of these unusual facilities (such as the hyperbaric chambers and flight simulators), but call ahead. With current military downsizing, Brooks AFB and its above-mentioned facilities may be curtailed or eliminated in coming years.

KELLY AIR FORCE BASE
General Hudnell, off US 90 • South • 925-1110 • W variable

(Note that this base is due to close sometime around the year 2001 because of the nation's downsizing of the military. Between now and then, Kelly is being slowly phased out, much to the regret of the large workforce there. Some of the areas have already been privatized into commercial aircraft business.)

Personnel at Kelly diligently kept some of the air force's biggest planes—C-5s and B-52s—in good running order. The C-5 is the world's largest cargo plane, and the B-52 isn't exactly small either.

In the past, Kelly's San Antonio Air Logistics Center laid claim to being the largest single industrial complex in the Southwest, with a workforce in the thousands. These workers maintained and repaired the big engines and electronic equipment of many aircraft. Kelly, dating from 1917, is the oldest military air base in Texas. During World War I, it served as a training school for pilots and ground personnel. Charles Lindbergh as well as James Doolittle graduated from here.

LACKLAND AIR FORCE BASE
Military Drive West at US 90 • South • 671-1110 • W variable

The kids will love Lackland, a haven for model airplane buffs but with the real thing rather than models on display. There's no landing strip here, but every air force recruit gets trained here. The base has about eighty older jets, missiles, and World War II planes that you can view close up.

At the Visitors Center, you can pick up a map that will guide you to the History and Traditions Museum (see **Museums**). Some older fighter jets are outside the museum, and more World War II bombers (B-17s, B-24s) are displayed at the parade ground on Bong Avenue.

Lackland is a rather nondescript base with endless barracks, needed for the thousands of recruits who pass through here yearly. It also houses the Wilford Hall Medical Center, the air force's largest medical complex, plus the Defense Language Institute. The base is open to visitors.

RANDOLPH AIR FORCE BASE
Pat Booker Road, off I-35 • Northeast • 652-1110 • W variable

Randolph used to proclaim itself the West Point of the Air because it had trained so many of the air force's pilots and crews over the years. The Air Force Academy has stolen its thunder a bit, but Randolph is still a showplace base with tree-lined boulevards and Spanish-style architecture, all kept neat as a pin.

Randolph, dating from 1930, is home to Air Education and Training Command Headquarters and air force personnel and recruiting services. In the 1930s, the film *West Point of the Air* was made here, and in the 1940s, *I Wanted Wings*, which introduced Veronica Lake and her then famous World War II peekaboo hairstyle.

Notice the local landmark, the "Taj Mahal" tower, and see the T-38s and T-37s taking off and landing. The Taj, a Texas Historical Landmark, is used as an administration building and actually hides a water tower. The base offers short group tours. Call ahead.

INDEX

W

Walking
    clubs for, 244; hiking areas, 94
Walking tours: downtown, 42–45
Water recreation park, 86
Wax museum, 21
Weaving guilds, 242
Wilderness preservation
    club, 243
Wildlife parks
    Friedrich Park, 83; Natural
        Bridge Wildlife Ranch, 84;
        Y.O. Ranch, 111
Wildlife rescue, 233
Wilford Hall USAF Medical
    Center, 231
Witte Memorial Museum, 49, 199
Women's services, 238
WPA, 13

Writers' guild, 243
Wurstfest, 13

Y

YMCA, 87, 225
Y.O. Ranch, 111
Young Men's Christian
    Association. *See* YMCA
Young Women's Christian
    Association. *See* YWCA
Yturri-Edmunds House and Mill,
    32, 46
YWCA, 88, 225

Z

Zoological Gardens and
    Aquarium, San Antonio, 85